In Defense of Women

IN DEFENSE OF WOMEN

Susanna Rowson (1762-1824)

Dorothy Weil

The Pennsylvania State University Press
University Park and London

Published with the help of the Charles Phelps Taft
Memorial Fund, University of Cincinnati

Library of Congress Cataloging in Publication Data

Weil, Dorothy.
   In defense of women.

   Bibliography: p. 185.
   1. Rowson, Susanna Haswell, 1762-1824. I. Title.
PS2736.R3Z9   813'.2   75-26963
ISBN 0-271-01205-6

Printed in the United States of America

Frontispiece:
Susannah Haswell Rowson and William Rowson. (Courtesy of the
Clifton Waller Barrett Library, University of Virginia Library)

Contents

1

Enter Mrs. Rowson

Prompter.–behind.
Come–Mrs. Rowson! Come!–Why don't you hurry?
Mrs. R.–behind.
Sir I am here–but I'm in such a flurry,
Do let me stop a moment just for breath,
Enter.
(Epilogue, Slaves in Algiers, Philadelphia, 1794)

Mrs. Susanna Haswell Rowson enters breathless to deliver the epilogue to her stage comedy *Slaves in Algiers*. She has written the play, acted a central role in its first performance, and now addresses the audience. Mrs. Rowson might well be breathless, although temporary lack of oxygen never stopped her for long.

Susanna Rowson is best known for having written *Charlotte Temple*, America's first best-selling novel, which conquered the American market in 1794 and has since been printed in nearly two hundred editions. But a complete view of Mrs. Rowson's activities shows this achievement to have been only a brief episode in her career. During her years as a writer, from 1786 to 1822, Mrs. Rowson also produced seven other novels, two sets of fictional sketches, seven theatrical works, two collections of poetry, six pedagogical works, and many occasional pieces and lyrics for popular songs. She also contributed to at least two early American magazines, acted with several theater companies, operated a school for young women, and took a leading role in her church and community. The modern reaction to such a career for a woman is to ask "Way back then?" And a recital of Mrs. Rowson's accomplishments generates interest in an author who has not in the past attracted much attention, although she has sometimes evoked strong feelings.

A list of Susanna Rowson's achievements suggests a personality unchecked by the traditional constraints of which women complain, and her literary efforts reflect the energy, vitality, and purposefulness displayed in the author's willingness to undertake so many activities.

The few chapters Mrs. Rowson has been awarded by literary scholars, which are usually based upon only a few of her novels, present Susanna Rowson as a purveyor of stylistic formulae and sentimental tears, but a look at her complete works shows that she aspired to be a serious writer and teacher as well as an influential force in promoting freedom for women. The scope and seriousness of her themes and her attitude toward her own work may entitle her to recognition as America's first professional writer of fiction.[1]

Mrs. Rowson undertook nothing less than the complete education of the young female, religious, moral, emotional, intellectual, and worldly. Her books are addressed to women, all her novels' protagonists are women, her subject is women; whether she is writing of the struggles of a fictional heroine, of biography, history, or the glories of the American republic, she addresses herself to themes important to the situation, education, and rights of women. Working before the formal suffrage movement, at a time when only a few European or American writers had taken a strong stand in favor of female emancipation, she anticipated many of the questions that would be formulated by later advocates.

In The Oven Birds, a selection of works by nineteenth-century American women writers, Gail Parker suggests that "the history of American feminism and literary history must be studied simultaneously if any sense is to be made of the rise and fall of the woman's movement in America."[2] The importance women have enjoyed in the literary arts (which is out of proportion to their contribution in other fields, even the performing arts), and especially the novel, suggests a strong link between the thoughts of various female writers and the demand for women's rights. A study of the work of Mrs. Rowson, an early and ardent observer and teacher of women, should contribute toward a picture of the feminist movement, as well as reveal this neglected writer to students of American literature.

In the following pages, Mrs. Rowson is considered as a literary personality. The motives and state of mind of the flesh-and-blood woman are not treated; however, the facts of Mrs. Rowson's life are relevant to particular themes and techniques, and a brief biographical sketch is in order.

Mrs. Rowson was born Susanna Haswell in Portsmouth, England, in 1762. Her early life was filled with dramatic events. Her mother died at her birth; then, as a young child, Susanna was brought to America by her father and her American stepmother, and the family lived in Nantasket until the Revolution forced them to return to England. William Haswell was a lieutenant in the British Navy; in spite of his friendship for America, he could not take the oath of allegiance required of him.

Eventually, his property was confiscated, and in 1778 the Haswells were sent back to England.[3] The family suffered financially, and as a young woman Susanna Haswell became a governess in the family of the fascinating Georgiana Cavendish, Duchess of Devonshire.[4] All her life Susanna Rowson found help and patronage from important people. As a child in America, she was taught literature by James Otis, who was a friend of William Haswell's. The Prince of Wales noticed her early work and granted a pension to her father.

In 1786, Susanna Haswell published her first novel, *Victoria*. She married William Rowson the same year. During the period following these events, and before the Rowsons emigrated to America, she brought out seven works: the two sets of fictional sketches, *The Inquisitor* (1788) and *Mentoria, or the Young Lady's Friend* (1791); a full-length poetical critique on contemporary actors and drama, *A Trip to Parnassus* (1788); a volume of poetry, *Poems on Various Subjects* (1788);[5] and three novels, *The Test of Honour* (1789);[6] *Charlotte: A Tale of Truth* (1791), which was renamed *Charlotte Temple* in the third (1797) American edition; and *The Fille de Chambre* (1792).

Little has been written about these years in England. The author's life was probably seldom serene. There is the interesting possibility of Mrs. Rowson's contact with various celebrated actors and theater personalities. Several biographers have noted that the marriage to William Rowson was undertaken more for practical than romantic reasons. Rowson, a friend of Susanna's father, was a member of the Horse Guards, a trumpeter, and a sometime hardware merchant. He was unable to support himself and his wife, and most accounts of him emphasize the point that he was not of his wife's caliber. As R.W.G. Vail writes, "he is always very much in the background" (p. 51).[7] And, according to a persistent rumor, he probably drank.[8]

In the season of 1792-1793, the Rowsons, accompanied by William's sister Charlotte, joined a theater company and toured the British Isles. In 1793, they were brought to America by Thomas Wignell to play the "New Theatre" in Philadelphia. Before the Rowsons left the stage in 1797, by then members of the Federal Street Theater in Boston, they had performed in Annapolis, Philadelphia, and Baltimore. During these years, Mrs. Rowson completed several more works. *Slaves in Algiers*,[9] a farce with music, and *The Female Patriot*[10] were performed in 1794. A four-volume novel, *Trials of the Human Heart*, and a musical entertainment based upon the Whiskey Rebellion, *The Volunteers*,[11] appeared in 1795. Two more dramtic pieces, *Americans in England* (1796)[12] and *The American Tar* (1796),[13] were completed during the years in the theater.

Mrs. Rowson was as versatile a performer as she was a writer. Julian

Mates notes that she "helped the range of pantomime's interest by becoming the first female Harlequin in America" (*The American Musical Stage Before 1800*, p. 161). He also notes the Rowsons' connection with the famous Rickett's Circus in which she "danced hornpipes in the part of a sailor" (p. 189). The many dramatic roles Mrs. Rowson played are listed by R.W.G. Vail; among them were the nurse in *Romeo and Juliet* and Mrs. Quickly in *The Merry Wives of Windsor*.

Contemporary reviews of Mrs. Rowson's acting were moderately approving. In his *History of the American Theatre*, George O. Seilhamer writes, "The Rowsons, it is apparent, were held in higher esteem in Boston than elsewhere, even Mr. Rowson being accorded some parts of some importance."[14] The estimate of Mrs. Rowson's plays, judging by the number of performances given them, was not high; according to Seilhamer, only *Slaves in Algiers* became "a popular stock piece" (pp. 182-183). It survives in printed form along with one song from *The American Tar* and the score of *The Volunteers*.

In Boston, in 1797, incredible as it seems for a British woman with a somewhat disreputable husband, and a career as an actress behind her, Mrs. Rowson opened her school for young ladies. According to several accounts, she began with only one pupil, the daughter of Mrs. Samuel Smith,[15] but managed to increase her enrollment rapidly and to run the academy successfully in several locations (Medford, Newton, and finally Hollis Street in Boston) until 1822. Mrs. Rowson's writing during these years included three new novels, *Reuben and Rachel* (1798), *Sarah* (run in serial form, 1803-1804, in the *Boston Weekly Magazine* as *Sincerity* and published in revised form in 1813), and *Charlotte's Daughter, or The Three Orphans, A Sequel to Charlotte Temple* (published posthumously in 1828). In addition to these efforts, Mrs. Rowson contributed to the production of at least two periodicals, the *Boston Weekly Magazine* and the *New England Galaxy*.[16] During her years as schoolmistress, Mrs. Rowson also produced the six pedagogical works designed for use in her own and other schools: *An Abridgment of Universal Geography* (1805), *A Spelling Dictionary* (1807), *A Present for Young Ladies* (1811), *Youth's First Step in Geography* (1818), *Exercises in History*, and *Biblical Dialogues* (1822). But these efforts did not exhaust Mrs. Rowson's zest for projects. She published a volume of poetry, *Miscellaneous Poems*, in 1804 and a final theatrical piece, *Hearts of Oak* (1810-1811),[17] as well as numerous odes, poems, and popular songs. In addition, she found time to devote to several adopted children, among them William's natural son, William, Jr., and to church and charity—including the presidency of the Fatherless and Widow's Society.

Mrs. Rowson seems to have been perpetually in motion, and her activities on the early American scene were widely known. A contemporary critic called her "the celebrated Mrs. Rowson."[18] The flavor of her fame is shown in a letter from her half-brother, Robert Haswell, written in response to one from Susanna requesting information about living conditions in Boston:

> of all the happy fellows in America I am the most lucky in my acquaintance; Williamson knows . . . he can describe to you my situation and some of the charming women with whom I spend part of my time who love you for your writing and me for being your Brother. . . .
>
> (19 May 1796)[19]

Of course, much of Mrs. Rowson's popularity at the time Robert writes was due to the great American success of *Charlotte Temple*, or *Charlotte* as the book was originally entitled, and the author is still primarily known for that novel. Even the informed and scholarly today are more likely to know the name "Charlotte Temple" than that of her creator. The Haswell memorial stone (Roxbury, Massachusetts) identifies Susanna as "the author of *Charlotte Temple*," and so do most literary studies that include Mrs. Rowson. Therefore, something must be said about the work's character and notoriety.

Charlotte Temple is one of the wonders of American literature. The story of the seduction and abandonment of young Charlotte by an American army officer, Lieutenant Montraville, it purports to be, as its subtitle indicates, "A Tale of Truth." It is supposedly founded upon facts gleaned by the author from the memory of a lady of her acquaintance.[20] The most remarkable fact about *Charlotte* is its popularity. It was widely read when it was first published in America in 1794 (over 25,000 copies sold shortly after publication), has since had close to two hundred editions, and is still in print. R.W.G. Vail contends that *Charlotte* [in 1932] had "been read by more persons than any other volume of fiction ever printed in this country" (p. 66). James D. Hart, in *The Popular Book*, calls *Charlotte* "the most popular of all eighteenth-century novels in America,"[21] and Frank Luther Mott, in his study of best sellers, *Golden Multitudes*, lists it as one of the overall best sellers in America.[22]

The book's fame has been increased by a cult that developed around Charlotte's supposed grave in Trinity Churchyard in New York City. Tradition, aided by various writers and newspapermen, established the idea that Charlotte was really Charlotte Stanley, a granddaughter of the eleventh earl of Derby, that Montraville was in reality a cousin of Mrs. Rowson's, Colonel John Montrésor, and that Lucy Blakeney (heroine of *Charlotte's Daughter*) was a real person who visited her mother's grave in New York's Trinity Churchyard (where a grave marked "Charlotte Temple" is still visited), to place a plaque bearing the family's coat of arms on the tomb.[23]

Besides the lure of legend to increase its popularity, the book has had a reputation for being immensely and prodigiously sad. The introduction to a very inaccurate and much shortened version, which is labeled *The Lamentable History of the Beautiful and Accomplished Charlotte Temple, With an Account of Her Elopement with Lieutenant Montroville [sic] and Her Misfortunes and Painful Sufferings, Are Herein Pathetically Depicted* (1865), says:

> The Publishers of this most painful and pathetic history deem it entirely unnecessary to say anything in reference to its authenticity, as most of the main facts connected with Miss Temple's unhappy fate, have been recited at almost every fireside. The house in which the unhappy girl sojourned for a time, and miserably expired, yet stands on the Bowery, New York City, a sad monument of her wrongs, and many indeed are those who have dropped the tear of pity as they gazed upon it. No work of fiction can possibly compare with this sorrowful and vivid portraiture of the feelings of a crushed heart. It having often been remarked that no one could read this truthful tale of woe without shedding tears, the writer of this preface recollects an incident which took place in this connection a few years since. A wager of one hundred dollars was made between two gentlemen, that one of them could not read the account of Miss Temple's unhappy fate, without shedding tears. The gentleman who undertook the task, had scarcely finished one half the affecting narrative, when he laid the book aside, and gave up the bet; his heart was filled with deep pathos and new and thrilling emotions, his voice became husky and tremulous, and tears of real affection and sorrow gushed from his eyes.[24]

In terms of sales and pathetic appeal, *Charlotte* was the *Love Story* of eighteenth- and nineteenth-century America and could probably still hold its own in the literary market.

Charlotte was immensely popular, yet it was not the only work by which Mrs. Rowson was known to her contemporaries. *The Fille de Chambre* (1792) was a very popular novel; Mott, in *Golden Multitudes*, lists it as a best seller (p. 40). According to Vail, *Reuben and Rachel*

(1798) also sold well (pp. 76-77); *Trials of the Human Heart* (1795) was read, if not by the enormous public who devoured *Charlotte*, by a large number of subscribers, and an important and socially prominent audience.[25] *Charlotte's Daughter* was published in over thirty editions, and Mrs. Rowson's fame as a writer of occasional pieces was considerable. "The Standard of Liberty," a poetical address to the army of the United States, performed in Baltimore by Mrs. Whitlock in 1795, was "enthusiastically received" (Vail, p. 70). Mrs. Rowson's pedagogical works were used in her own school, and all were published. Her poetry reached the periodical reader through the *New England Galaxy*, and her opinions through her contribution to the *Boston Weekly Magazine*. The songs and libretti were set to music by the most celebrated composers of the day, among them Gottlieb Graupner, Alexander Reinagle, and John Bray.

The public eagerly read Mrs. Rowson. Only one of her works, *Poems on Various Subjects* (1788), was treated harshly by the critics. Both the *Monthly Review* and the *Critical Review* suggested that the author was not ready for the rigors of poetry (Vail, p. 141). The other works enjoyed at least moderate success if not a consensus of praise.[26] Of course the standards of late-eighteenth-century English and American critics were based largely upon moral rather than aesthetic judgments.[27] This situation prevailed also in nineteenth-century attitudes toward Mrs. Rowson. Samuel Knapp in his "Memoir" praises Mrs. Rowson for her "uniformly moral tendency" (p. 11), and Whittier in his 1828 review of *Charlotte's Daughter* recommends her work for its "moral beauty" (*On Writers and Writing*, p. 17). In addition, both men credit Mrs. Rowson with the ability to handle pathos, and they endorse the simplicity and realism of her style. Mrs. Rowson's biographer, Elias Nason, is enthusiastic about both style and moral content. Begun as a paper delivered in 1859, and based upon interviews with Mrs. Rowson's surviving relatives, friends, and school pupils, Nason's *Memoir* (1870) provides extensive evaluation of Rowson's works. An educator himself, Nason approves of Mrs. Rowson's instructional volumes; he writes of *Biblical Dialogues*:

> Taking her listeners gently by the hand, she leads them pleasantly along through the labyrinths of biblical history; always telling the "good old story" gracefully, and sustaining her narrative by apt and appropriate references to geography and chronology.
>
> (p. 181)

Nason "waxes poetic" about *Charlotte* and Mrs. Rowson's poetry. Of the former, he writes: "The plot of the story is as simple and as natural as Boileau himself could desire; the denouement comes in just at the right time and place; and the reader's interest is enchained, as by magic, to the very last syllable of the book" (p. 48). *Charlotte's* popular appeal, which to Nason proves its worth among "works of genius," is described as follows:

> It has stolen its way alike into the study of the divine and into the workshop of the mechanic; into the parlor of the accomplished lady and the bed-chamber of her waiting maid; into the log-hut on the extreme border of modern civilization and into the forecastle of the whale ship on the lonely ocean. It has been read by the grey-bearded professor after his "divine Plato;" by the beardless clerk after balancing his accounts at night; by the traveler waiting for the next conveyance at the village inn; by the school girl stealthfully in her seat at school. It has beguiled the woodman in his hut at night in the deep solitudes of the silent forest; it has cheated the farmer's son of many an hour while poring over its fascinating pages, seated on the broken spinning wheel in the old attic; it has drawn tears from the miner's eye in the dim twilight of his subterranean dwelling; it has unlocked the secret sympathies of the veteran soldier in his tent before the day of battle.
>
> (pp. 50-51)

Mrs. Rowson has never, before or since Nason, enjoyed such unqualified esteem. Her contemporary and friend, Samuel Knapp, added in his *Memoir* that she was not "a consummate artist" (p. 11), and later nineteenth-century critics tend to agree.[28] Twentieth-century writers have been, for the most part, unsympathetic to Mrs. Rowson although many have granted her fiction some redeeming qualities.[29]

Herbert Ross Brown is among those who devote significant attention to Susanna Rowson. In his study *The Sentimental Novel in America 1789-1860*,[30] Brown ridicules the sentimental tradition in general, using Rowson as a prime example of all its faults. Henri Petter in *The Early American Novel* contends that Mrs. Rowson's fiction represents the "deliberate collection of the ingredients that went into the making of an average novel designed to be fashionably successful and derived from earlier successes" and that she "remained strictly within the limits of such novel-writing."[31]

The most vociferous reactions to Mrs. Rowson have come from critics reacting to her feminist views. From William Cobbett, Mrs. Rowson's contemporary, to Leslie Fiedler, these critics have adopted a passionate tone. In a review of Mrs. Rowson's works, part of *A Kick for a Bite* (1795), Cobbett criticizes the feminist assertions in *Slaves in Algiers*. He objects to these lines of the heroine, Fetnah:

> But some few months since, my father (who sends out many corsairs,) brought home a *female captive*, to whom I became greatly attached; It was she, who nourished in my mind the love of liberty, and taught me, woman was never formed to be the abject slave of man. Nature made us equal with them, and gave us the power to render ourselves superior.
>
> (I. 1, 9)

And he was equally incensed by a passage in the epilogue of the play:

> "Women were born for universal sway,
> "Men to adore, be silent, and obey."

Cobbett rails that "Sentiments like these could not be otherwise than well received in a country, where the authority of the wife is so unequivocally acknowledged . . ." (pp. 23-24). Cobbett goes on to attack Mrs. Rowson's writing style. He calls her work in general his "*materia medicae*"; *Rebecca*, his "philtre"; *The Inquisitor*, his "opium"; and *Slaves in Algiers*, his "emetic" (p. 27).

Helen Waite Papashvily, in her 1956 study *All the Happy Endings*, cites Mrs. Rowson as an important source of feminist views, which in the hands of her successors constituted a "witch's brew" designed to "destroy their common enemy, man."[32] The sentimental novel, contends Papashvily, was an underground "manual of arms" for the "quiet women" (p. 24); she quotes Mrs. Rowson's epilogue to her play *Slaves in Algiers* (1794) as being particularly outspoken against male domination (p. 34). Papashvily argues that American women, brought up on sentimental novels like Mrs. Rowson's and their modern counterparts, are prone to play the role of the sentimental heroine, which includes unwholesome martyrdom and a sense of moral superiority, among other undesirable traits (p. 212).

In *Love and Death in the American Novel*, Leslie Fiedler states that Mrs. Rowson's novels were inspired by "a feminist attack upon the male," which is abetted (shades of William Cobbett!) by American willingness to allow the "downfall of the male" and the castration of "father."[33] According to Fiedler, Mrs. Rowson was a "pioneer" in American literature who popularized mutant formulae from the Richardsonian novel (p. 67). Thus she helped disseminate a "Sentimental Love Religion," which has as its secret articles of faith the ideas that "tears are . . . a truer service of God than prayers, the Pure Young Girl replaces Christ as the savior, marriage becomes the equivalent of bliss eternal, and the Seducer is the only Devil" (p. 27). Fiedler agrees with Papashvily that the view of women presented by Mrs. Rowson and her successors is unwholesome and limited. Fiedler writes, "In Mrs. Rowson's version . . . it [the Richardsonian story] succeeded in projecting once and for all the American woman's image of herself as the long-suffering martyr of love—the inevitable victim of male brutality and lust" (p. 81).

These writers make many points with which any reader of Mrs. Rowson must agree. Yet their interpretation of the picture of the female Mrs. Rowson tried to project is inaccurate, principally because their evaluations are based on a very small sample of work. When her total canon is looked at, Mrs. Rowson appears in a different light. She tried to suggest a lively and active rather than domineering or martyred personality for the female. Her concentration on this goal gives her work a certain vitality—as Constance Rourke suggests in her sketch in The Roots of American Culture.[34]

If Mrs. Rowson's stated intentions and themes are traced from the first to the last of her work, coherence emerges, and a more solid image of the author appears than that of a dabbler in lachrymose romance, or an unconscious purveyor of sexual warfare. Instead, we see the robust teacher who stresses the Christian religion, democratic ideals, reality over fantasy, and sense over sensibility, and who tries to tie these teachings to a realistic and practical view of life.

Mrs. Rowson's devotion to her audience is reiterated in her stated intentions and carried out in the content of her works. Her religious views and her literary treatment of women, as well as her preoccupation with various related themes and issues, bear out her interest in her own sex. Even the Rowson style, which is a seeming "grab-bag" of literary modes, was determined by her dominant goal. She worked at a time when fiction as well as poetry and belles-lettres offered little that could help her cause. The novel in England awaited the purifying irony and realism of Jane Austen, and in America there was almost no tradition of native fiction; little predates Mrs. Rowson. The prevailing mode in most writing was sentimental and genteel, and there was no real criticism. Still, Mrs. Rowson attempted to practice realism. Most important, she successfully created a literary self that served as both model and mentor for her readers.

2

Aims and Achievements

My whole soul was engaged in my duties, my pupils became to me as my
children, and few things were of consequence to me that did not contribute
to their improvement, their present and eternal happiness.
(Biblical Dialogues, 1822)

Mrs. Rowson wrote these words in 1822, just two years before her
death. She had operated her school for young ladies for twenty-five
years, a fact that she notes in another work of the same date. But she had
adopted the female young as her pupils long before she opened an
academy to provide for their formal education. Her critical poem, *A
Trip to Parnassus* (1788), and the prefaces appended to most of the
fictional and pedagogical works provide a running commentary on her
literary goals and aspirations.

The complete education of the young female was the consistent aim
of Mrs. Rowson's literary life. From the beginning of her career, the
author selected critical principles that underlined and supported her
rhetorical purpose. Three topics recur in Mrs. Rowson's discussion of
literary standards and goals: concern for the young female audience,
the importance of instructing this audience, and the necessity to provide a realistic or natural picture of life.

In *A Trip to Parnassus* (1788),[1] Mrs. Rowson's only wholly critical
work and one of her earliest efforts, her lifelong artistic standards are
suggested. *A Trip* is a humorous dramatic poem, in light anapests, in
which the poet is taken in a dream to Parnassus to observe the judgment
of Apollo upon the popular playwrights and actors of the day. The
piece is dedicated to Thomas Harris, manager of the Covent Garden
theater; the personalities criticized were associated with Covent Garden or the Drury Lane. The judgments of Apollo coincide with the
judgments of Susanna Rowson as they are revealed in her fiction and
other works.

Apollo's two most important canons are morality and naturalness,
the two qualities for which Mrs. Rowson aimed in her own works, and

for which she was often praised. Among the playwrights accepted by Apollo in *A Trip* is George Colman the Elder, "Who, pourtraying the heart of a *Freeport*, has shown/ The honour and virtue which glow in his own" (p. 3). Sheridan receives honors for his desire to "instruct and improve" (p. 4), and the younger Colman is narrowly saved from being sent back to earth by the "virtue" of his play *Inkle and Yarico* (p. 5). The author of "*Baron Kink-van*—I can't think of his name" sends modesty fleeing in embarrassment, and he is therefore consigned to a lower region. Mrs. Hannah Cowley, the famed woman playwright, is also rejected—an act unusual for Susanna Rowson, who customarily defends women colleagues in the professions. But she has Apollo declare,

"Hold, woman . . . approach not too near,
"I dictate no line that can wound the chaste ear;
"When your sex take the pen, it is shocking to find,
"From their writings, loose thoughts have a place in their mind."

(p. 4)

In contrast, Mrs. Brooks, author of *Rosina*, is praised for the "innocence" of her work (p. 4). So the drama must teach high moral standards, not just provide a good cry or be able to wring the tear of sensibility from the audience. The specific qualities some of the approved playwrights possess are the harder virtues, for example, "wit, sense, and humour" in the case of Mrs. Inchbald (p. 9).

Mrs. Rowson's standards for the art of acting correspond to those recommended for the writing of drama. As important as morality, *A Trip to Parnassus* demonstrates, is naturalness. The words "nature" and "natural" occur over and over in the poem. The actor Charles Machlin is placed "at the Head of the band" of Thespians for, as Apollo says,

. . . "To dame Nature, you've paid due regard,
"And trod in the steps of my favorite bard."

(p. 9)

Mrs. Rowson dislikes overacting and calls for performances that realistically express the emotion the playwright is trying to convey. She has Apollo scold Stephen Kemble, Joseph Holman, and John Edwin for their excesses. Of John Edwin, Apollo says,

"Then his limbs he'll distort, and he'll screw up his face,
"And for humour he'll constitute pun and grimace.

"But EDWIN (he cried) you must mend this fault soon,
"Tho' I honour true genius, I hate a buffoon."

(p. 14)

The god advises the actor to "Make Nature your copy, you'll always do well" (p. 14).

Although several performers are advised to undergo further study, Mrs. Rowson scorns artifice and affectation. Apollo praises Elizabeth Kemble (Mrs. Stephen) for her freedom from these qualities:

Apollo, with smiles, call'd her up to this throne,
And mark'd the fair dame for a child of his own.
He clad her in native simplicity's dress,
And taught her to tell a soft tale of distress;
Banish'd vile affectation and strip'd her of art,
Then bade her, in *Yarico*, ravish each heart.

(p. 19)

The good actor will convince his audience of the truth of the character he plays, for the role of drama is to reflect a true picture of the world and exhibit the human types to be laughed at or scorned. Apollo praises Macklin highly in this regard:

"When *Macsycophant* teaches to get an estate,
"By *bowing* and servilely flatt'ring the Great;
"When he talks of religion and turns up his eyes,
"And puts on hypocrisy's specious disguise;
"So well the vile heart is unfolded by you,
"And the base fawning sycophant held up to view."

(p. 10)

Sincerity is a quality revered in both playwright and performer. As the references to Mr. Holman and others reveal, the virtues and feelings in a work of art reflect those of the artist—a maxim important to Susanna Rowson, and one that she insisted upon in all her own efforts. This principle underlies her adherence to "Method Acting," which can be seen in Apollo's advice to a Miss Tweedale:

"You must have animation, must feel what you speak,
"Call a tear to your eye, or a blush to your cheek.
"It is wrong, on the stage, when performing a part,
"Like a school girl, to con o'er your lesson by heart.

"The merely repeating a speech will not do;
"You must feel it yourself, and make others feel too."

(p. 18)

Conceit, pride, and emptiness on the part of the artist are projected in his craft. And the artist, in Mrs. Rowson's works, is in direct communication with the audience, a relationship Mrs. Rowson successfully exploits in her own career.

In outlining her aims for her own work, Mrs. Rowson continues to develop the canons advocated in *A Trip to Parnassus*, and she adheres to these aims. Her concern for "modesty" evolves into exclusive concentration upon the young female as her audience. The protagonists of all but one of the fictions are young women, the action consists of problems faced by women, and the point of view rarely departs from that of the protagonist or a female friend. The textbooks were written in response to student needs observed by Mrs. Rowson as an educator of girls.

The desire to teach is the organizing principle of Mrs. Rowson's work. She states this idea in her prefaces and follows it in practice.[2] Each of Mrs. Rowson's fictional works aims at and is organized by a moral lesson (or two) with the author's brand of Christianity as the controlling doctrine. The textbooks carry on the teachings of the fiction and offer moral reflection as well as instruction in specific subject areas.

Much has been written about Mrs. Rowson's claim that *Charlotte Temple* is a "Tale of Truth." Many other works of the period, Mrs. Foster's *The Coquette*,[3] for instance, include similar claims. This practice supposedly gave the novelist a defense against the pervasive distrust of fiction—a distrust that has been variously attributed to the disapproval of puritanical American society of mere amusement, the suspicion of the imagination aroused by the ascendant school of philosophy in America, Scottish Common Sense, and the subordination of creative art to action and utility produced by American political exigencies. These forces supposedly represented such strong opposition to fiction from community powers that novelists claimed to be writing nonfiction in order to survive. The popularity of the claim to truth in fiction could, on the other hand, arise from the titillation inherent in the *roman à clef*. Both *Charlotte* and *The Coquette* are generally believed to be based upon actual occurrences, with the participants still living at the time as the subject of gossip.

There may be some element of self-defense or catering to the literary market in Mrs. Rowson's use of the popular claim of authenticity. However, these theories must be put into perspective. While the tag "founded on fact" is frequently encountered in early American fiction, it also appears at a much earlier period in English literature.[4] It is not an exclusively American phenomenon, and cannot be explained by any historical situation exclusively American, nor is this tradition a surprising tendency in a literary form so closely linked to the diary, memoir, and journal. Mrs. Rowson's insistence upon the factual in *Charlotte*, when placed in context, can be seen as inchoate realism, part of her avowed method, and the product of aesthetic choice. For Mrs. Rowson did not confine her claim to authenticity to *Charlotte*. She asserted that all her works were reflections of reality. She never labeled a fictional work "romance"—a popular term undergoing definition, and used in Mrs. Rowson's day, as it was later used by Hawthorne and James, to indicate wider scope permitted to the imagination. Mrs. Rowson called all her extended fictional stories "novels," indicating that she meant them to be held to the higher standard of verisimilitude and probability. Her projected design for her texts was that they too should describe the real world and combat the errors of fancy, imagination, and false doctrine. Her whole didactic scheme rests upon the idea that everything she writes is based on actuality.

The young woman must be taught certain religious and moral principles, but this task must never be accomplished by holding up visionary or chimerical pictures of the world. Mrs. Rowson's rôle as the young woman's guide requires that she give her audience an honest look at what they might experience in reality. A comparison of Mrs. Rowson's prefatory remarks with the content of her fiction and a summary of the aims and achievements of her pedagogical works show how consistent she remained in trying to carry out her self-imposed task.

Victoria (1786),[5] Mrs. Rowson's earliest novel, contains no preface, but the author's intention to teach her young female audience by representation of the actual is projected clearly in the full title: *Victoria, A Novel. In Two Volumes. The Characters taken from Real Life, and calculated to improve the MORALS OF THE FEMALE SEX, By impressing them with a just Sense of THE MERITS OF FILIAL PIETY.* A quotation from Milton on the title page emphasizes the central religious theme of *Victoria*:

> Your Bodies may at last all turn to Spirit,
> Improved by Tract of Time; and winged ascend
> Etherial.—

Here, or in Heavenly Paradises dwell;
If ye be found obedient, and retain
Unalterably firm his Love entire,
Whose Progeny you are.

Victoria tells the story of the melancholia and death of the protagonist. The young girl disobeys the direct orders of her mother to avoid Harry Finchly, the lover by whom Victoria conceives a child and is abandoned. Harry is of a higher social standing than Victoria, and her mother, who knows the ways of the world, is aware that the couple would not receive the blessing of the Finchlys. Several parallel plots emphasize the clear lesson: obey your parents. There is a "Miss C." who marries a fortune-hunter against her father's wishes; she also has a child, and dies. By contrast, "Charlotte R.," in a story-within-the-story, accepts an undesired suitor picked by her parents, and although the man is too "rustic" for her tastes, lives happily ever after. The central character, true to her name, achieves redemption because she repents her actions and does not become corrupted mentally. However, Mrs. Rowson has declared her concern for "the present *and* eternal happiness" [italics mine] of her "pupils," and Victoria's actions incur suffering for herself and her family. Victoria is not a model of beauty or refinement, but a sad example of youth assuming decisions too complex for its understanding.

In *The Inquisitor* (1788),[6] Mrs. Rowson describes the adventures of a rambling dilettante, a man who possesses a magic ring that enables him to become invisible and thus eavesdrop on the lives of others. He goes about London observing the behavior of his countrymen, and at times helping the poor or unfortunate. Written in what Mrs. Rowson takes to be the style of Sterne, *The Inquisitor* is heavily didactic even though it is the only work Mrs. Rowson ever claims to have "written solely for my own amusement" (p. viii). The author continues to insist upon a connection between her fiction and reality; she writes in the preface that while the sketches are "merely the children of Fancy; I must own that the best part of them originated in facts" (p. vii).

The Test of Honour (1789)[7] tells the story indicated by the title: the protagonist proves her honor by rejecting a marriage not approved by the father of the man who loves her. At the conclusion, Mary Newton, who has established her integrity as well as her resilience, marries her beloved. In contrast, Mary's best friend, Emily Elwin, marries secretly and suffers a fate similar to that of Victoria.

In the preface, Mrs. Rowson states her didactic purpose: to show other young women the superiority of Mary's character and behavior to that of Emily:

> *If the character of Mary should interest or please any 'f my fair readers, let them reflect, that she is not merely the child of fiction, but an amiable woman, who, taking reason and religion for the guide of all her actions, and keeping her passions under due controul, sunk not beneath the pressure of adversity; but, supported by that Providence who delights in virtue, passed through life with honour and applause.—Should the sorrows of Emily Elwin melt the heart of sensibility, Oh may it warn them to avoid her errors, and never suffer themselves, or those who may call themselves their lovers, to act contrary to the dictates of filial duty! for few, very few, are happy in the married state, who enter into it without reflection; and sure no person, who reflected for a moment, would take a partner for life, whose chief dowry would be the curses of their offended parents!*
>
> (pp. iii-v)

Besides noting that Mary is "not merely the child of fiction," Mrs. Rowson insists upon the verisimilitude of her tale by describing it as "a simple recital of some facts, here and there embellished by the hand of fancy," which contains "no outré characters, no elopements, duels, or any of those common-place incidents found in almost every novel now extant . . ." (pp. ii-iii).

Mentoria, or the Young Lady's Friend (1791),[8] Mrs. Rowson's second volume of fictional sketches, is designed like the earlier efforts, around a central message addressed to the young female. In the preface, Mrs. Rowson delineates her intention to help her "dear country-women" to become "as truly amiable as they are acknowledged beautiful" (p. ii). The sketches, most of which are in the form of letters from Mentoria to her charges, teach various moral principles such as filial obedience and charity, but most insistently they stress the false allure of social ambition. Mentoria, the central character, leads an exemplary, useful life, and avoids the perils of social climbing. She refuses to marry the son of her employer, Lady Winworth, and later becomes governess to his children. The tragedies of Dorcas and her daughter Marian, narrated in one of the lengthier episodes, are precipitated by Dorcas's submission to passions "improper and improvident" in a girl of "humble station" (I, 89). Dorcas secretly marries Lord Melfont only to be rejected by him when he finds someone he prefers. Her marriage is annulled, and Dorcas is left with two young daughters and very little income.

"Fatima and Urganda: An Eastern Tale" points up the same moral that Dorcas tries to communicate to her daughter: "be humble, be innocent, and be happy." Fatima, lured by the luxury at the court of the vizier, allows the fairy Urganda to help her become the favorite, only to find her life one of "splendid slavery" (II, 97). She aspires then to become the favorite of the emperor, succeeds in doing so, and is again disappointed, for the emperor is old, ugly, and jealous. Fatima is overheard expressing these sentiments and is saved from death just in time by Urganda who delivers her back to her humble home and advises her to "envy not the superior lot of another, but humbly take the blessings within thy reach, enjoy them and be happy" (II, 101).

The preface to *Charlotte* (1791)[9] projects the didactic design followed in the most popular of Mrs. Rowson's novels. The author states that she wishes to divert young ladies from the errors committed by Charlotte, whom she views as one of many girls "deprived of natural friends . . . spoilt by a mistaken education . . . thrown on an unfeeling world without the least power to defend themselves from the snares not only of the other sex, but from the more dangerous arts of the profligate of their own" (p. 21). The résumé of *Charlotte* in chapter 1 of the present study shows how faithfully Mrs. Rowson follows this plan. While Charlotte, like Victoria, embraces Christ, repents, and is presumably saved "in futurity," she suffers mental and physical tortures, and inflicts awful pain on her doting family. *Charlotte* was alleged to have been told to Mrs. Rowson by an acquaintance who knew the facts and to have been embellished by only "a slight veil of fiction."

In the preface to *The Fille de Chambre* (1794),[10] Mrs. Rowson reiterates her dedication to teaching and to realistic treatment. She states her desire to stand against "vice and folly" and to portray virtue in all her "transcendant beauties" (p. vi). Rebecca Littleton, the protagonist, is forced into the world to earn her own way without the help of parents, guardians, or friends. But unlike Charlotte, she possesses strength of character and a practical turn of mind, and she survives, among other hardships, a trip to America, where she undergoes experiences very similar to Mrs. Rowson's own (and acknowledged as taken from life). *The Fille de Chambre* proves the point Mrs. Rowson makes in her preface—that virtue is not related to social rank (p. v). Rebecca contrasts with many aristocrats who are shown to lack common decency; a poem on the title page celebrates contentment with a comfortable, not showy, rank in life. In the story, Rebecca refuses advances from the son of her patron, Lady Mary Worthy, for she has taken a vow not to marry this young man who is above her socially.

Mrs. Rowson develops her preference for the actual in the preface to *The Fille de Chambre*. She imagines an interview between herself and a Mr. Puffendorf, who likes to read only about aristocrats. The author argues that "a woman may be an interesting character tho' placed in the humblest walks of life" (p. v), and proclaims her intention to portray such a character even though Mr. Puffendorf warns her that her story will not sell. Mrs. Rowson calls Rebecca a "true child of nature," and warns the reader to expect no "wonderful discoveries, of titles, rank and wealth, being unexpectedly heaped upon her" (p. v).

Mrs. Rowson explains in her preface to *Trials of the Human Heart* (1795)[11] that she has chosen her presentation for its effectiveness in teaching. Meriel is to be taken as a model for other young women. Mrs. Rowson writes, "My Heroine, though not wholly free from error (for where shall we find the human being that is so?), I trust is not altogether unworthy of imitation" (p. xiii). She quotes Dr. Johnson as her authority for the dictum that fiction should represent virtue, but with human proportions so that the fictional model can be emulated (p. xii).

This novel stresses the importance of trusting Providence and practicing Christian morality in spite of the grim vicissitudes of life. Meriel is a girl of eighteen. She has been receiving her education in a convent in Bologna, when she is called home to England because of the imminent death of her godmother. She returns to her supposed parents, whom she has not seen since early childhood. The couple are really her aunt, who had adopted Meriel when the girl's real mother was unable to acknowledge her, and the aunt's husband. The latter tries to seduce Meriel; he fails in the attempt, but succeeds in cheating her out of the bulk of her money. Meriel is then cast into the world to care for herself and her "mother," and she meets a variety of trials over a period of sixteen years before she is permitted reunion with her beloved Mr. Rainsforth.[12]

Reuben and Rachel (1798),[13] Mrs. Rowson's next novel, was published after she had begun her school for young ladies. In the preface, Mrs. Rowson announces her intention—one that she fulfilled—to write a whole series of books for the formal education of young women. She notes, "It is observable that the generality of books intended for children are written for boys" (p. iv).

The subject of *Reuben and Rachel* is the discovery of America, first by Columbus, and then by his modern descendants, the Reuben and Rachel of the title. The lesson of *Reuben and Rachel* has to do with the nature of various traditions and governments. The reader sees the fifteenth-century Spanish explorers who scheme, plot, and murder for gold. These plunderers are contrasted with the good man of adventure, Columbus. Then come the English during the Civil Wars, in whose machinations a later generation of Columbus' family is caught. Next one sees the earliest American settlers and the Indians by whom a subsequent branch of the family is massacred, followed by English types of the late eighteenth century such as conniving lawyers, greedy relatives, and lecherous males, who nearly cause the ruin of the modern Reuben and Rachel. Finally come the Americans of the New Republic who, while imperfect, inhabit a fresh world where the protagonists settle. In this book, too, Mrs. Rowson intends to stress the actual over the imaginary. *Reuben and Rachel*, claims the author, in striving to interest the young in history, will not fill their heads with the "wonderful and indeed impossible," but will point out the "real wonders and beauties of nature" (p. v).

In *Sarah, or the Exemplary Wife* (1813),[14] Mrs. Rowson tackles the subject of marriage. She states her didactic purpose in the preface:

> Beware, ye lovely maidens who are now fluttering on the wing of youth and pleasure, how you select a partner for life. Purity of morals and manners in a husband, is absolutely necessary to the happiness of a delicate and virtuous woman. When once the choice is made and fixed beyond revocation, remember patience, forbearance, and in many cases perfect silence, is the only way to secure domestic peace. What, in all marriages? asks some young friend. Why, in truth, there is seldom any so perfectly felicitous, but that instances may occur where patience, forbearance, and silence, may be practised with good effect.
>
> (p. iv)

Her story remains concentrated on this theme, the problems that her protagonist Sarah encounters upon undertaking a loveless marriage of convenience, and the endurance and forbearance required of her. Sarah is respectful of her marriage vow; in addition to the absence of divorce and the force of social pressures maintaining the institution of marriage, this vow prohibits Sarah's breaking free. "Beware, ye lovely maidens"; proceed slowly and do not idealize marriage.

The premise that knowledge of the actual is more valuable than ascent into imaginary realms underlies *Sarah*. Here, too, Mrs. Rowson chooses faithfulness to life in order to teach more effectively. In the preface, she eschews the "happy ending." She will give Sarah "her reward in a better world" in order to "avoid every unnatural appearance" (p. i). Mrs. Rowson writes, "Characters of superlative excellence, tried in the furnace of affliction, and at length crowned by wealth, honor, love, friendship, every sublunary good, are to be found abundantly in every novel, but alas! where shall we find them in real life?" (pp. i-ii). She argues that such stories are positively harmful to the young reader because they fill her mind with the visions of rewards instead of encouraging her to adopt the Christian virtues. Further, if the promised rewards are not forthcoming, the reader is liable to consider the "character portrayed to be as chimerical as the happiness represented as its reward" (p. ii).

Mrs. Rowson adds that she believes pain no less than goodness makes up reality, and thus she will be more faithful to life if she portrays both. Further, Mrs. Rowson claims that many of the scenes in *Sarah* are "drawn from real life" (p. iii). She discusses the fate of Mr. Darnley, the boorish husband, as a real person, but here she is beyond *Charlotte* and the tale of truth, and she blurs the link to actuality by insisting that the events occurred "in another hemisphere, and the characters no longer exist" (p. iii). Mrs. Rowson states that her protagonist will not be a "faultless monster," and by her choice of words—the phrase is probably borrowed from the prefatory poem in *Evelina*—she aligns herself with Fanny Burney and other writers who paved the way for the realism of Jane Austen.

Charlotte's Daughter, or the Three Orphans (1828)[15] is not accompanied by a preface, but the novel follows in the pattern set by the earlier fiction. It is a cautionary tale for young women in which the fates of three young orphans, Aura Melville, Lady Mary Lumly, and Lucy Blakeney, the wards of kindly Reverend Matthews, are traced as the girls reach marriageable age. Two of the girls, Aura and Lucy, follow the advice of their guardian and are cautious about entering relationships with young men. Lady Mary rushes into life, goes off with her fiancé without the permission of her guardian, a commitment to marriage, or a property settlement, and is seduced and abandoned. Aura makes a conventional marriage, while Lucy, the protagonist, is saved from the disaster of marrying her own half-brother only by her prudence and her obedience to Reverend Matthews.

In Mrs. Rowson's later years of writing, school activities over-shadowed her devotion to fiction. Her conversion to schoolmistress at the age of thirty-five, however, was perfectly consistent with her earlier literary career. Mrs. Rowson was always concerned with the formal education of young women; the subject is a ubiquitous theme in the fiction. Women characters are universally the victims of fashionable, shallow schools where "accomplishments" are stressed over understanding, morals, and solid intellectual fare. If they rise above their education, it is only by force of character and reli-gious training. Mary Newton, in *The Test of Honour*, is an examplary young woman even though her ignorant guardian, Mrs. Fentum, packs her off to boarding school, where she "learnt to jab-ber bad French, and sing worse Italian" and where

> the more essential branches of needlework were totally ne-glected, that she might learn embroidery, clothwork, and fifty other things, equally as useless; drawing, or rather scrawling, was not forgot; and to dance with ease and elegance, was a thing of the greatest consequence.
>
> (I, 20)

Rebecca, in *The Fille de Chambre*, is grounded in the "tenets of the protestant religion," preparation that allows her to enjoy drawing and other fine arts as "pastime" (p. 20). Almost every fictional work has its satirical passage on the typical female education; *Mentoria* contains a lengthy treatise appended to the letters entitled "Female Education" in which Mrs. Rowson elaborates many of her ideas.

But even more important than this pattern, which is a familiar one in fiction and treatises on women, is the strong similarity of the prefaces and goals of her pedagogical works to those of the fiction. Her audience continues, of course, to be the female young. While the lessons include much objective material, they significantly ex-tend the religious, moral, and psychological teachings of the fiction. Mrs. Rowson now finds models of good and bad for her pupils in historical characters and situations rather than in fictional ones. Whereas formerly she had presented "authentic" fiction, she now uses real histories and "geographical" studies to teach her lessons in new but familiar ways.

An Abridgment of Universal Geography (1805)[16] consists, says the preface, of exercises Mrs. Rowson had used successfully in her school. It is made up of a main text with two substantial appended sections, "Geographical Exercise" and "Historical Exercise," which recapitulate many of the original lessons. Mrs. Rowson's prefatory defense of her moral purpose and her allegiance to truth recalls those of the novels:

> In my accounts and descriptions, I have endeavoured to be accurate, and throughout the whole, I have been careful that not a syllable should drop from my pen, that might militate against the morality, religion, or good government of any society whatever. I am of opinion that instructors of every kind, particularly those who give their labours publicity, are strictly accountable to the highest of all tribunals, for the sentiments they inculcate; that it is their duty, as far as in them lies, to impress upon the minds of youth a love of order and a reverence for religion. If therefore the minds of the rising generation are not improved by my exertions, I have been studious that their imaginations should not be misled, or their judgements perverted, by the dissemination of absurd opinions, or corrupt and pernicious principles.
>
> (p. iv)

The preface also states that the author will blend "moral reflections" with her descriptions of various countries. The exercises that follow this statement cover the globe, moving from country to country and through all the United States. Mrs. Rowson explains topology, resources, climate, and industry; she comments upon the government, the religion, the character of the people, and the social habits of the various regions—including the treatment of women.

Mrs. Rowson begins her studies with Europe because "EUROPE though the least extensive quarter of the globe, is in many respects that which most deserves our first attention. There the human mind has made the greatest progress towards improvement, and there the arts whether of utility or ornament, the sciences both civil and military, have been carried to the greatest perfection" (p. 15). She also stresses the spread of Christianity in Europe. The continent of Asia is praised for its huge size and resources; and also, "as being the seat of the creation of the world" where "our all wise Creator planted the garden of Eden, and placed in it our first parents, from whom sprang the whole race of mankind" (p. 101).

In *Abridgment*, Mrs. Rowson provides abundant facts about the globe, and at the same time teaches familiar lessons. A flattering portrait of New England by a geographer, which stresses the region's hospitableness, learning, and humaneness, evokes an aside to the pupils: "This is a charming portrait; may the fair daughters of Columbia ever study to copy it and preserve the likeness" (p. 197). Again, in studying the behavior of a people, Mrs. Rowson remarks, "Were vice but once unfashionable, it would soon be ashamed to shew its head" (p. 117).

Mrs. Rowson's next effort was *A Spelling Dictionary* (1805).[17] Her preface shows that she thought seriously about teaching methods. And on her title page she says,

> When we have taught children to read, however accurately they may pronounce, however attentive they may be to the punctuation, we have done nothing towards the information of their minds, unless we teach them to associate ideas; and this can never be done if they do not understand the exact meaning of every word.

In her preface, Mrs. Rowson contends that her book is offered to advance the storing of "the young mind with ideas." She stresses "meaning" and "association" of ideas: "Children study with more cheerfulness when the lesson is short and determined," and if they are taught to associate ideas can continue their reading throughout life, for reading will be pleasurable and amusing. "It is my fixed opinion," Mrs. Rowson continues, "that it is better to give the young pupil one rational idea, than fatigue them by obliging them to commit to memory a thousand mere words." The short dictionary is made up of a small number of words and brief definitions; the part of speech is abbreviated, and the etymology omitted. Many of the terms are words likely to be unfamiliar to children and encountered in the other Rowson texts; for example, "mandarin," used in her explanation of Chinese culture, is not likely to be an everyday term for New England children. There are quite a few religious terms, and appended is "A Concise account of the Heathen Deities and other Fabulous Persons with the Heroes and Heroines of Antiquity," which would aid young readers with classical and mythological references.

A Present for Young Ladies (1811)[18] is a collection of "poems, dialogues, and addresses" recited over a number of years at the annual Rowson Academy exhibitions—occasions when the handiwork and lessons of Mrs. Rowson's girls were displayed to parents and interested local citizens. In her "Advertisement by the Author," Mrs. Rowson offers these sketches—which include some of her most insistently didactic and assertive statements—as "bagatelles for the amusement of very young minds." This less than ingenuous prefatory statement ushers in the miscellany cited above, as well as three sections entitled "Outline of Universal History," "Sketches of Female Biography," and "Rise and Progress of Navigation."

The poems and dialogues in *A Present* are replete with preachments to young women, with insistence upon the factuality of the subject matter. The "Second Dialogue for Three Young Ladies," written in verse, includes a debate on the dangers and virtues of reading fiction; the wisest of three young virgins notes that the "true history of the world" does not contain romantic Cinderella stories (p. 39). "Outline of Universal History" is introduced with the same rationale as that of the novels; history is a "school of morality" that contains "useful Lessons" (p. 53). History contains examples of persons worthy of imitation as well as cautionary figures. In regard to the former, Mrs. Rowson asks "pardon" if she "brings forward those of my own sex"; there follows an account of the career of Sappho—a favorite figure from secular history—as well as other accomplished women. Among various men who are lauded is Demosthenes, "worthy of imitation" for his "persevering industry in correcting the defects of nature . . ." (p. 67). "Sketches of Female Biography" is made up of portraits of women in history who possess traits worth copying. In her school-oriented works Mrs. Rowson begins to emphasize the Bible. Scripture is "the most authentic history and should precede the study of all others. . . . It is the history of God himself . . ." ("Outline," *A Present*, p. 55).

Youth's First Step in Geography (1818),[19] which followed *A Present*, is a similar blend of fact, moral judgment, and religious indoctrination. Mrs. Rowson wrote no preface for it, but only a short note "To Instructors," advising them on its best use. The book is a geography for beginners and simplifies much of the material presented in *An Abridgment*. Written in the form of questions and answers, *Youth's First Step* provides scientific detail such as:

> It [the earth] has two motions, one round the sun, which it performs in a year; this is called its annual revolution; and another on its own axis, which it performs in 24 hours; this is called its diurnal motion. The annual motion occasions the change of seasons; the diurnal, day and night.
>
> (p. 2)

The book also contains "geographical" descriptions like the following:

> Mecca . . . is said to have been the birthplace of the impostor Mahomet.
>
> (p. 144)

and

> The northwestern parts of Asia are remarkable for having been the scene of the Creation, and that part called Palestine, for the birth, miracles, sufferings, and death of Jesus of Nazareth, the Saviour of the World.
>
> (p. 144)

Of special interest to Mrs. Rowson's female audience is her description in *Youth's First Step* of a unique ceremony in France. Mrs. Rowson points out that Oise, in Beauvais, is

> remarkable for having been defended by the women, under the conduct of Joanne Hatchette, in 1463, when it was besieged by the duke of Burgundy. They obliged the duke to raise the seige; and in memory of their exploits, the women always walk first in the procession on the 10th of July, the anniversary of their deliverance.
>
> (p. 101)

Youth's First Step contains somewhat less editorializing than *Abridgment*, although many recurring heroes and villains are introduced: Columbus and Luther are praised; Napoleon is condemned. The book contains a great deal of objective information, which, once again, lends an air of authenticity to Mrs. Rowson's ideas. She advises instructors to have the pupils use the material two times a week with the maps before them, and then "according to their several capacities," memorize it. At the end of a section on France, Mrs. Rowson writes: "Note. The pupils during the study of this exercise, should be accustomed, when any historical circumstance is mentioned, to turn to the part of history where they may have a full account of it. Thus by being interested in the incident, the place where it occurred will become impressed upon the memory, and they will insensibly form a habit of associating ideas" (p. 101). Mrs. Rowson stresses the use of maps and the globe, and tries to make the lessons concrete for the pupils by encouraging them to visualize various facts and relationships. She asks frequent questions that force the student to enter the movement from place to place;

for example, if you travel north from Baltimore, what state will you be in?

In 1822, Mrs. Rowson brought out the two last efforts published in her lifetime, *Exercises in History*[20] and *Biblical Dialogues.*[21] The first, like *Youth's First Step*, is in the form of questions and answers, and traces the history of the world from biblical times to the founding of the American republic. In the preface, Mrs. Rowson looks back upon twenty-five years "devoted to the cultivation of the minds of the youth of my dear adopted country, America; in particular the young females of Boston and its vicinity" (p. iii). She restates her desire to teach only "religion, virtue and morality" (p. iii). The opening exercise defines history as "A narration of well authenticated facts and events, related with clearness and perspicuity" (p. 5); of course, to Mrs. Rowson, the Bible *is* fact, and she begins with the events depicted in the Scriptures. She then moves on to the secular histories of Greece, Rome, England, Modern Europe, and Asia—well-worn stops by now—and ends once again with the American republic. *Exercises*, like the earlier texts, reiterates Mrs. Rowson's reliance upon Christianity as the hope of the world, and provides value judgments about various civilizations and historical personalities.

Women are not forgotten. Although many of the great personages described in *Exercises* are men, the presence of an outstanding female in a particular period is pointed out with special force by means of questions put directly. In presenting the history of the Roman Empire, Mrs. Rowson writes,

> Q. What illustrious female lived about A.D. 1081?
> A. Anna Commina, daughter to the emperor Alexius Commenus, whose elegant writings gave celebrity to her father's reign. About this time the Turks invaded the eastern empire, and they finally conquered Asia minor, A.D. 1084.
>
> (p. 56)

and in the section on English history,

> Q. Was there not a celebrated female warrior about this time? [when the Druids were routed].
> A. Boadicea, queen of the Iceni, having been highly injured by the Roman procurator, headed an army of 100,000 men, took and burnt London; but being at length defeated, killed herself, A.D. 61.
>
> (p. 59)

Biblical Dialogues, Mrs. Rowson's most ambitious pedagogical work, is an attempt, in the form of dramatic conversations between a father and his family, to resolve the questions that children might ask about the biblical stories. In the preface, Mrs. Rowson writes of her continued involvement with the young female audience,

> When I became engaged in the momentous business of instructing females of the rising generation, whose future conduct as wives and mothers was to stamp the moral and religious character, and ensure in a great measure the virtue and consequent happiness of another age, I could not but feel the great responsibility of the undertaking. My whole soul was engaged in my duties, my pupils became to me as my children, and few things were of consequence to me that did not contribute to their improvement, their present and eternal happiness.
>
> (p. iv)

By now, Mrs. Rowson is teaching The Truth, not just tales of truth that exemplify religious teaching. She has two sets of characters, those of the Bible and the members of the Alworth family, an exemplary group of evening Scripture readers. The lives of the biblical characters illustrate the central messages of the fiction—that humanity is dependent upon God, that reward and punishment are not always forthcoming in the present world (II, 360).

As to method in *Biblical Dialogues*, vice and folly can be painted best in their natural colors, and Mrs. Rowson shows her continuing respect for the natural over the exaggerated, which she had first stated in *A Trip to Parnassus* and adhered to in the fiction, by presenting the biblical *dramatis personae* as believable human beings with everyday motivations rather than as extremes of vice and virtue. The father and children engage in lengthy discussions of the morality and psychology of such characters as Abraham, Esther, and Judith. They often try to reduce the situations in Scripture to the everyday proportions of their own lives by finding analogies between biblical episodes and the doings of the children in the neighborhood.

Still concerned with authenticity, Mrs. Rowson has the father in *Biblical Dialogues*, Mr. Alworth, explain to his children that he does not expect them to accept the sometimes bizarre occurrences in the Christian story "upon trust," and reminds his children that "We have before us authentic records of our Saviour's life and actions" (II, 184). There is an exchange in which the trustworthiness of the Bible is debated, a problem raised by the many translations and transcriptions the books have undergone. Mrs. Rowson cites the sources of biblical authenticity, just as in *Charlotte* she cited the source of her story.

There is a parallel relationship between Mrs. Rowson's stated goals in literature and the form given her work, between the design of Mrs. Rowson's novels and that of her pedagogical efforts. Thus, while her books may not be models of style (although they were once considered so in certain quarters), they exhibit coherent purpose and the employment of a process of selection based on principles other than literary fashion.

These qualities as well as Mrs. Rowson's main didactic purpose—to offer a complete education to the young female—are also evident in her dramatic efforts insofar as these are known, and in her poetry and songs—a preponderance of which contains religious and moral advice, often directed to young women.

Of course, didacticism was a strong element in most late-eighteenth- and early-nineteenth-century fiction, and women have been the traditional buyers of fiction, so that the dedication of novels as instruction to the female reading public was not a novelty. Of the British writers of fiction to whom Mrs. Rowson paid tribute, Edgworth, Burney, and More ("Dialogue for Three Young Ladies," *A Present for Young Ladies*, p. 45), Hannah More compares most closely with Mrs. Rowson in didactic purpose, but as will be seen later, she was more cautious in her concept of proper female activity. Although anthologists now are making conscientious efforts to recover the writings of early American women who taught the female to aspire to accomplishments beyond the domestic, they produce few before Mrs. Rowson.[22] Anne Bradstreet in the seventeenth century,[23] and Judith Sargent Murray,[24] a contemporary of Mrs. Rowson's, made strong public statements; several others in Mrs. Rowson's period took some interest in the education of women, but none could match Mrs. Rowson in volume of work, and singleness of purpose.

3

Inferior to None

The union of masculine virtues, feminine softness, and christian meek-ness, form the most illustrious assemblage. . . . The name of christian unites in it all that is lovely and amiable in nature. . . .

(A Present for Young Ladies, 1811)

Under the banner of Christianity and with a battalion of literary forms at her command, Mrs. Rowson met the major issues concerning women, and claimed freedom for her sex. She did not deal with specific political rights; Mrs. Rowson died when Elizabeth Cady Stanton was nine years old—twenty-four years before the Women's Rights Convention held by Mrs. Stanton and Susan B. Anthony at Seneca Falls, New York, in 1848. But at a time when the prevailing ideal for women in both Britain and America was that of "a gentle but capable mistress in a sheltered home,"[1] Mrs. Rowson attacked the myths and stereotypes that surrounded women and taught her reader that she could be the equal of the male in most of the important spheres of life, and that she should see herself as a person capable of great achievement. Mrs. Rowson's attempt to work through the problems that such a belief entails, and her recommendations for social change, are her major themes.

A glance at the situation of women in the period in which Mrs. Rowson worked places her feminist ideas in perspective. Many English women novelists had complained of the narrowness of their world and the masculine attempt to confine them to the domestic scene.[2] In America, as well as England, women were much discussed: their fundamental nature, their proper social rôle, and their rights.

The literature that dealt explicitly with women was pretty much the same in England and America during Mrs. Rowson's writing years. In her study *Women in Eighteenth-Century America*, Mary Benson divides the writers into those who denied women equality with men and saw them as objects to please the male (the Rousseau-Chesterfield point of view); those who might grant women equality with men, but still based their worth on their influence upon husbands and children (Hannah More and Mrs. Chapone); and, in a category by herself, Mary Wollstonecraft, who argued that women were responsible to themselves and that virtue was worth attaining for a woman's *own* self-respect. Writers on the subject crossed these divisions, of course; some argued that women were inferior, but granted them a "higher" destiny than that of pleasing the male. Some even argued that women were morally superior to men, but this approach still led to defining their worth according to their uplifting effect on men. These elementary areas of discussion had been established by European writers, and the various writers were available to American readers.

Mary Wollstonecraft, while not at first attacked in America, lost favor due to fear of radicalism and her connection with the ideas and thinkers of the French Revolution (Benson, p. 86). On the other hand, the works of Hannah More were very popular; and More, notes William Wasserstrom, "urged women to respect themselves and women's work, avoid encroaching upon masculine interests or entering the 'theatre of masculine activities.' "[3]

Education for women was generally approved of in America; the distinguishing feature of the genuine advocate for women is often a matter of tone. The clergy favored female education, but as Mary Benson points out, their concern had the effect of forestalling the influence of Mary Wollstonecraft and other advanced thinkers (Benson, p. 145). Further, some of the most enthusiastic supporters of feminine intellectual development phrase their ideas in patronizing language. James Neal, an educator himself, wrote in defense of scientific, rigorous education for women, yet apparently regarded it as a form of beautification. In his *Essay on the Education and Genius of the Female Sex* (1795), in which he praises the Ladies' Academy of Philadelphia, and even approves Mary Wollstonecraft, he advises the pupils to "adorn and beautify your minds."[4] Neal uses the words "ornament" and "ornamental" over and over until his original premises appear in doubt. The commencement address delivered by a pupil at the academy (such pieces were generally written by teachers) also belies to some degree Neal's enthusiasm for the female mind. The young lady attempts to refute certain myths about feminine temperament, then goes on to say in support of separate roles and education for men and women,

> To undergo the fatigues and toils of war, to tread the thorny path of politics, and to move in the more active scenes of life, belongs to men.

"Nothing," says Milton, "is lovelier in a woman, than to study household good."

(Neal, p. 18)

For all the talk, women were the "second sex." Whether the ideas of women were "high or low," says Mary Benson, the vision of the woman's proper rôle was that of "a gentle but capable mistress in a sheltered home." In the periodicals, for example,

> Women . . . save for some unconvincing fiction, were not idealized figures on pedestals, but more ordinary creatures whose moderate education gave them a taste for the milder forms of literature but did not lead them to deep reasoning or serious study. They formed a part, and a most important one, of the community in their relation to men's pleasures and in their specialized duties as mistresses of families. Their character was a subject of interest and study rather in social than in intellectual aspects although interest in the latter was increasing. Despite these signs of change women remained, for most of the men who wrote popular essays and sketches, objects to be smiled at, scolded, loved, perhaps praised, but rarely to be treated as men's equals.

(Benson, p. 222)

Frank L. Mott, in his *History of American Magazines*, examines the periodicals' interest in the rôle and education of women. Notes of counsel and advice were ubiquitous; several periodicals, among them the *American Magazine* and *Massachusetts Magazine*, were designed for, and explicitly appealed to feminine readers.[5] Mott points out one instance of a discussion of the equality of the sexes, but most of the excerpts he provides from the periodicals of the day involve the education of women. These consist of suggestions for curricula and warnings that women must not drink too deeply of learning. Noah Webster and Benjamin Rush agree on teaching females English, Arithmetic, and Geography, and in forbidding them novels (p. 64).

The "learned woman" faces much opposition, and the magazines increase the prejudice against her. Mott quotes Webster's *American Magazine* (1788) as advising women to "be mild, social and sentimental" and to avoid the "profound researches of study" (p. 64). The *Ladies Magazine* (1792) says of women writers that "We admire them more as authors than esteem them as women" (Mott, p. 66), while the *American Moral and Sentimental Magazine* (1797) paints a completely traditional view of "Domestic Felicity" (Mott, p. 65).

Charles Brockden Brown and Judith Sargent Murray, who according to Mary Benson in Women in Eighteenth-Century America represented "radical thought" (p. 177), brought out portions of their works in periodicals. Parts I and II of Brown's Alcuin, a dialogue between a pedantic male teacher and a somewhat cynical bluestocking who discuss the issues of sexual equality, was published as a book and serialized (in altered form) in the Weekly Magazine in 1798. The final two parts, however, in which the narrator, Alcuin, describes a utopia in which the only difference between the sexes is the biological function, were not published until 1815, after Brown's death.[6] Judith Sargent Murray's The Gleaner (1798), a collection of miscellaneous writings begun in 1792 in the Massachusetts Magazine, defends independent lives for women.[7]

Brown and Murray aside, the magazines continue to express doubts about the strength of the female mind. The Portico (1816) refuses intellectual equality to women, for their minds "were never designed to soar into the higher regions of literature and science" (Mott, p. 143). The notion of women as beings of superior sensibility and capacity for civilization lives on in the Literary Magazine in 1805, and the idea that the highest female rôle is that of a companion to and an influence upon the male survives in 1816 in Portico (Mott, pp. 141, 143). Physical education joins music and dancing as possible threats to female domesticity; the American Journal of Education (1826) finds it "unfeminine" (Mott, p. 143).

Studies of early American fiction and drama also reveal few examples of liberal treatment of the female. Mrs. Benson discovers a mild note of feminism in Sally Wood's Dorval (1801)[8] while arguing that the novel is basically adverse to the ideas of Mary Wollstonecraft; she grants a few unusual female portraits to Charles Brockden Brown (pp. 194, 198), but finds almost none in early American drama. The heroines' lives, according to Benson, culminate in marriage, and there is little variety in the type of female presented.

In her study The Stereotype of the Single Woman in American Novels, Dorothy Yost Deegan finds in the early fiction mainly disgust for any feminine type but the happily married woman:

> In fact, it was in this early period that this concept of spinsterhood was translated and took deep root in American fiction. Only one novelist, Charles Brockden Brown, influenced by the radical theories of Godwin, dared to present the unmarried woman as somewhat admirable. But he too adopts the Richardsonian suicide motif, and in some of his minor characters, makes the gossiping spinster the villain.

There can be little doubt or question as to the social attitude toward single women in this early period of American fiction. Herbert Ross Brown in his recent study on the sentimental novel, observes that the "new woman" who entertained ambition outside the home was regarded as the moral horror of the time. He summarizes tersely the prevailing opinion: if happiness beyond the bonds of wedlock was criminal in a man, it was the unpardonable sin for a woman.[9]

The actual situation of the woman in the late eighteenth and early nineteenth centuries was akin to limbo. The single woman might be an outcast socially, but she was better off economically and legally than her married sister. The married woman, though accepted socially, was economically and legally a slave. If a woman married—and marriage was practically forced upon the female—she suddenly found the oppressive law of "coverture" descend upon her and herself deprived of control of her property, her earnings, her ability to engage in contracts, collect debts, or enter a business. Husband and wife had been declared by Blackstone to be a legal unit, and that unit was the husband. American law followed the British in this regard, so that until the mid-nineteenth century, when married women's property laws were passed, these restrictions of coverture (as well as others equally demeaning to the wife) prevailed here. The husband chose the place to live, and the wife had to follow. He had the right to inflict punishment upon his wife as long as he used a small stick. Torts and crimes committed in the presence of the husband were presumed to be his responsibility.[10]

At the time that Mrs. Rowson wrote, divorce was almost impossible to obtain in England. No secular court divorce was instituted in England until 1857 with the Divorce and Matrimonial Causes Act. During the late eighteenth and early nineteenth centuries, the only relief from a bad marriage was a "legislative" divorce; that is, dissolution of a marriage required an act of Parliament concerning the specific case. This process was expensive, time-consuming, and was available only to the privileged. In America after the Revolution, legislative divorce existed alongside newly emerging judicial divorce (with strict, explicit grounds) as the various states instituted new laws on the subject. The difficulty of obtaining a divorce was viewed as a protection for the female, and it may have operated as such in a society that provided so few options. Still, the difficulty of the process, reinforced by social disapproval of divorce, made it virtually impossible for a woman to break the "bonds" of matrimony.

In other areas women were equally disadvantaged. Although, as

Mary Benson notes, some women had participated in the Revolution (through economic boycotts, for example), they were left out of the Constitution. Several important women had exerted political influence with their husbands and brothers—Mercy Warren, Hannah Winthrop, and Abigail Adams are cases in point—but politics was still considered beyond the feminine sphere (Benson, p. 258). Women were not, of course, permitted to vote, to serve on juries, or to hold public office. An item in the *Monthly Magazine and American Review* illustrates the feeling of one writer about females in politics. It describes a case of a young woman who denies herself an interest in the political arena in favor of "tranquillizing" her husband. Literature is open to her, judges the writer, but not the "agitation" of politics.[11] The opinion of Thomas Jefferson was that "the tender breasts of ladies were not formed for political convulsion" (Benson, p. 246). John Adams's answer to Abigail when she suggested that the Constitution guarantee rights to women as well as to men was even less liberal.[12]

In her study *Economic Feminism in American Literature Prior to 1848*,[13] Augusta Violette confirms the fact that no really radical or profound moves were accomplished in behalf of women until the convention at Seneca Falls, New York, in 1848, although there were pro-feminist forces (the Quakers, for instance) from the beginning, and the anti-slavery movement somewhat later, working in that direction. The Fanny Wright societies[14] and writers such as Thomas Paine and John Neal, says Violette, contributed to the eventual changes.

Thelma Smith, in her article "Feminism in Philadelphia, 1790-1850,"[15] concurs in seeing little movement toward emancipation during Mrs. Rowson's period. While the leisure attained by many Philadelphia women, the interest in European ideas, and the Quaker influence encouraged change, such forces as the rise of romanticism in literature and the lack of educational opportunities kept feminism at a low ebb (p. 245).

This is the atmosphere into which Mrs. Rowson, with her emancipated ways, arrived in 1793. Mrs. Rowson was thoroughly aware of the controversies concerning women and had already begun to chip away at what she considered misconceptions about the nature of the female. She emphatically rejected the advice to be "mild, social and sentimental," and although she described the contemporary woman's rôle as inevitably one of influence upon the male, she insisted that women are capable of high intellectual development and success in "any profession whatever."

One aspect of woman's basic nature upon which Mrs. Rowson never wavered was her sex's equality with the male. She states her view clearly in "Sketches of Female Biography," a series of vignettes of famous women in history who excelled in various ways. These sketches are part of *A Present For Young Ladies* (1811), the collection of pieces in prose and poetry written by Mrs. Rowson and recited by her students at the annual exhibitions of her academy. In this work, Mrs. Rowson declares, "It would be absurd to imagine that talents or virtue were confined to sex or station" (p. 88). She believes, then, in both intellectual and moral equality of the sexes, and she supports this view in all phases of her literary work.

The matter of sex and temperament is somewhat more complex for Mrs. Rowson. She has been included among writers who perpetuated the myth of the delicate, sensitive, passive woman, and the lustful, brutal, active male; she does tend at times to present this view. She often uses phrases like "the delicacy natural to our sex." On the other hand, Mrs. Rowson devotes a good deal of energy to refuting feminine stereotypes. As noted, she resolves such problems by resorting to a religious standard. A Christian, she argues, should combine the softer female virtues and the harder masculine ones. She cannot quite bring herself to drop the male-female dichotomy, so she retains it and still asserts a non-sex-linked personality for women. The Christian female person will conform to the pattern outlined in the following passage:

> A woman who to the graces and gentleness of her own sex, adds the knowledge and fortitude of the other, exhibits the most perfect combination of human excellence; and since innumerable instances may be produced of female courage, fortitude, talent, and virtue of every description, why should not we start forward with generous ardour in the pursuit of what is praiseworthy, and substitute for the evanescent graces of beauty the durable attractions of a cultivated mind.
>
> ("Female Biography," *A Present*, pp. 84-85)

Mrs. Rowson manages to come to at least compromise terms even with the notion of sex-associated emotional patterns. As early as her second novel, *The Test of Honour* (1789), Mrs. Rowson was dealing unequivocally with the idea that women were morally special. The story attempts to show that women may possess virtue and character equal to that of men. Mary, the protagonist, is fifteen when her parents die; she is moderately well-off financially and is left with two sets of guardians. Mary has spirit and integrity, and she leaves Mrs. Fentum, one of her guardians, when she discovers that the lady intends to marry her to her son, Harry Fentum. The main action of the novel turns upon Mary's refusal of a paragon of a suitor, Frederick Stephens, because he does not have his father's blessing to propose to her. Mr. Stephens wishes Frederick to marry a wealthy young girl. He cannot believe that Mary, because she is a female, could want Frederick for other than mercenary reasons and he sees her behavior as a strategem to catch a husband. Mr. Stephens's dislike of women is general. He expostulates to his son, "I tell you Fred you know no more of women than an ideot. Why, I'll be d—d if there ever was a generous disinterested woman in the world; they are all as artful as serpents; they study every look, word, and action, and are ever laying plans to compass some favorite end" (I, 134). But Mary's actions prove her to be above art.

On receiving a letter from an uncle in Jamaica, Mary leaves the country to avoid Frederick. Frederick follows and is captured by Algerians. After several years, during which she meets many trials with courage and sense, Mary returns to England. She is approached by Mr. Stephens, who despairs of Fred's ever being returned to his home. The broken old man apologizes for having parted the lovers and brought on Fred's captivity. He is sickened by the venality of his son's acquaintances, who have tried to ingratiate themselves with him. To expiate his own guilt, and because Mary was loved by his son, he offers to adopt Mary and make her his heir. Mary refuses the offer, of course. She extends Mr. Stephens her affection only, so that the old misogynist is forced to admit that "there might be true generosity, even in a woman" (II, 160).

In a story within the story, Frederick's tale of his adventures in Algiers, a woman, Semira, saves her father and sister by marrying the chief of the Algerians, Hali, and swearing that she will embrace the Mohammedan religion. Semira fulfills her promises, but then produces a dagger, and is about to kill herself when the infidel, moved by her filial love as well as her religious and moral integrity, releases her from her vows and arranges for passage for the entire English group back to England (chapter XX, "Female Fortitude and Filial Duty Rewarded," II, 196). Twice Frederick is returned to his father through the efforts of a woman. Two unbelievers, Hali and Mr. Stephens, are converted to a new and respectful view of women.

Mrs. Rowson's heroines tend to combine the "graces and gentleness" of their own sex and the "knowledge and fortitude of the other" rather than to possess a rare, specifically feminine, religious and moral sensibility. Weak, passive vessels like Charlotte and Victoria may be in good standing "in futurity," but cause themselves and others great distress in the present. The heroines Mrs. Rowson presents as models to copy possess an active moral sense, and they face up to the tribulations involved in their choices as well as any man. Rebecca, who must support herself financially, faces poverty and ignominy when she refuses on two occasions to assist her employers in immoral intrigues. In several instances the power of Christian women to influence others is given special focus. Meriel's example is an inspiration to Rooksby and Clara to repent; but Meriel has had to struggle, as a man would, to attain a Christian frame of mind.

In *Slaves in Algiers* (1794), which is ostensibly organized around a patriotic theme—the enslavement of Americans by the Barbary Pirates—the courage and fortitude of women takes precedence. The plot is very similar to that of Frederick's narrative of his captivity in *The Test of Honour*. A group of Americans enslaved by the Dey of Algiers escape, partly through the efforts of two women. Olivia promises to marry the Dey in exchange for her fellow prisoners' lives. Olivia has resolved, of course, to kill herself after the ceremony, but is saved when a slave revolt intervenes. The slaves have been incited by Fetnah, a courageous young woman who has been given to the Dey by her father in exchange for pecuniary advancement.

Fetnah explicitly rejects the concept that women are inferior to men. She has learned to appreciate liberty in spite of being the daughter of Ben Hassan, a Jew and keeper of slaves. She says, "Woman was never form'd to be the slave of man. Nature made us equal with them, and gave us the power to render ourselves superior" (II.1.9). Fetnah also rejects the notion that the character of a woman should express itself differently from that of a man. When she, Frederick, Henry, and others who encourage the revolt are hiding in a cave and Frederick tells her to retreat to the back of the grotto while he goes off to rescue Olivia, she refuses. She intends to accompany Frederick on his mission. Fetnah asserts,

> A woman!—Why, so I am; but in the cause of love or friendship, a woman can face danger with as much spirit, and as little fear, as the bravest man amongst you.—Do you lead the way, I'll follow to the end.
>
> (III.1.47)

In response, Sebastian, a servant, who has witnessed Fetnah's performance, exults,

> Bravo! Excellent! Bravissimo!—Why, 'tis a little body; but ecod, she's a devil of a spirit.—It's a fine thing to meet with a woman that has a little fire in her composition. I never much lik'd your milk and water ladies; to be sure, they are easily manag'd—but your spirit'd ladies; require taming; they make a man look about him—dear, sweet angry creatures, here's to their health.
> (III.1.47)

Fetnah is Mrs. Rowson's version of a Shakespearean comic heroine, the girl who shows her spirited, active side. In helping the plot along, Fetnah must dress in men's clothing, thus underlining her relationship to Rosalind, Viola, et al.

In the epilogue to the play, Mrs. Rowson not only assumes equality with men, but incites her female audience to claim precedence:

> Well, Ladies tell me—how d'ye like my play?
> "The creature has some sense," methinks you say,
> "She says that we should have supreme dominion,
> "And in good truth, we're all of her opinion.
> "Women were born for universal sway,
> "Men to adore, be silent, and obey."

In character and virtue, Mrs. Rowson asserted, women could rival men, and their morality should be judged by similar standards. As to intellect, men may appear superior to women, but Mrs. Rowson viewed this situation as a function of society, not nature. She made conventional apologies for the artistic quality of her own intellectual efforts in several prefaces, but usually accompanied these expressions with a plea for better education for the female. In the preface to *Mentoria*, Mrs. Rowson writes,

> a-well-a-day for me, I must also be judged by some sage male critic, who, "with spectacle on nose, and pouch by's side," with lengthened visage and contemptuous smile, sits down to review the literary productions of a woman. He turns over a few pages, and then
>
> > Catching the Author at some that or therefore,
> > At once condemns her without why or wherefore.

Then alas! What may not be my fate? whose education, as a female, was necessarily circumscribed, whose little knowledge has been simply gleaned from pure nature, and who, on a subject of such importance, write as I feel with enthusiasm.

(p. iii)

In the preface to *Slaves in Algiers*, Mrs. Rowson writes of the disadvantages of "a confined education" and heads off the male critics by adding that she does not expect to be found equal to masculine playwrights who have "from their sex or situation in life" had the advantage of a classical education (p. ii).

The works themselves exhibit men and women of about equal mental ability. The heroines of the fiction are great readers and writers. The examples of the original poetry written by Victoria, Meriel, Rebecca, Charlotte, and Sarah do not impress the reader with the quality of the intellects that produced them; still these efforts are introduced to create minds for the protagonists as well as to provide an elegant artistic effect. Several women in the fiction are attracted to literature and learning; Rebecca, Sarah, and Lucy are well enough educated to teach. Several women writers and artists appear in *The Inquisitor*.

In the nonfiction, Mrs. Rowson makes a strong claim for the intellectual ability of women. "Female Biography" (*A Present*) is replete with examples of women who developed their minds to a high level. Among many others, Mrs. Rowson cites Hypatia, a fourth-century Egyptian who was educated by her father and succeeded him as head of his school after he died (pp. 85-86), Lucretia Cornaro, a Venetian who attained a doctor's degree in the seventeenth century and excelled in mathematics (p. 86), and Mrs. Macaulay, the English historian, whose work was "inferior to none" (p. 88).

These stories are echoed in the pages of the *Boston Weekly Magazine*. The types of women celebrated in the biographical department of the paper parallel those in "Female Biography" and the texts, and thus suggest the hand of Mrs. Rowson. The issue of 17 November 1804 (vol. 3) includes a sketch of the life of Donna Maria Agnesi, a prodigy and professor of mathematics and philosophy in Bologna. The writer refutes the idea that great talents appear only in men. On 29 December 1804, four columns are devoted to a Miss Linwood, an artist in needlework whose copies in tapestry of famous paintings had been praised by Sir Joshua Reynolds as well as the president of the Royal Academy. Volume 3, 26 January 1805, brings a sketch of the religious insight of Catherine Paar, wife of Henry VIII.

There are praises for Mrs. Johnson, the "Stella" of Swift (13 April 1805, vol. 3), and for Mrs. Chapone, the famed writer on women (25 May 1805). The biographical subject for 28 September 1805 (vol. 3) is Ann Eliza Bleecker, the American writer known as a poet and author of the 1797 novel *The History of Maria Kittle*.

In her poetry, Mrs. Rowson underlines her belief in the natural intellectual equality of the sexes. Her poem "The Birth of Genius," a long and ambitious dramatic piece that appears in *Miscellaneous Poems* (1804), personifies "Genius" as a male, but the young fellow is told by Apollo,

> A few words beside! And, my son ever mind them,
> Love talent and merit, wherever you find them.
> To no sex, to no station, no climate confin'd,
> They ever will reign uncontroll'd in the mind.
>
> (p. 25)

Queen Elizabeth, a favorite figure with Mrs. Rowson, as she was with Anne Bradstreet, appears in a manuscript poem "Commemorative of the Genius of Shakespeare." Mrs. Rowson celebrates the Elizabethan age as the greatest for literature and art. She writes of the Queen,

> Elizabeth, who in retirement bred,
> Had drank of Wisdom at the fountain head,
> Whose high taught mind, discriminating eye,
> Knew native worth and genius to discry;
> Who called the tuneful Nine around her throne,
> And made the muse of Shakespeare, all her own.
> Drew all his talents forth her reign to adorn,
> Then gave his works to ages yet unborn.[16]

If men and women are born with an equal capacity for moral and intellectual growth, are there any intrinsic differences besides gender? As has been stated, Mrs. Rowson tended to answer this question ambiguously. In her analysis of Catherine II in *An Abridgment of Universal Geography*, she ascribes the queen's penchant for murder (Mrs. Rowson says she ordered the death of the emperor John) to Catherine's "masculine understanding, ambitious, haughty, and revengeful" (p. 287).

In poems like "To Anna," which appears in both *Victoria* and *Mentoria*, women are called "Weak womankind" and "the helpless fair." The "tyrant" man is compared to a hawk and woman to a small bird liable to be devoured:

> Be circumspect, be cautious then,
> Beware of all, but *most* of *men*.
> For they will study to betray,
> And make our helpless sex, their prey,
> From virtue's bright, refulgent, throne,
> With baleful hand, will drag you down.
> Dishonor first, then leave to mourn
> Those blessings, which can ne'er return.
> As the young bird, who from the nest,
> Its mother's fost'ring wings and breast.
> Timidly ventures through the air,
> Far from the tender parents' care,
> If chance some hawk beholds it fly,
> He views it with an eager eye,
> Pursues, & clench'd within his power
> It falls poor bird to rise no more.[17]

This picture of the sexes is echoed in other passages in Mrs. Rowson's work. In *The Test of Honour*, she speaks of woman's character as being soft and tractable, for "nature formed them friendly, affectionate, noble, and unsuspicious" (p. 61). Her poem "Maria, A Fiction" in *Miscellaneous Poems*, a dramatic piece about a seduction, reflects the same point of view; the woman is passive, while the man is "the cruel spoiler." In a more playful vein, in the song "He is Not Worth the Trouble," Mrs. Rowson writes,

> Ye Maidens then beware of men,
> They're all alike believe me,
> They all proceed on Damon's plan
> And flatter to deceive ye.
> Then let not love your senses blind,
> And be not made their bubble,
> For should you meet one to your mind,
> And marry! ten to one you'll find,
> He is not worth the trouble.[18]

Such warnings in Mrs. Rowson's work tend to suggest that she conceived women—if treated properly—as naturally gentle, tractable, and affectionate, and men—if unchecked by religion and morality—as exploitative, destructive, and irresponsible. Mrs. Rowson often quotes Milton's line about women as "nature's last, best gift"; yet in the fallen world she writes of, she must grant the sexes an equal propensity for vice and virtue. In general, she does. In *The Inquisitor* she presents us with "Lassonia":

> It is such women as Lassonia, who cast an odium on the whole sex; and such women are not only objects of contempt, but detestation. I am not of [the] opinion that women would never degenerate into vice, were they not at first seduced by man; certain I am . . . that there are many women, who are abandoned to all manner of wickedness, entirely through the depravity of their inclinations.—Oh! how my soul rises with indignation, to see the fairest works of the Creator's hand so far forget their native dignity, as to glory in actions which debase them beneath the lowest reptile that crawls upon the earth!
> (III, 232)

In the novels, both sexes can both be exploitative and destructive. Victoria is not a victim simply of "male scheming." A haughty, ambitious female, Lady Maskwell, who has married an aged earl for money, captures Victoria's Harry. This same woman nearly allows her mother and sisters to starve in order to devote herself to her social schemes. There is no implication that Lady Maskwell's nature is a result of a "masculine understanding." Mademoiselle La Rue in *Charlotte*, even more the villain than Montraville, is a prime mover in Charlotte's seduction—she is a go-between for Montraville and urges fifteen-year-old Charlotte to see the young man against her school's and her parents' wishes. Mrs. Bellamy in *Sarah*, more persuasively than the male, urges Sarah to lower her moral standards for financial security. The analogy of the hawk and the small bird is not meant to be confined only to sexual nature, either. Here too, the woman can be as predatory as the male. Lady Ossiter of *The Fille de Chambre* matches her husband's affairs with her own, and Clara of *Trials of the Human Heart* seduces poor Rooksby, the heroine's young man, in his own home.

Mrs. Rowson often attributes a specifically feminine twist to the vicious behavior she satirizes. In *The Inquisitor*, she presents an episode about a young girl whose literary aspirations are squelched by an older woman. The woman, Mrs. Greenham, encourages Ellen, the aspiring writer, to recite some of her poems in public so that she will be ridiculed. First hearing of Mrs. Greenham's encouragement, the narrator muses, "It is rather surprising . . . that one woman should be so liberal in the praises of another" (II, 143). When Ellen's humiliation proves his cynicism accurate, the Inquisitor declares,

> Friendship is a word universally used, but little understood; there are a number of people who stile themselves friends, who never knew that it was to have an anxious thought for the person for whom they pretend this violent friendship, in the female world in particular. I make no doubt but there are numbers of women who, should they be informed whilst at cards, of the greatest misfortune having befallen one of their most intimate friends, would cry, Poor thing, I am vastly sorry—I had a great regard for her—and then inquire what is trumps? or how gows [sic] the game?
>
> (II, 148)

When out of patience with some supposedly female foible, Mrs. Rowson will give the advantage to men. In *Sarah*, Ann, with whom Sarah exchanges letters, writes to Elenor, "It is a humiliating circumstance to confess, that beauty, wit and talents, are by no means possessions to secure a friend in our own sex. Why is this? Why do women suffer that degrading quality envy, to predominate in their bosoms? Men naturally esteem those who are most worthy esteem . . ." (p. 35).

For the most part, Mrs. Rowson works from the theory that human temperament, guided properly, can be the same in both sexes. The virtuous male, like the virtuous female, would aspire to a similar goal, a combination of the "knowledge and fortitude" of his own sex and the "gentleness" of the other. As a Christian he would make the best of the two sides of his nature.

The narrator designated in the title of *The Inquisitor* is a male, the typical man of feeling. He is interested in others, helpful, and compassionate. Like Mackenzie's man of feeling, his compassion extends to prostitutes and persons of other races, as well as to animals and old soldiers. The heroes of the fiction are men of action, but they all possess understanding and some degree of sensitivity. Columbus appears in *Reuben and Rachel* as both a man of feeling and an intrepid adventurer. The masculine types who dominate Mrs. Rowson's poetry are such men as Washington and Adams.[19] These figures are praised for their deeds as well as their intellects. In her 1799 tribute to John Adams, in *Miscellaneous Poems*, Mrs.

Rowson puts Adams above the mythical Alcides, for he "took rigid honour for his guide," and "Firm to her cause,/ Enforc'd the laws,/ That made his country free" (p. 39). Washington is praised as a soldier but is certainly not cast in the Miles Gloriosus mold. In her "Eulogy," also in Miscellaneous Poems, Mrs. Rowson has "wisdom" say,

> "Yet martial ardour go with wisdom hand in hand.
> There was a man who has this wonder done;
> A man! my much lamented darling son!
> Columbia's guardian genius—WASHINGTON!"
>
> (p. 48)

In her "Commemorative" on Shakespeare, the poet is praised for his moral influence as well as for his artistic style. The best types of each sex use the full range of their potentialities. In spite of her slips in splitting temperamental characteristics into feminine and masculine, Mrs. Rowson finds the sexes capable of the same emotional responses.

To underline her view, Mrs. Rowson questions the stereotypes of female temperament. In the fictional works, she frequently pauses to question whether men or women are the worse gossips or the more capable of true friendship, and so on. In Reuben and Rachel, she comments,

> Curiosity, when once awakened, is hard to be repelled, at least in women, say the opposite sex. Whether we are more troubled with the impulse than our fathers, brothers, or husbands, I will not now dispute; it is a certainty Dinah stopped to listen to a conversation which had powerfully excited her's.
>
> (II, 281)

Of course, the novels provide one long argument that the female is not the weaker sex. Mrs. Rowson's heroines confront physical as well as moral dangers. Mary survives being marooned on a desert island (a female may share Robinson Crusoe's adventures), Rebecca endures near starvation on the voyage to America, and helps to bury a dead Revolutionary soldier, Meriel is shipwrecked, and Sarah courageously faces a storm at sea. In Reuben and Rachel, Rachel Dudley (aunt of the modern day Reuben and Rachel), and her Indian sister-in-law, Oberea, accompany their men into war (I, 161). Even demure little Lucy Temple, Charlotte's mother, shows her grit; she helps support her father by taking on needlework and painting (*Charlotte*, p. 34). Isabelle, granddaughter of Christopher Columbus, closes the gap between conformity to standards of feminine delicacy (which Mrs. Rowson could not quite relinquish) and the qualities needed to endure and survive in real life. In *Reuben and Rachel*, she says to Columbia, her daughter, when they face life alone,

> I have a trifle, my child . . . and we must summon all our fortitude to brave even hardship and danger without shrinking. We are women it is true, and ought not to forget the delicacy of our sex; but real delicacy consists in purity of thought, and chastity of words and actions; not in shuddering at an accidental blast of wind, or increasing the unavoidable evils of life by affected weakness and timidity. How many of our sex are obliged by hard and daily labour, to procure for themselves and children the bare means of existence!"
>
> (I, 113)

In "Female Biography" (*A Present*), Mrs. Rowson questions the idea that women are weak by nature:

> They [women] are generally called the weaker sex, and perhaps through constitution, habit, and education in some degre [sic] they are so; but there have been numberless instances of women who have proved themselves adequate to every trial, that proves their attachment to their husbands, children, parents or country.
>
> (p. 90)

She follows this statement with examples from history of female fortitude: there is Chelonis, daughter of a king of Sparta, who accompanies her husband "into perpetual exile" (p. 91), and Eponina, a Roman woman who lives in a subterranean vault for nine years to help her husband evade his enemies, and when he is finally caught, demands to be executed with him (pp. 92-93). In *Exercises in History* and *Biblical Dialogues*, Mrs. Rowson tells the stories of many other such women.

Mrs. Rowson also attacks the myth that women cannot keep secrets. She cites in "Female Biography" (*A Present*) the story of Tymicha of Lacedemonia, who is threatened with torture by an enemy who, in attempting to pry state secrets from her, relies upon woman's propensity to talk. Tymicha bites off her tongue and spits in the tyrant's face. Leona, an Athenian woman who follows suit, was honored, Mrs. Rowson tells us, by a monument erected to her that bore the inscription "a lioness without a tongue" (p. 97). Surely, there could be no greater conscientiousness in secret-keeping than these women showed!

With all these virtues and talents, the female might be expected to claim almost any social rôle, but Mrs. Rowson does not suggest such a sweeping program. The prevailing social ideal envisioned woman as a good influence upon the male, with marriage as the principal means of influence. Susanna Rowson defers to this trend, even while she recognizes that marriage will not be the lot of every woman and will provide none with an eternally comfortable haven. She does not preclude the participation of women in any other kind of activity.

Mrs. Rowson sees the rôles of men and women as complementary. She advances in "Outline of Universal History" (A Present) the importance of history in teaching the sexes "as in a faithful mirror their respective duties" (p. 53). In all the pedagogical works, Mrs. Rowson stresses the importance of women as an influence upon men and children. In the "Concluding Address For 1808" (A Present) she speaks of "reforming" the opposite sex as the job of the woman (p. 148). Her rationale for the education of women is often based on the uplifting effect educated women will have on their families; as she states in "Female Biography," such women become "friends and rational companions to our fathers and brothers" (p. 122). Still, she stresses the value of the works of individual women, and offers some alternatives to marriage.

In the fiction, the destiny of most of the protagonists is marriage. Only a few escape husbands for useful single lives. Of course, Mrs. Rowson's novels, aside from Victoria and Charlotte, are comic in the sense that there are alternatives for the protagonists, and the final reversal of fortune moves from bad to good; and marriage is the traditional resolution of the comic plot. The Inquisitor contains a little paean to married love as exhibited in the royal marriage, in which Mrs. Rowson envisions Hymen "triumphant o'er the British nation" (III, 176). The assertive epilogue to Slaves in Algiers continues in a similar vein:

> True, Ladies—bounteous nature made us fair,
> To strew sweet roses round the bed of care.
> A parent's heart of sorrow to beguile,
> Cheer an afflicted husband by a smile.

To bind the truant, that's inclined to roam,
Good humour makes *a paradise at home.*
To raise the fall'n—to pity and forgive,
This is our noblest, best prerogative.
By these, pursuing nature's gentle plan,
We hold in silken chains—the lordly tyrant man.

(italics mine)

The poem "Rights of Woman" in *Miscellaneous Poems* also stresses the domestic scene. Addressed at the outset to a masculine audience, it proclaims:

Poor woman has her rights as well as you [men];
And if she's wise, she will assert them too.
If you have patience, and your wrath forbear,
In a few words I'll tell you what they are.

(p. 98)

The "rights" are to be competent in the household (p. 99), to make a "paradise at home," and to share the woes of "father, brothers, friends, oppress'd with care" (p. 100). The widow, the orphan, and the sick are to share the good woman's ministrations, but the influence upon the male is paramount.

Mrs. Rowson's enthusiasm for the domestic rôle is laid on a little thick in this poem; she ends with a paean to "Domestic duty—oh how blest we are!" (p. 103). But many of the individual pieces in *Miscellaneous Poems* were written years before the 1804 publication. "Rights of Woman" is probably a very early effort, for under full sail Mrs. Rowson tempers her enthusiasm for domesticity with emphasis upon intellectual attainment. In this poem, knowledge makes only a brief appearance as the poet concludes, now addressing her own sex,

Then ever let it be our pride, ye fair,
To merit their [the good and brave man's]
   protection, love, and care;
With useful knowledge be our heads well stor'd,
While in our hearts we every virtue hoard.
These rights we may assert, and tho' thought common
These, and these only are the RIGHTS OF WOMAN.

(p. 104)

Mrs. Rowson's poem "To Anna" and many of her other works contain advice on how to maintain a good marriage, but there is little joy held out for the woman. She tells a young woman about to marry,

If e'er your heart feels joy sincere,
Twill be to dry affliction's tear
To visit the distress'd and poor,
And chase pale famine from their door.

(7379-a, Rowson Collection)

The joys of matrimony are also seen from the man's point of view in her poem "Women As They Are" in *Miscellaneous Poems*:

The happiest lot that can to man be given,
To smooth the rugged path, and sweeten life,
Is an affectionate and faithful wife.

(p. 115)

For the woman, marriage is one more possible briar in that "thorny path of life" Mrs. Rowson offers to her audience. It may be fulfilling: one feminine type frequently encountered in the works is the generous, philanthropic, happily married woman. She is embodied in Victoria's best friend, Arabella Hartley Selton, in *Victoria*, and in Mrs. Beauchamp in *Charlotte*. Both these women are more compassionate toward the disgraced heroine than is society at large. Rebecca in *Slaves in Algiers*, Mrs. Rooksby in *Trials of the Human Heart*, and Lady Mary Worthy in *The Fille* conform to this pattern. They are not only happily married but extend the blessings of their enviable state to people outside their homes. At best, marriage can be a fine institution, good not only for the participants but for the rest of society.

At worst, marriage is legalized prostitution. This idea is stated in *Charlotte*, where marriage forced upon women as their only alternative is quietly attacked. Mrs. Rowson's language in this passage conveys her disgust with such a system:

Mr. Temple was the youngest son of a nobleman whose fortune was by no means adequate to the antiquity, grandeur, and I may add, pride of the family. He saw his elder brother made completely wretched by marrying a disagreeable woman, whose fortune helped to prop the sinking dignity of the house, and he beheld his sisters legally prostituted to old, decrepid men, whose titles gave them consequence in the eyes of the world, and whose affluence rendered them splendidly miserable.

(p. 26)

Mrs. Rowson continues this argument against society's insistence upon marriage in *Charlotte*, *Trials of the Human Heart*, and *Sarah*. The virtue of a woman who does not marry or retain masculine protection is open to assault and gossip. In *Charlotte*, the father of Montraville enunciates the difference in the situations of the sexes:

> "My daughters," said he, "have been educated like gentlewomen; and should I die before they are settled, they must have some provision made to place them above the snares and temptations which vice ever holds out to the elegant, accomplished female, when oppressed by the frowns of poverty and the sting of dependence: my boys, with only moderate incomes, when placed in the church, at the bar, or in the field, may exert their talents, make themselves friends, and raise their fortunes on the basis of merit."
>
> (p. 52)

In *Trials of the Human Heart*, the unmarried Meriel is frequently accused of illicit relationships. If she attempts to establish a friendship with a man, the gossips assume she is having an affair. She is fair game for the machinations of married employers and the suspicions of their wives. Near the conclusion of the novel, when Meriel is living with her father, she is safe. Mr. Kingly states that he is free to visit her without censure—"For under the shelter of paternal protection, who shall dare to arraign her conduct?" (IV, 158). Without this protection, Meriel, who has no practical training, sinks according to the elder Montraville's prescription, to the lowest level of the job market and is almost forced into prostitution.

Sarah provides a strong case against marriage as the only respectable rôle for a woman. Sarah marries because her mother is dead and her father has abandoned her. She and her husband are completely incompatible; but when Sarah tries to escape and live apart from her husband, she is defeated. Her reputation suffers; an earl who is infatuated with Sarah makes a false judgment about her availability. She faces poverty. Sarah puts it thus to her beloved, Frederick:

"My separation from him was enforced by necessity: but had I known the misery of a state of separation, how forlorn, how desolate, how totally unprotected a married woman is, when separated from her husband; how every one thinks he may insult her with impunity, and no one will take the trouble to defend her, but rather unite in aspersing and depressing her, even to the very earth—I would have never thrown myself into so deplorable a situation. I will make no overtures towards a reunion; but should he solicit me to pardon his unkind neglect, and again share his fate, I shall certainly do it. . . . I am convinced I shall never again appear respectable in the eyes of the world, until I am again under my husband's protection."

(p. 182)

The subtitle of *Sarah, The Exemplary Wife*, contains an ironic twist. Sarah has no legal recourse against her husband; she has few skills; there is little she can do but passively endure the marriage. In doing so, she is the "exemplary" wife, that is, worthy of imitation, but she is also exemplary to serve as a warning. Mrs. Rowson sounds both notes in her preface.

In making Sarah's confidante, Anne, a single woman—and a likeable one—surely Mrs. Rowson comments upon the possibilities for happiness in and out of the married state. Anne is well off by contrast to Sarah, and Mrs. Rowson develops her to some degree as a character in order to bring out this point. Anne is not only sympathetic, concerned, and fond of Sarah, but has a witty, analytical attitude toward life—including her own single state—which is far from the stereotype of the dried-up, vicious spinster. In *Sarah*, Anne jokes to Elenor as she extols the virtue of patience:

... in the married state, I believe a double portion is absolutely necessary. I cannot speak from experience, as I have never entered the holy pale, and being now on the wrong side of thirty-five, in all probability never shall, unless some spruce young squire of twenty-one (I would not marry one older) very rich and gallant, should fancy me the *Ninon* of the age and fall in love with me. But this is not very likely; it does not happen very often that men become seriously attached to women considerable older than themselves, though often that they are deeply enamoured of their fortunes. Now and then indeed, a woman appears, who, like the celebrated madam Maintenon, maintains her sovereignty over the young, the wealthy, the no-

ble, the learned; and is beloved and courted to the very verge
of her grand climacteric; but never was such a phenomenon
known as such a woman being an old maid—

(p. 234)

Anne is typical of Mrs. Rowson's treatment of the single woman.
While she presents a few portraits in the early fiction that conform
to the pattern outlined by Dorothy Deegan, Mrs. Rowson is usually
kind to the unmarried. A "superannuated" female appears in *Victoria*,
and Miss Abigail Prune in *The Fille de Chambre* is an example
of the grotesque old maid; but these portraits are outweighed by
Mentoria, the epitome of feminine wisdom, a widow who does not
remarry; Meriel's friend Celia, a nun; Fetnah in *Slaves in Algiers*,
and Aunt Rachel, who guides and helps the two young protagonists
of *Reuben and Rachel*.

In her school-oriented works, Mrs. Rowson did not forget the
unmarried. She makes a distinction that many people fail to recog-
nize as they advocate the home or the job market as the place for
women: not all situations are alike. In her "Concluding Address,
1810" (*A Present for Young Ladies*), Mrs. Rowson writes that most
women must be domestic, but that the wealthy and single have
time to learn and should therefore develop themselves to the fullest
(p. 151). In "Female Biography" (*A Present*), she provides an interesting example of a woman who—though not unmarried—proved
that marriage was not the only honorable estate. Catherine of Cline,
an actress, managed to live separately from her husband and still
maintain "a spotless reputation." Furthermore, she was buried in
Westminster Abbey (pp. 89–90).

What social rôles outside of marriage are available to women?
Mentoria takes on the traditional governess role. Fetnah will remain
in Algiers to devote herself to the care of her father, and to instruct
the dey in morality (Fetnah's escape from marriage may be due
simply to Mrs. Rowson's reluctance to unite her Christian hero with
a girl of Jewish ancestry). Lucy Blakeney is the only really successful career girl in the fiction. When Lucy's enamored is discovered to be her very own half-brother, son of the notorious Montraville who seduced her mother, Lucy turns to her natural altruism
and uses her inherited wealth to open a school for girls.

The incest theme in *Charlotte's Daughter* and the belated
punishment of Montraville (he grows faint with guilt when he first
beholds Lucy, and eventually dies) has been used by Leslie Fiedler
as a prime example of the dire treatment in American literature of

the trespassing male. In *Love and Death in the American Novel*, Fiedler places Montraville among dejected hulks ruined by excess sexuality.[20] Helen Papashvily would agree and see the near incest and the guilt suffered by Montraville as part of the "witches broth" cooked up by the early American women writers.[21] In the context of Mrs. Rowson's time, however, this kind of situation was one of the few acceptable ways to excuse a heroine from matrimony. An insurmountable problem would be needed to justify a single life for a heroine. What more irrefragable obstacle to marriage than the threat of incest?

Other women in Mrs. Rowson's fiction besides Lucy aspire to careers, but they do not attain them because the attitudes of society toward women prevent success. Mrs. Greenham's ill treatment of Ellen in *The Inquisitor* is due to these attitudes. Mrs. Greenham confesses, "I should like to see her heartily laughed at—I am sure women have no business with pens in their hands, they had better mend their cloaths, and look after their family" (II, 143-144).

Meriel, in *Trials of the Human Heart*, is discouraged from pursuing a writing career. She is told by a Mr. Friendly, the attorney of her benefactor, that she is not only too obscure socially to win praise, but also of the wrong gender:

> "burn your pens and paper, and believe me, a woman makes as awkward a figure engaged in literary pursuits, as a counsellor would do seated at a tambour frame or busied in assorting colours for embroidery."
>
> (II, 68)

Meriel takes Mr. Friendly's advice. However, one of the interesting aspects of Meriel's struggle is that she does not write to enrich family life or help a man's career; she simply likes to write. She tells Celia, her confidante,

> "I would like to obtain a living by the exertion of my natural talents, than by following the straight-forward path of the plodding world of business . . . ."
>
> (II, 58)

Careers for women are defended by Mrs. Rowson. An "old gentlemen" stands up for Ellen in *The Inquisitor*:

And pray, why not, Madam, said an old gentleman, who had

listened attentively to this loquacious harangue, why may not a woman, if she has leisure and genius, take up her pen to gratify both herself and friends. I am not ashamed to acknowledge that I have perused the productions of some of our female pens, with the highest satisfaction; and am happy when I find any woman has so large a fund of amusement in her own mind. I never heard a woman, who was fond of her pen, complain of the tediousness of time; nor, did I ever know such a woman extravagantly fond of dress, public amusements, or expensive gaiety; yet, I have seen many women of genius prove themselves excellent mothers, wives, and daughters."

(II, 144)

The Inquisitor himself defends a professional actress whose character has been questioned. He contends,

I have frequently been engaged in disputes concerning women of this profession—it puts me beyond all patience to hear people advance an opinion so very contracted and illiberal, as that of supposing no woman can be virtuous who is on the stage—I know many at this time who are ornaments not only to their profession, but to the sex in general: even the lady I have just mentioned, is generous, humane and prudent, pride is her only fault—Charming woman! I have often said, when I was enchanted with her performance of some amiable character—conquer but that one foible, and our admiration will rise into veneration.—I am confident a woman may, if she is so inclined; be as virtuous as Lucrece behind the scenes of a theatre.

(I, 71)

Two social rôles are consistently downgraded in Mrs. Rowson's work, the woman of fashion and the household drudge. Neither of these rôles permits expression of the total woman. The fashionable female—that is, one who devotes her life to being ornamental and to her own pleasure—may be noble or poor, she may work or not. Her identifying characteristic is her selfish pursuit of personal aggrandizement. This type is represented by Lady Maskwell in *Victoria*; she takes on West Indian hue in *The Test of Honour* where she appears as the indolent Jamaican wife of Mary's scheming cousin. La Rue plays the role in *Charlotte*. Lady Ossiter in *The Fille de Chambre* is one of the best-drawn portraits of the heartless society woman. She and Rebecca appear in a scene not unlike Proust's between Swann and Madame de Guermantes in ironic intention. Lady Ossiter's absorption in her mourning clothes is played off against Rebecca's genuine sorrow over the death of Lady Ossiter's mother. Knapp quotes the scene in full in his 1828 *Memoir*, so impressed was he with the writing.[22]

These women see their function in society as ornamental only. They are castigated in Mrs. Rowson's "Women As They Are" in *Miscellaneous Poems*:

> The girl, who from her birth is thought a beauty,
> Scarce ever hears of virtue, sense or duty;
> Mamma, delighted with each limb and feature,
> Declares, she is a fascinating creature;
> Forbids all study, work, or wise reflection;
> 'Twill spoil her eyes, or injure her complexion.
> "Hold up your head, my dear; turn out your toes;
> Bless me, what's that? a pimple on your nose;
> It smarts, dear, don't it? how can you endure it?
> Here's some *Pomade divine*, to heal and cure it."
> . . . .
> Thus, ere one proper wish her heart can move,
> She's taught to think of lovers, and of love;
> She's told she is a beauty, does not doubt it;
> What need of sense? beauties can wed without it.
> And then her eyes, her teeth, her lips, her hair,
> And shape, are all that can be worth her care;
> She thinks a kneeling world should bow before her,
> And men were but created to adore her.
>
> (pp. 105-108)

The purely domestic woman is portrayed as equally incomplete. She appears in the fiction as Mrs. Penure (née Prune) in *The Fille de Chambre* and in *Reuben and Rachel* as Tabitha who hates all forms of literature and is interested only in "pickles and preserves" (II, 220). This female too is ridiculed in "Women As They Are" in *Miscellaneous Poems*:

> "Dear," cries mamma, whose only merit lies
> In making puddings, good preserves, and pies;
> Who rises with Aurora, blythe and cheery,
> Feeds pigs and poultry, overlooks her dairy,
> Brews her own beer, makes her own household linen,

And scolds her girls, to make them mind their spinning—
"Dear, surely Tom was blind; what could he see,
To think of marrying such a thing as she?
She was a beauty; what is beauty? pshaw!
I never knew a *beauty* worth a straw.
She's so eat up with pride, conceit, and folly,
I vow she knows no more than little Molly,
Whether a pig were better roast or boil'd;
I warrant many a dinner will be spoil'd.
But I'll take care, whoever weds my daughter
Shall find a different lesson, I have taught her.
My Bett's fifteen next May; I'd lay a crown,
She'd cook a dinner with the best in town;
To roast, or boil, make pudding, pye or jelly,
There's not her equal far or near, I tell ye.
Then at her needle, making, mending, darning,
What is there else that's worth a woman's larnings?
With my good will, a girl should never look
In any but a pray'r or cook'ry book:
Reading 'bout kings, and states, and foreign nations,
Will only fill their heads with proclamations."
If of these documents a girl's observant,
What is she fit for, but an upper servant?

(pp. 108-109)

Mrs. Rowson's rejection of a narrow or reduced rôle for women is underlined by the comments in her texts. In *An Abridgment of Universal Geography*, Mrs. Rowson disapproves of the Thibetans' treatment of women because "They consider women as very inferior to men; that they were created only to people the world, and to look after household affairs" (p. 110).

Ideally, the woman who has a family would combine the practice of the household arts with the attainment of knowledge. Intellectual or cultural activities must be curtailed only if they are incompatible with one's financial and social situation, if they interfere with domestic and family duties, or if they are carried to "extremes." If the motive of the learned woman is simply to show off, Mrs. Rowson disapproves, for she believes that knowledge should be useful. In "Concluding Address, 1810" (*A Present for Young Ladies*), she states that "pedantry and presumption in a woman is more disgusting than an entire want of literary information" (p. 152). But in the same passage, she had defended the maligned bluestocking:

Many are the prejudices entertained, and the witticisms thrown out against what are called learned women; but surely a woman will not be less acceptable in the world, or worse qualified for performing her part in it, for having devoted a large portion of her early years to the cultivation of her understanding.

(p. 151)

Some areas of endeavor appear to be outside the woman's province. In "The Rights of Woman" in *Miscellaneous Poems*, Mrs. Rowson may be haunted by Dr. Johnson's simile describing the performing female, for she declares,

But know you not that woman's sphere
Is the domestic walk? To interfere
With politics, divinity, or law,
As much deserved ridicule would draw
On woman, as the learned, grave divine,
Cooking the soup on which he means to dine;
Or formal judge, the winders at his knee,
Preparing silk to work embroidery.

(p. 103)

But this sentiment does not represent Mrs. Rowson's final judgment on this issue. In her later work, "Female Biography" (*A Present*), she notes,

Though few of our sex are called to sway the regal sceptre; yet among those who have filled the important station of queen, many might be mentioned as examples of their political abilities; amongst whom may be reckoned preeminent, Elizabeth queen of England.

(p. 98)

The many stories of other female monarchs bring home Mrs. Rowson's point. Besides that of Elizabeth, the careers of Anne of Austria, Catherine the Great of Russia, and Catherine the Second are sketched in "Female Biography." Elizabeth appears in nearly all of the historical surveys. In *Exercises in History*, Mrs. Rowson praises Margaret of Denmark, a fourteenth-century ruler, for her "great qualities for government and policy" (p. 138), Queen Christina of Sweden for her support of learning (p. 143), and Queen Anne of

England for having achieved one of the "most illustrious" reigns in the history of Britain (p. 99). In *Abridgment of Universal Geography*, Mrs. Rowson points to Catherine II of Russia: Catherine was "successful in her military pursuits, and her reign has been the admiration of all Europe"; she is also praised for abolishing torture to elicit confession of crime and for encouraging commerce (p. 287). Mrs. Rowson underlines the implications of her historical examples by noting in "Female Biography" that "The exercise of brilliant talents in *any profession whatever*, does not prevent the practice of virtue" (*A Present*, pp. 88-89, italics mine).

As to the rights of women, education is certainly first. This point needs little further development, except to note that while Mrs. Rowson admits that all women need not "study with the closeness of application which is essentially requisite in the education of a boy" ("Concluding Address, 1808," *A Present*, p. 153), she makes no concession to the male pundits who advised women to avoid the "profound researches of study." In "Female Biography" she emphasizes the encouragement she has offered women to go beyond dabbling in intellectual pursuits; she argues, "when literature, or the study of the fine arts, can be engaged in, without neglect of our feminine duties, why may not we attain the goal of perfection as well as the other sex?" (*A Present*, p. 85). The forcefulness of Mrs. Rowson's statements on this subject can be illustrated best by comparing her language to that of others who supposedly advocated female intellectual attainment. The commencement speaker at the Philadelphia Ladies' Academy (1794) assures the girls that "A sprig from the top of Parnassus would certainly be allowed a pleasing and fragrant decoration for a lady."[23]

Mrs. Rowson says little about specific legal rights, although in the novels she shows her single heroines exercising their property rights, and her married heroines deprived of redress to law. In *Sarah*, the heroine endures even the ignominy of physical abuse (as does Meriel in *Trials*) rather than seek legal help. She writes to Anne of her husband,

> "D—n," said he, in an under voice, and being on the opposite side to my female companion, he actually struck my arm with his open hand. The blow was not heavy, but it was a blow; and I felt that it had broken the last small link that remained between us. Dishonored—insulted—struck! Anne, Anne! I am a woman; the law will not redress my grievances, and if it would, could I appeal publicly? No; I can suffer in silence, but I could not bear to appear

openly as the accuser of the man I had once sworn to honor.

(p. 94)

Charlotte's Daughter also touches upon the legal rights of women. Mary Lumly is an example of the sorrows that overwhelm a female foolish enough to surrender not only her body but her property to a man. Her guardian, the Reverend Matthews, tries to convince Mary to cool her ardor for her fiancé long enough to allow him to negotiate a sensible property settlement for her. But Mary gives her all; she says, "When I make him master of my person, I shall also give him possession of my property, and I trust he is of too generous a disposition ever to abuse my confidence" (p. 83). Mary is, of course, seduced, abandoned, and robbed.

The rights of woman begin, Mrs. Rowson believed, with changes in the attitudes of society. She calls for abandonment of the stereotypes that confine the woman's world educationally and professionally, in the way men view women, and in the treatment of women by the social mores.

All that has been said to this point shows Mrs. Rowson's disapproval of the limited world of the average female. Ellen's and Meriel's stories of blighted ambition make this point. One after another, the women in the fiction find that there is practically no work obtainable except teaching as a governess or assisting in a hat shop. Meriel works as a milliner's assistant and attempts prostitution. Rebecca is mistreated by the children she is assigned to teach; as a governess, she is only a step from being a maid. Sarah is also treated badly in her attempt at teaching. Such conditions are criticized in other important feminist works. In *A Vindication of the Rights of Woman* (1792), Mary Wollstonecraft complains of the menial and demeaning work open to the female. The rôle of governess amounts to "degradation," for the woman does not receive the respect given a male tutor; the job of milliner's assistant "could sink them [women forced to earn a living] almost to the level of those poor abandoned creatures, who live by prostitution. For are not milliners and mantua-makers reckoned the next class?"[24]

The rights of women also include treatment from men as the equals they are and the abandonment of the image of women as children or "sex objects." One small episode in *Reuben and Rachel* makes this point. Dinah, wife of Jacob Holmes, presumes to offer her opinion that Reuben is an honest young man, and she is chided by her father for judging "on her own" (II, 282). Of course, her opinion is correct.

Sarah states the woman's right to adult status most clearly. She tells Anne in *Sarah*,

"You have never been married, Anne; so cannot inform me whether it is so or not, but if every married man is so captious, and petulant, so angry at their wives' only expressing a difference in opinions in the mildest words: I wonder how any woman can be so passionately attached to them. But, perhaps, that passionate attachment prevents their seeing any fault in them, and they, supposing all the man, thus idolized, says, does, or thinks is right, never take the trouble of contradicting him; assent implicitly to his opinions, however absurd, and will not exert their own mental powers to think or decide for themselves."

(pp. 43-44)

The same heroine writes to Frederick, describing her friendship with Reverend Hayley:

"Of my own sex, I have seldom met with any who are formed for more than the companion of an hour. Your sex, in general, accustom themselves to consider women in so inferior a light, that they oftener treat us like children and playthings, than intelligent beings. I must be candid enough to confess, it is too frequently our own fault, that we are not held in higher estimation. How gratifying, then, was it to my self love, to be considered by a man of sense and erudition as an equal, and to be conversed with as a rational companion."

(p. 258)

To Anne, Sarah emphasizes her point; when trying to escape her husband, she says, "but to be treated either like a child, an idiot, or a slave, is what I cannot, will not submit to" (p. 114). The friendship between Sarah and Mr. Hayley is unique in Mrs. Rowson's fiction. Other characters dream of such a relationship, but societal pressures intervene.

Women, claims Mrs. Rowson, have the right to be judged on a par with men. The sexual double standard is implicitly criticized throughout her works. In *Victoria*, she attempts to formulate her disgust with this phase of society's mores. Her heroine says to her best friend, Arabella Hartley,

How cruel is it, that if one of us poor weak mortals only once step aside from the path of rectitude, we are never suffered to return. Penitence may make us acceptable in the sight of Heaven, but the world will never pardon us; while man may plunge into every idle vice, and yet be received in all companies, and too often caressed by the brave and worthy. Can you tell me why this is, Bell? Are crimes less so when committed by men than women? Are not they allowed to be wiser than we? Ought not they then to be better?"

(I, 131-132)

Mrs. Rowson's unflagging championship of the "fallen" woman is an important part of her plea for change in society's attitudes toward women. She never forgot the figure of the "fallen woman," and her compassion for the plight of such women is illustrated forcefully by the appearance of this motif even in her early critical piece *A Trip to Parnassus* (1788). Apollo, bestowing plaudits upon various playwrights and actors, praises Harriet Lee for her compassion:

"You my kindest protection shall share;
"For the woman who stoops, a fall'n sister to raise,
"Shall find her own temples encircl'd with bays."

(p. 6)

The type of the fallen woman appears in *The Inquisitor* (1788). The narrator writes to the prostitute Annie, whom he finds begging for a drink near a tavern, "Now let the icy sons of philosophy say what they please. I could no more have left this poor girl . . . than I could travel barefoot over the burning deserts of Arabia" (II, 160). With the help of the narrator, Annie's reformation is brought about (III, 178).

Mary's best friend Emily (little Emily?) in *The Test of Honour* (1789) is seduced by Harry Fentum, who marries and then abandons her. Mary later finds the girl wandering about and takes her in. Harry repents, and Mary hopes to see the couple and the child reunited. But the good news of Harry's return is too much for poor Emily, and she expires. In *Trials of the Human Heart*, as has been noted, the protagonist herself nearly indulges in prostitution to support her starving mother.

The besmirched protagonists, Charlotte and Victoria, must die—but more by society's and the reader's decree than Mrs. Rowson's. Through the many secondary characters, Mrs. Rowson argues for compassion for the erring female, and in some cases presents us with examples of full recovery from the supposedly fatal effects of seduction. True Christianity demands forgiveness of the fallen; mankind is fallen. In both *Victoria* and *Charlotte*, there is a sympathetic woman to defend the transgressor. Arabella Hartley (now Lady Selton) writes to a friend of the difference between her own and her husband's attitudes toward Victoria. Lord Selton, who is in general a very decent man, sees only

Victoria's disobedience to her mother. Bell sees and writes of the unfairness to Victoria:

> How well does it teach us to be careful how we confer favours on the unworthy of the other:—Strage beings! who at the moment we are giving them the highest proofs of affection, despise us for those very errors themselves have urged us to commit.
>
> (I, 189)

Mrs. Beauchamp in *Charlotte* argues that Charlotte might "in spite of her former errors, become a useful and respectable member of society" (p. 82).

Two women in *Charlotte's Daughter* who encounter Mary Lumly at an inn where her seducer has left her exhibit the proper attitude toward the fallen woman:

> These truly virtuous, respectable women did not think that the commission of one fault was sufficient to banish a human being from society, or excuse in others the want of humanity or kindness.
>
> (p. 136)

Chastity is very important in Mrs. Rowson's system of values; in one passage she calls chastity the cornerstone of virtue; but if, as Margaret Wyman contends in her article "The Rise of the Fallen Woman," Mrs. Rowson conceived of "a Providence upholding the absolute value of feminine chastity,"[25] she surely emphasizes the spiritual meaning of chastity. Mrs. Rowson's belief in the ability of the individual female to recover from sexual mistakes shows that bodily purity is not her prime concern. Only when the mind becomes corrupt is "purity" lost. Charlotte bears the surname "Temple," which represents in Christian symbolism the body as a reflection of the soul rather than an entity valuable in itself. To emphasize sexual chastity would be indeed to reduce the female to an object, and Mrs. Rowson's purpose is to avoid such reduction.

Women are entitled to be judged as whole personalities rather than by one virtue alone, argues Mrs. Rowson. She teaches women that they are equal to men in virtue, intellect, emotional range and fortitude, and that the ideal they should strive for is not feminine as defined by society, but androgynous, combining the best of the "masculine" and "feminine" traits. She points out the unfairness of narrowing the female's sphere of activity to the domestic, emphasizes her right to education and decent employment, and calls for the abandonment of stereotypes along with the treatment of women as children and objects.

The exact boundaries of Mrs. Rowson's feminism are impossible to establish. Other writers examined one phase or another of the problems of women, and some of the recommendations Rowson made appear in a variety of sources. Further, as more early British and American women writers are rediscovered, we find feminist concepts and phrases appearing in earlier and less publicized texts. Even a lurid romance like *The Happy-Unfortunate* (1732) by Elizabeth Boyd[26] protests masculine preemption of the arts. Mary Wollstonecraft, as noted, considers several of the same issues as Mrs. Rowson, but the latter had already published seven books dedicated to female emancipation before *A Vindication of the Rights of Woman* appeared.

4

True Christianity

> O where's a nobler theme
> To call forth all our pow'rs!
> He came, he suffer'd to redeem
> A race so fall'n as ours.
> > ("Come Strike the Silver String,
> > A Sacred Song," 1818-1825)

Susanna Rowson's religion is the controlling system from which the author's main concerns take their shape and support. As we have seen, Mrs. Rowson uses a Christian standard as the basis for her concept of temperament. Religious themes and character types recur in her work, and her treatment of these elements supports her feminist views. Mrs. Rowson's theology is a timely reaction to male-inspired church traditions demeaning to women.

Mrs. Rowson believes in the unity of Christian doctrine, and stresses the power of Christ to redeem fallen mankind. In accepting the doctrine of original sin, she takes a harder view of human nature than literary scholars have ascribed to the typical female novelist of her period. She accepts the basic sacraments and forms of the Anglican Church, but stresses the spirit over the letter of the law. Nevertheless, she does not advocate religion based purely on emotion, as many nineteenth-century sentimentalists did, but insists on the need for intellectual as well as emotional understanding of the Scriptures.

According to Mrs. Rowson, the relationship between man and God is the orthodox one of weakness on the one hand and omnipotence on the other, with Christ as the mediating force. In *Abridgment of Universal Geography*, Mrs. Rowson states of the plethora of sects and factions that have arisen in the Christian Church,

> all unite in the great fundamental point, that we must depend on an omnipotent and omnipresent God, for life, health, and security, and on the merits of a crucified Redeemer, for eternal salvation.
> > (p. 15)

She never drifts toward belief in an in-dwelling God, nor toward doctrines of inner light. In *Victoria*, Mrs. Rowson has Lucinda Harlow, a character whose rôle is to comment by means of her poetry, write: "Then on Thee let us feeble worms depend,/ And rest securely on thy mighty arm" (II, 150). God is outside man, and intervenes directly in his affairs. Furthermore, whatever Providence decrees is right, although it may first appear unjust or unduly harsh. In *Charlotte* Mrs. Rowson argues that "the cup of affliction is poured out for wise and salutary ends, and they who are compelled to drain it even to the bitter dregs, often find comfort at the bottom; the tear of penitence blots their offences from the book of fate, and they rise from the heavy, painful trial, purified and fit for a mansion in the kingdom of eternity" (pp. 106-107).

The nature of man is depraved. Mrs. Rowson states this dogma directly and forcefully in her religious songs, poetry, and pedagogical works; for example, her questions in *Exercises in History* include,

> Q.   What is the first great event recorded in history?
> A.   The creation of the world.
> Q.   The second?
> A.   The fall of man from his state of innocence and happiness by disobedience to the commands of his Creator.
>
> (p. 6)

Strong statements such as these are prepared for in the fiction. In her earlier efforts Mrs. Rowson uses satire to dramatize the difference between the ideals of Christianity and life as it is.[1] She presents a world marred by the activities and attitudes of a fallen race. There is a smattering of practicing Christians who keep the world from becoming a desert, and to these the author often bows and apologizes for her harsh statements; still, human society as a whole is corrupt—the world is a Vanity Fair where the majority engage in heartless barter and the worship of false idols, especially money and rank.

This is the background against which naive Victoria tries to assert her belief in romantic love. The Finchlys, who reject her because of her lack of wealth and status, are shown to be typical of the society of which they are a part. Lady Maskwell, a woman who diverts Harry from his obligation to Victoria, devotes her life to scheming for money and a title. The majority of her peers are busy with cards, gossip, and fashion. Although Mrs. Rowson is not adept at rendering social scenes, she presents in several satirical passages a glimpse of the un-Christian and frivolous world of fashion. Arabella Hartley (Lady Selton), Victoria's best friend

and the embodiment of common sense as opposed to Victoria's sentimentalism, provides the satirical comment.

She describes playing cards as "mottled deities" (I, 78), and writes to
Alicia Finchly of the man of fashion:

> Oh I have it then; you have got a new lover? Pshaw, nonsense; I see
> none of the tinsel gentry of the times worth a moment's notice. A
> fine gentleman, charmingly dress'd, just new from the taylor and
> frisseur's hands, is a charming thing tho', Alicia? Divine, my Lady!
> but I think they are too nice for the rude wind to blow upon, and
> should be put in a glass-case; for some complexions will fade with
> the least rude blast. O you wicked creature, to say such mortifying
> things of the lovely Adonisses. Nay Madam, the ladies of the
> present age are as much indebted to art as the gentlemen, and a
> modern beauty, instead of addressing a hymn of thanks to Venus
> for making her beautiful, should offer her thanks and praises to the
> inimitable M—.
>
> (II, 105-106)

Arabella follows this passage with a poem deriding society's worship
of youth and beauty:

> Ye virgins and matrons whoe'er felt the pow'r,
> Of M—'s cosmetics, come round and adore,
> For the widow of sixty, and nymph of sixteen,
> Both alike with a blooming complexion are seen,
> And all must be lovely whose cheeks still discloses,
> Like nature's fair bloom, M—'s Bloom of Roses.
>
> Some men have been fam'd for their prowess and glory,
> And Wolf, Hawke, and Manners live still in each story,
> And peace to their mem'ries, their names are still dear,
> Each true loyal heart mourn their loss with a tear;
> But I sing of one that is greater than they,
> For he can drive age and its wrinkles away.
>
> Come praise this dear man, who can make you so fair,
> Give complexion and brows, change the hue of your hair,
> And when with his fathers he sleeps in the dust,
> Raise a tomb to his mem'ry, and worship his bust,
> Inscribe it with verses, adorn it with posies
> Engrave at the bottom, this sad tomb discloses,

That death takes no heed of the best Bloom of Roses.

(II, 106-107)

Similarly scornful critiques of modern society appear regularly in the works that follow *Victoria*. The narrator of *The Inquisitor* writes of the contemporary scene:

> The modern man of honor . . . must have his pleasures whether he can afford to pay for them or not; he will steal his friend's fortune at the gaming table; debauch his wife, or ensnare his daughter, and then run him through the body by way of reparation.

(III, 182)

Innocence and sincerity in the artist are pitted against commercial interests; in "The Printing Office" the Inquisitor watches a young woman author trying to get a book published. The printer tries to persuade the author to steal from the works of others and publish anonymously, a suggestion she indignantly refuses. The narrator observes "Mr. C [the printer] . . . wondered, no doubt, how an author could study any thing but her own emolument" (I, 53).

Mary in *The Test of Honour* is originally unacceptable to Frederick's father because she is neither rich nor highly placed socially. Mr. Stephens recommends to his son the daughter and heiress of Sir Thomas Watson. He says of Mary, "Miss Newton! why, who is she? I never knew but one family of that name in the neighborhood; and sure you have not been such a fool as to fall in love with Farmer Newton's daughter?" (I, 78). The Fentums, on the other hand, want Mary for their son because of her "respectability and fortune" (I, 16); lower in the social scale than the Stephenses, they see Mary as a step up.

The world of *Charlotte* is dominated by the twin idols of status and wealth. In a flashback to the events before Charlotte's birth, the elder Mr. Temple, Charlotte's paternal grandfather, tries to coerce his son into marrying a Miss Weatherly, who has "three thousand pounds per year" (p. 36). When the son objects, the young lady marries Mr. Temple's father, the Earl of D——, out of pique and the desire for a title (p. 38). In America, and temporarily out of touch with her family, Charlotte is rejected by all but one person when her situation as a kept woman is revealed; until a humble family finally takes her in, one person after another refuses to help as she wanders through a snowstorm to find Montraville. These examples of false values and lack of compassion derive from the limits of human nature. Mrs. Rowson writes,

Alas poor Charlotte, how confined was her knowledge of human nature, or she would have been convinced that the only way to ensure the friendship and assistance of your surrounding acquaintance is to convince them you do not require it, for when once the petrifying aspect of distress and penury appear, whose qualities, like Medusa's head, can change to stone all that look upon it; when once this Gorgon claims acquaintance with us, the phantom of friendship, that before courted our notice, will vanish into unsubstantial air, and the whole world before us appears a barren waste. Pardon me, ye dear spirits of benevolence, whose benign smiles and chearful giving hand has strewed sweet flowers on many a thorny path through which my wayward fate forced me to pass; think not, that, in condemning the unfeeling texture of the human heart, I forget the spring from whence flow all the comforts I enjoy: oh no; I look up to you as to bright constellations, gathering new splendours from the surrounding darkness; but ah! whilst I adore the benignant rays that cheared and illumined my heart, I mourn that their influence cannot extend to all the sons and daughters of affliction.

(p. 110)

Rebecca's story in *The Fille de Chambre* repeats the pattern of virtue overlooked in favor of money and rank. Rebecca's first employers, Lord and Lady Ossiter, relations of the Worthys, who consider themselves too good for Rebecca socially, vie with one another in indulging in flirtation and seduction. The high as well as the low are relentlessly venal, preoccupied with the ever-present desire for the "coach and six" and the prospect of "elegant equipage." Even a humble old couple in the country is tainted and bribed by another of Rebecca's employers, Mr. Barton, into allowing him to visit their granddaughter for immoral purposes. Rebecca's own mother and her stepfather steal her trunk. Meriel in *Trials of the Human Heart* undergoes similar experiences. The fact that she saves her landlady's children from a fire does not prevent the woman from taking Meriel's furniture as payment on her rent. Meriel writes to Celia: "Some few years since, I believed every heart glowed with humanity . . . but very lately I began to perceive how erroneous my opinion was . . ." (II, 85).

And so it goes: thieves, fortune hunters, seducers, social climbers, flirts, embezzlers—the wicked, the foolish, the frivolous make up the majority of "the sons and daughters of affliction," while a few "spirits of benevolence" occasionally appear to help a fellow Christian.

Reuben and Rachel, with its combination of historical tales and the lives of fictional characters, provides a transition to the pedagogical works, in which a similar propensity for evil marks the activities of both nations and individuals. Mrs. Rowson tells the story of the Spanish conquest and exploitation of South America and Mexico. Using an emblem to summarize the many instances of robbery and seduction of the innocent, Mrs. Rowson laments,

> Alas! Avarice had discovered this new world was an inexhaustible mine of wealth; and, not content to share its blessings in common with the natives, came with rapine, war and devastation in her train; and as she tore open the bowels of the earth to gratify her insatiate thirst for gold, her steps were marked with blood.
>
> (I, 25)

The worship of gold is illustrated by the experience of Roldan, a Spaniard who returns to Spain rich, where once he had been poor and despised, and experiences sudden respect from his countrymen. They now "received him with open arms, applauded every word he spoke, and like summer flies around a vessel which contains honey, swarmed with a fond, officious, greedy hum, in hopes to share the sweets that it contains" (I, 57).

One passage in Reuben and Rachel appears to question the notion of human depravity. Of the modern-day brother and sister, Mrs. Rowson rhapsodizes, "Nature, Blessed Goddess, the minds of Reuben and Rachel were blanks" (II, 176); but this temporary confusion—not unusual in Mrs. Rowson, who had a tendency to pick up the latest shibboleth—is outweighed by the depiction of characters universally prone to error, as well as by her other comments on this subject. Probably Mrs. Rowson was trying to express the sense of hope that the new world and young people offer mankind to model society along more ideal lines. Elsewhere in Reuben and Rachel, Mrs. Rowson states,

> Revenge is a principle inherent in human nature, and it is only the sublime and heavenly doctrine of Christianity that teaches us to repel the impulse, and return good for evil.
>
> (I, 142)

The textbooks reinforce the picture of the world projected in Reuben and Rachel, often by using similar historical eras and personalities. Mrs. Rowson repeats certain episodes from history over and over: the Spanish conquests, which appear in almost every history and geography, sacred as well as profane, and Napoleon's conquest of France and the rest of Europe. The former illustrates the thirst for gold and the second unlimited ambition. Mrs. Rowson introduces "Sketches of Female Biography" (*A Present for Young Ladies*) with this view of human history:

> ... history with a pen dipped in the blood of millions wet with the widow's and orphan's tears, records the struggles of contending powers, and decks the conqueror with such gorgeous robes as hide the sanguinary stains which stain his polluted soul; while she relates the rise and fall of empires, tracing the steps of those who striding over heaps of their slaughtered fellow creatures, mount to the regal seat, and snatch the diadem from royal temples to place it on their own.
>
> (p. 83)

In *Biblical Dialogues*, Mrs. Rowson's view of human nature is repeated many times. Mr. Alworth frequently speaks of "the ignorance and imbecility of human nature" and the "depravity of the human heart." Mankind needs more than social reform, instinct, or the "light of nature" to improve his conduct. The Alworth family, like the best of human types described in the Bible, share the flaws of all humanity. Mrs. Rowson makes this point quite dramatic—and sounds like a good seventeenth-century Puritan—in the following passage:

> We are none of us without fault, we are all prone to evil from our very childhood. You, my children, young as you are, if you will reflect a moment, and question your own hearts, will know that you are more inclined to evil than good, and that the seeds of sin, even of the most heinous kind, are lurking in them. For instance, Amy, when you snatched your cousin Lucy's doll, broke off its legs, and threw it into the fire, punching it with the tongs, and crying in a passion, "there, burn, burn, ugly doll, you are not half so handsome as mine," would, if you had dared, have pushed your cousin in after it. And you, my son Horatio, when you so unmercifully whipped the poor little playful dog that tore your kite, would, in an equal fit of passion, have fallen upon a play-mate, and perhaps by an unlucky blow have occasioned his death.
>
> (I, 36)

Mrs. Rowson's view of human nature and society has been developed at length because it is a key point upon which rest several theories about the early American novel, and Mrs. Rowson's relation to the genre. The critics who have placed Mrs. Rowson at the vanguard of American sentimentalism argue that belief in human perfectibility is one of the basic characteristics of the sentimental tradition. As J.M.S. Tompkins asks, "what better evidence can there be of the innate goodness of the human heart than spontaneous sensibility?"[2] In *Love and Death in the American Novel*, Leslie Fiedler argues that the "denial of the Calvinist belief in human depravity" supports the sentimental tradition's acceptance—established in America by Mrs. Rowson—of a "Sentimental Love Religion," which views American women as "absolutely pure" and capable of doing "Christ's work in the world."[3]

Mrs. Rowson's choice of plot elements, use of language, and other aspects of her work coincide in some respects with that of the sentimental writers, but she does not share the optimistic view of human nature ascribed to them, nor—as we have seen—their portrayal of women as instinctively purer and better than men. According to Fiedler in *Love and Death*, "the sentimental myth of the Seducer and the Maiden . . . projects the image . . . of the head attempting to lead the heart astray"; Fiedler writes of "The anti-intellectualism of the sentimental code, its theory that simple feeling is closer to God's truth than educated intelligence" (p. 63). He has earlier noted the lack of respect in the sentimental tradition for the institutions and forms of religion, an attitude he interprets as a resurfacing of darkness and irrationality in religion, elements that he thinks of as feminine. Applied to Mrs. Rowson, this theory leads to an exaggeration of the dominance of emotion over reason in her presentation of religion and to a distortion of her concept of women. Although in several instances one of Mrs. Rowson's heroines is the agent for someone else's conversion to Christianity, in general the resemblance of the protagonists to Christ is that of every Christian: Imitation of Christ is the orthodox way to acceptance and salvation. Further, Christ is evident in the novels, doing his own work, as in *Charlotte*, where he presumably responds to Charlotte's prayer to him (p. 122).

Mrs. Rowson does recommend a return to the simplicity of early Christianity. Her idea of "real religion" is stated in *The Inquisitor*; the agreement of the later description in *Biblical Dialogues* with this early formulation shows that she did not change her essential view. In the earlier fiction the narrator describes genuine religion as

> A cheerful, contented disposition—a heart grateful for every blessing, and resigned to the all-wise dispensations of Providence—and a hand ready to bestow on others parts of the bless-

ings we enjoy ourselves;—these are the results of pure religion—
these are the acceptable sacrifices in the sight of our Creator.

(II, 105)

In answering his son Horatio's question about the "pomp and ceremony" of the "Jewish religion," Mr. Alworth in *Biblical Dialogues*
argues,

> The christian religion, requires neither bulls, nor goats, for offer-
> ings; neither gold nor embroidery for the decoration of their tem-
> ples; neither precious stones, or golden ornaments, for their
> priests' vestments. Its sacrifice is a contrite heart; its incense is a
> meek and quiet spirit; its richest pillars and best ornaments, are
> faith in the Redeemer's blood; and that charity which at once
> enlargeth the heart, and openeth the hand; and that love to God
> which evinces itself in purity of life, in sincerity, humility, and
> grateful obedience.

(I, 217)

In the two works quoted, as in the intervening ones, Mrs. Rowson
argues for a simple religion based upon faith. Membership in a particular sect and the observance of ritual and rite are unimportant beside the
fundamental and inward condition of the soul. She excoriates religious
"enthusiasm," hypocrisy, and Phariseeism. She tries to adhere to a
principle of religious tolerance, but in this regard does not completely
succeed.

In *The Inquisitor* Mrs. Rowson's narrator observes a ranting Methodist preacher. At one moment he is arousing a public gathering with
his haranguing, and damns all those who do not agree with him. In the
following scene he is revealed as a heartless landlord demanding
exorbitant rents from his tenants (II, 106).

Overzealous devotion to the rules and observances of the various
Christian sects is often satirized. The presence of factions in the church
disturbs Mrs. Rowson throughout her career. In *An Abridgment of
Universal Geography*, she calls the differences between the multifarious protestant sects "trivial" (p. 15). Reuben in *Reuben and Rachel*, a
Quaker, argues that rules are only justified if they cause a man to be
more religious. His uncle Hezekiah, a particularly pious Friend, thinks
over Reuben's remarks and is forced to agree that "a man might be a
very good Christian, though he wore a button to his hat, and ruffles to
his shirt" (II, 211). Tabitha, a female relative of Hezekiah's who keeps
house for him, is shown to be overly strict in her religious practice, and

Rachel condemns her "hatred and malice" (II, 222). Jacob Holmes, a Quaker cousin of Reuben and Rachel's, is the most strongly satirized figure in the novel. He is as fanatical about dress and demeanor as Tabitha, and at the same time he mismanages and steals from the elder Reuben Dudley American landholdings that he had been hired to oversee. Young Reuben arrives in Philadelphia after his father's death to claim his inheritance, and finds that Jacob has not only embezzled from him, but blackened his father's name in the community. Upon meeting Reuben in Philadelphia, Jacob quibbles, "How is it young man, that I see thee in the garb of the children of vanity? thy father wore it not" (II, 275).

Strong feeling is not a substitute for persuasive argument, and "enthusiasm" is ridiculed. Engaged in a discussion with a zealot, Reuben meets frustration:

> Here a dispute ensued, in which Reuben evidently lost ground with his antagonist; for Reuben argued with coolness, and took reason for his monitor; whereas his opponent was wild, enthusiastic, and extremely ignorant. He had adopted some eccentric ideas in regard to religion, and he asserted that his opinions were right, "because they were," and that all who did not think exactly as he did, were in the high road to destruction, for the same unanswerable reason, "because they were."
>
> (II, 267)

The principle of religious tolerance to which Mrs. Rowson often pays tribute prompts her to provide examples of worthy members of the groups she satirizes. She reminds us in *The Inquisitor* that there are good Methodists as well as some who may resemble her hypocritical minister. Reverend Matthews, the guardian of the three orphans in *Charlotte's Daughter*, delivers a sermonette on religious tolerance to Mary Lumly when he hears his ward use the term opprobriously:

> "And now, Mary, let me advise you, never to use the term methodist in this way again. Dame Lonsdale and her husband are good pious members of the church of England . . . there are many roads to the foot of the cross, and whichever may be taken, if it is pursued with a pure and upright heart, is safe, and He who suffered on it, will remove every burthen from us whether it be earthly affliction, or sorrow for committed offences."
>
> (p. 60)

In *Reuben and Rachel* Stedfast Trueman, an honest, upright Quaker, is contrasted to Jacob.

To Mrs. Rowson, some kind of religion, even the non-Christian, is preferable to no religion at all. In "Outline of Universal History" (*A Present for Young Ladies*), she tries to conclude on a tolerant note by saying merely,

> . . . Empires have been, men of all ages have abounded in wealth, power, and pleasure; but where are they now? gone—vanished as a dream. Swallowed in the gulf of oblivion; but religion, and particularly the christian religion, holds out the most blessed hopes. . . .
>
> (p. 62)

But at the conclusion of this paragraph, she refers to her religion as "the true faith"; throughout textbook passages on history and geography, she refers to other world religions as "gross idolatry" and ridicules their modes of worship.

Further, the "true faith" is protestant. Mrs. Rowson must include Catholicism in the fold of Christianity, and she tries to moderate her remarks about the Roman form of worship; the individual practicing Catholic Christianity is often praised and shown in a good light, but the church structure is an immovable obstacle in her acceptance of Catholicism—a point that will be developed later. Important here is the fact that part of Mrs. Rowson's dislike of the Catholic Church is its priesthood and its emphasis upon forms and rituals as a key to salvation. A good Christian will perform deeds in imitation of Christ, but he does not need to fulfill elaborate duties nor be subservient to the priesthood in communicating with God. The relationship between man and God is direct.

The primary formal requisites for religious worship are noted at the conclusion of *Biblical Dialogues*: the sacraments, hymns, and a minister (II, 372). These are the requisites suggested in the fiction as well. In her hour of repentance and death, Charlotte calls for a clergyman and she "joined fervently in the pious office"—presumably communion (p. 123). Sarah also receives communion from a minister friend, Mr. Hayley. Otherwise there is very little emphasis in the fiction upon formal religion. Mrs. Rowson's heroines, although devout, spend little time in church. The ministers of the church are infrequently available to serve the troubled heroine. But this feature of Mrs. Rowson's work does not represent a substitution of tears for prayer and for orthodox beliefs. The heroines of the fiction pray constantly and, as in the foregoing examples, observe the basic rites. Mrs. Rowson does de-emphasize the male-dominated church structure. Her girls must solve their own problems, think as well as feel their way through the difficult situations in life—not depend on masculine guidance. Mrs. Rowson's religious outlook conforms in some respects to Gail Parker's description of the religion of the sentimentalist:

> . . . underlying the morally unexceptionable writings of the Sentimentalists was a fundamentally feminist reinterpretation of Calvinism. . . . Sentimental authors undercut the monopoly on the word of God that orthodox Christians had awarded to an all-male ministerial corps.[4]

Rather than trying to assert feminine "blackness" or "irrationality" in religion, Mrs. Rowson attempts to establish a basis upon which women might share religious life free from the many anti-female traditions of the church, which ranged from the use of Scripture to insist upon feminine inferiority to related rules giving women inferior seating and prohibiting them from preaching.[5] But rather than confront and combat these traditions directly as Elizabeth Cady Stanton did at a riper time, Mrs. Rowson stresses the aspects of her religion likely to encourage respect for the female.

Mrs. Rowson's emphasis on the spirit over the letter of the law, her insistence, as in *Biblical Dialogues*, that God's requirement is "the pure, humble and contrite spirit" (II, 353), serves Mrs. Rowson's purpose, whereas slavishness to formal religion would give too much support to entrenched, unexamined traditions.

While she derides formalism, Mrs. Rowson does not go to the other extreme of putting all her emphasis upon feeling in her treatment of religion. Gail Parker's further point in *The Oven Birds* about the religion of the sentimental tradition does not apply to Mrs. Rowson. Mrs. Parker writes that it "restructured the Calvinist model of salvation, making the capacity to feel, and above all to weep, in itself evidence of redemption," a course that, as the author explains, gave American women "a potentially revolutionary ideology"—but one that backfired (p. 13). Mrs. Rowson may have foreseen the "counterproductive" element in this ideology that made strength of emotion the sole basis of the right of women to express opinions on religion and society: that it could be used to picture women as "ever at the mercy of their impulses" (*Oven Birds*, p. 14).

Whether or not her foresight extended so far, Mrs. Rowson combines the concepts "reason and religion." Faith may be a relatively simple matter, and God may examine the "temple of our hearts" (*Biblical Dialogues*, II, 386) rather than our exact theological positions, our prayer books, and our style of life to determine our future destination, but maintaining our faith requires sense, the use of the intellect, and the faculty of reason.

In *Reuben and Rachel*, Columbia, the great-granddaughter of the explorer, meets "Bloody Mary," who attempts to convert the young woman to Catholicism. The queen announces that she will send ecclesiastics who will examine her and her mother for religious heresies. Columbia replies that she "will listen to them with patience; and if my reason is convinced—" (I, 101).

Mrs. Rowson stresses the importance of "the educated intellect" for both sexes. She writes in *The Inquisitor*, "So, place a man of education in ever so obscure a situation, you will always discover the manners of the gentleman, though obscured by the garb of the beggar" (III, 180). The importance of wide reading for women is one of Mrs. Rowson's main preoccupations in the fiction. She suggests a broad spectrum of authors and fields of interest, and condemns only books that might deflect young women from their religion. Abigail Prune in *The Fille de Chambre* and Tabitha in *Reuben and Rachel* are both satirized for their narrowness in reading only the Bible. The latter,

> Ignorant in the highest degree . . . valued herself on that ignorance; she understood nothing of polite literature; and whenever she saw our heroine engaged in any book, whether of instruction or amusement it mattered not, by her they were all termed vanity and vexation of spirit. The productions of the best poets were called blasphemy. History was of no use; for of what consequence was it to her what was done in the world before she was born? And works of fancy, however excellent in their kind, were all a pack of nonsense, and served only to fill young people's heads with proclamations. To be seen with a book on any day except Sunday, was highly against her creed.
>
> (II, 219-220)

Without education, even religious people are led into superstition as they were in early America. Mrs. Rowson provides a scene in *Reuben and Rachel* in which two rustics think they see the ghost of their employer:

> It need hardly be mentioned, that in those early days, superstition (the natural attendant on ignorant minds and contracted educa-

tions) pervaded the understandings of almost every class of people.

(I, 150)

Two of Mrs. Rowson's shiniest paragons in the fiction are well-educated clergymen, Mr. Hayley in *Sarah* and Reverend Matthews in *Charlotte's Daughter*; they combine religious faith and force of intellect. Mr. Alworth in *Biblical Dialogues* is their counterpart in the texts.

In the latter works, of course, the importance of the educated intelligence is clear. History and other disciplines are necessary for the clear understanding and practice of religion and morality. Various historical personages are commended for their contributions to learning. Peter the Great, for example, is mentioned in *Abridgment of Universal Geography* (p. 33), as well as in the other histories, for his encouragement of education and learning in his country.

Mrs. Rowson is not anti-intellectual, but she opposes a particular point of view: skepticism. It is not an adventitious combination of traits that makes so many of the male "seducers" in the fiction freethinkers. These men cause the "ruin" of the female only if she is corrupted by their philosophy. Mrs. Rowson does not set up an opposition between the head and the heart in these encounters, but the opposition of two points of view, both of which claim reason for their side. The male seducer tries to induce his target to use her reason to justify her passions, while Mrs. Rowson tries to convince the reader to use her reason to resist such arguments and maintain her faith (purity).

The Christian needs "a strong rational faith," Mr. Alworth's goal for his children in *Biblical Dialogues* (I, 113). In this book as well as in the fiction, a skeptic is on hand to "seduce" the Alworth children. He is George Walker, the boy down the street, a local scoffer who asks the Alworths embarrassing questions such as his "sneering and ludicrous interrogatories, concerning the size of the ark" (I, 51). Many of the children's questions, whether inspired by George or hatched in their own minds, are matters of probability. John, for example, raises the point that "naturalists in general describe the whale as having a small gullet" (II, 6). Although his basic religious principles are based upon "the heart," Mr. Alworth is prepared to defend the tenets of Christianity with logic and science. In many instances he provides everyday explanations for biblical occurrences; in others he stresses the metaphorical nature of the Scriptures or refers to modern science for corroboration of his ideas. The burning of the golden calf, he explains, probably took place by a process recently discovered by the Royal Academy at Paris in experiments with a "burning glass" (I, 197). Mrs. Rowson has Mr.

Alworth offer the Deist's image of the clock and clockmaker to describe the relationship between God and creation (I, 61-62). While the children are reminded that man's discoveries concern second causes, they are taught respect for them.

The beliefs and practices of the Christian must be reconciled with the rest of human knowledge. The mind, with or without George Walker, will conceive questions and will not easily retain its faith. The boys in *Biblical Dialogues* are more prone to these kinds of questions than the girls, and Charilea and Amy are occasionally given credit by the father for asking reasonable questions as opposed to the "cavilling of your brothers"; but the girls also ask the father for rational explanations. Amy wonders, "How could persons who were dead many years before our Saviour was born, be benefitted by his death and suffering—how could they believe on his word?" (II, 266).

In her treatment of the religious training of women, Mrs. Rowson shows much more trust in the feminine intellect than a typical contemporary, Hannah Foster. In *The Boarding School*, a series of letters and dialogues between a schoolmistress and her pupils, Mrs. Foster writes that women should confine their reading of the Scriptures to those passages that "mend the heart" rather than to use their heads on more complex problems of the Bible.[6] But Mrs. Rowson thinks they should be prepared to do just that. Like her other works, *Biblical Dialogues* was written *for* women; the questions discussed are for them to consider, and the book gives them an image of themselves as thinking and feeling Christians able to withstand the pressures of a scientific and skeptical age.

But the prejudice against female participation in religious matters was strong. While Judith Sargent Murray found it the *reductio ad absurdum* of discrimination to deny women "future existence,"[7] it had been only a century in America since Samuel Sewall had thought it necessary to defend the idea that women in the afterlife would have a recognizable form just as men did.[8] In Mrs. Rowson's day, only the Quakers allowed women to speak in church, and a move to change restrictions against women in Protestant churches was still being resisted by Lyman Beecher and others in the 1820s.[9]

Mrs. Rowson's encouragement of women in public speaking (as shown in her academy's commencement exercises, *A Present*) may be seen as an assault on these restrictions, for the fear of church participation was linked to the suspicion of women engaging in any form of public vocal expression—a suspicion expressed in John Cotton's defense of women's right to join in the psalm-singing in church. Cotton carefully distinguishes singing, which he approves of as "praises of the

Lord" (with precedence set by Miriam), from teaching or asking questions, which might "open the door to some of her [woman's] own weak
and erroneous apprehension, or at least soon exceed her bounds of
womanly modesty."[10]

While other schools besides the Rowson academy offered young
women a chance to address audiences, the hesitant tone of the students
illustrates how tentative a claim the schools made for their practices. A
pupil at the Philadelphia Ladies' Academy confesses in her commencement address:

> Were I voluntarily to offer myself a candidate for the purpose of
> addressing so respectable an audience, through any other motive
> than that of complying with the rules of the institution, I should
> consider the most elaborate apology, insufficient to extenuate such
> a violation of female delicacy.[11]

Defenses like this and the restrictions behind them must have seemed
illogical to Mrs. Rowson. She never apologized in the addresses she
wrote for her students, and in fact had the girls recite the stories of great
women in "Female Biography." Such eminent clergymen as Edward
Everett asked Mrs. Rowson to write religious musical pieces to be
performed in public, and she complied.

The anti-female traditions of the church were still entrenched, but
Mrs. Rowson might help weaken them with her brand of Christianity.
Further, her emphasis on the Christian virtues, which anyone could
practice, with or without privileges in church life, underline the equality among all people, and give support to her teaching—so necessary to
the complete education of her audience—on the proper arrangement of
society.

5

Independent and Free

> So woman when by nature drest,
>   In charms devoid of art;
> Can warm the stoic's icy brest,
>   Can triumph o'er each heart.
> Can bid the soul to virtue rise,
>   To glory prompt the brave,
> But sinks oppress'd, and drooping dies,
>   When once she's made a slave.
>
> (Slaves in Algiers, 1974)

During the 1790s and early 1800s, Mrs. Rowson wrote several theater pieces on American subjects, as well as numerous poems and songs eulogizing George Washington and John Adams and celebrating American values, virtues, and victories. At first glance "The Standard of Liberty," "America and Liberty," and "On the Birthday of George Washington" may appear to depart from Mrs. Rowson's central purpose. But this view fails to reckon with Mrs. Rowson's ability to relate every subject to her particular audience. The importance of national ideals and their significance for women is a theme that runs through Mrs. Rowson's entire canon. The values she praises in her patriotic American efforts, democracy and freedom, are extensions of those she always advocated. A Christian society, argues Mrs. Rowson, will be a democratic society, and a democratic society recognizes the female as a participating, rational individual. She establishes this equation through her literary treatment of various nations and groups, and makes her point especially trenchant by emphatically condemning dictatorship and slavery.

Mrs. Rowson's views on society are rooted in her condemnation as a Christian of the false idols society worships. Material wealth and social status are inferior to the "inner" wealth of faith and virtue and the "true nobility" of the Christian. Individuals may be virtuous regardless of their worldly possessions or their social position, and Mrs. Rowson dramatizes this idea by praising the charitable acts of persons from both ends of the social scale. The humble family of servants who help Charlotte when she is about to have her baby, and a group of sailors who share their food with Rebecca and the Abthorpes when the latter are starving are truly "rich" and "noble"—as are the Duchess of Devonshire who is praised for her virtue in *Victoria*, the Marquis H—, who helps Sarah financially, and Lady Chatterton in *The Fille de Chambre*.

On the other hand, Mrs. Rowson presents a plethora of wealthy and high-ranking people who believe that their worldly station makes them better than other people, but who are found to be inferior to persons of lower standing. Pride in one's wealth and lineage is an unfailing sign, in Mrs. Rowson's work, of moral degeneracy. Geoffry Talbot, the cousin who tries to cheat Mary of her estate, is a good example of such a relationship (*The Test of Honour*, II, 82). Lord and Lady Ossiter in *The Fille* betray contempt for the poor and the middle class, and their son thinks himself above the weaknesses of ordinary people. He tells Rebecca that he will never want because he is "a Lord's son" (p. 68). In *Charlotte's Daughter*, Lady Mary considers herself superior to the other two orphans because she is of noble rank. In each case, material wealth and the title to nobility are shown to be of little help to the possessor, while "true" worth and nobility carry the day. Lady Mary, for example, is seduced and abandoned, and she dies insane, while Lucy Blakeney overcomes the sad blow of falling in love with her half-brother and continues to live a useful and purposeful life. As Mrs. Rowson's Inquisitor reflects,

> A well-a-day, said I, 'tis a strange thing, but to me, poverty of ideas and meanness of spirit are greater afflictions than poverty of purse and meanness of birth.
>
> (II, 158)

A short step takes Mrs. Rowson from belief in a democracy of virtue to enthusiasm for democracy as a social standard. In celebrating the glories of the American republic, she selects specific aspects of the nation: prosperity, the desire for peace, the love of freedom, liberty, and independence. She does not recommend class equality and social mobility.[1] Although Mrs. Rowson celebrates America in her patriotic songs and poems, she does not denounce England. In fact, England is the predominant setting of the fiction; it is Susanna Rowson's original home, and in many ways remains her spiritual home. In *Charlotte's Daughter*, Mrs. Rowson praises a British rather than American concept of social relations between the classes. Aura Melville's wedding is described as celebrated after the fashion of the good old times when the poor not only looked up to the gentry for protection and friendship, but took a lively interest in their domestic affairs, were depressed at their misfortunes, and proud and happy in the fame and happiness of their patrons.

(p. 177)

Mrs. Rowson excoriates snobbery. In *The Inquisitor*, she criticizes an actress for thinking herself too good to speak to a barber. It is "the height of folly," she argues, for a woman who spends her life trying to please all ranks of people in her profession to mind meeting someone of lower status (I, 70). But the author allows little social mobility in her pages. Her religious viewpoint recommends content with one's station—for a Christian can pursue his goals in any social rank. Cinderella stories, in which young people meet and marry persons above them socially, are un-Christian because they set up unworthy goals, and are unrealistic in that they seldom happen in real life. In a neat reversal of the frog-to-prince transformation, George Worthy in *The Fille de Chambre* proves by means of a certain strawberry mark that he is a commoner rather than a rich lord before he is allowed to marry Rebecca.

George's metamorphosis is a step in the author's celebration of democracy. Mrs. Rowson had begun a satirical attack upon hereditary wealth and rank in *The Inquisitor* (III, 182); she continues to denigrate the concept in the many instances cited above in which the wealthy and aristocratic emerge as spiritually threadbare and ignoble. Mrs. Rowson's efforts culminate in *Reuben and Rachel*, in which she emphatically champions the American ideal of each man earning his own way and proving his own worth. As the novel ends, Reuben is married to Jessy, Rachel to Auberry; the two couples settle down to lives of felicity such as may be obtained in this "rocky path of life." The scheming Quaker, Jacob Holmes, is dead, and the family home, Mount Pleasant, has been restored to Reuben and his sister. The families receive a visit from Mr. Allibi, the attorney of the elder Dudley's creditor, who brings the news that Reuben and Rachel have finally inherited the English Dudley holdings and that Hamden is entitled to the estate of his aunt, Lady Anne. In a gesture that symbolizes the protagonists' rejection of the English system of aristocracy, the young people turn down these bounties. Reuben dismisses Allibi and states,

"You may think, Mr. Allibi, that by bringing us this intelligence you have greatly heightened our felicity; and in one respect you have, as it extends our power of serving our fellow-creatures. As to titles, both my brother Auberry and his wife Rachel, join with me to renounce them; they are distinctions nothing worth, and should by no means be introduced into a young country, where *the only distinction between man and man should be made by virtue, genius and education.* Our sons are true-born Americans, and while they strive to make that title respectable, we wish them to possess no other. Let the titles then go, and such of the estates as are annexed to them, to more distant branches of our several families, or in case of default of heirs, let them sink into oblivion. Of the immense property of which we are become possessors, we shall retain no more than will set our sons forward in business, and give our daughters moderate portions; the residue shall be equally divided amongst the indigent relatives of both families."

(II, 363-364, italics mine)

In his attack on Mrs. Rowson, William Cobbett alleges that the author's celebration of America is insincere, a concession to her residence in America and to her changed audience. Certainly there is a shift of primary allegiance in Mrs. Rowson's works from Britain to America,[2] but it is a shift of loyalty and a movement from one country to the other as the main symbol of equality, independence, freedom, and humane treatment of the individual, rather than a reversal of fundamental principles. Although there are no perfect societies in this imperfect world, and both English and American society are satirized, England and America represent the best social ideals, and other countries and groups are approved or disapproved as they conform to their standards.

In *The Inquisitor*, although England does not perform her duty—according to an Arabian captive in "Sadi and Zelia" (I, 125 ff.)—she still symbolizes the ideals of freedom and equality. The narrative of Sadi, the slave, reveals how he was sold into captivity by some English "Christians." He remonstrates, "I heard that England was the land of freedom" (I, 129), but he is charged for his passage there, and put into prison. After his release, he is allowed to starve in the street until some "Christian women" sympathize with his plight and give him money to buy food (I, 130). His ironic admonition, "Go tell the tale to all the Eastern world—go warn them beware of trusting Christians" (I, 130), reminds us that the situation should be reversed.

Mrs. Rowson's schematization of national and social virtue is neatly expressed in *The Test of Honour*. Christian nations are contrasted to pagan, and Protestant to Catholic. England, an example of both the former, holds out the hope of human rights, and is a better place for women than any of the other cultures appearing in the book, although treatment of women is on an ascending scale from pagan to Protestant.

The events that lead up to Frederick's captivity by the Algerians include a series of naval coups symbolic of Mrs. Rowson's hierarchy. First, the English ship carrying Mary and Frederick to Jamaica is boarded by Spanish privateers, and its course is changed to Cadiz (II, 48 ff.). Mrs. Rowson notes that "However disagreeable such a change in their circumstances might be," the English dread to a greater degree the threat of Algerian piracy, now imminent. The English join their Spanish captors in trying to drive the pirates away. Although Frederick is taken by the Algerians, the ship goes free because of the appearance on the scene of a "large ship, bearing British colours" (II, 52). The Algerians "knowing that all christian powers, however at war with each other, would join unanimously against them . . . crouded all their sail, and left the Spaniards an easy prize to the English" (II, 52). Frederick, separated from Mary, "gathered some comfort from the reflection, that she must undoubtedly be much better in the hands of the Spaniards, who, in general, were *attentive and honourable to the fair sex*, than if she was, like himself, at the mercy of the infidels" (II, 52-53, italics mine). Mary's ship is taken by the lately arrived second British ship, however, and the Spanish privateers "now chearfully resigned themselves prisoners to the British arms, and thought Providence had visibly interfered, in allotting them to an enemy so humane and generous as the English" (II, 54).

Mary returns home to England to gain her rights against her scheming cousin in Jamaica. She bases her right to reject Harry Fentum on her status as a "free born English woman" and claims "spirit enough to assert those rights which nature and my country allow me" (I, 34).

In contrast to Britain, the non-English, non-Christian societies are shown to be tyrannical and cruel. In Jamaica Mary observes slaves turning a gristmill, and sympathizes with their plight. The Algerian Dey who becomes Frederick's master when he is sold into captivity has absolute power of life and death over his subjects and slaves. There are no "rights" granted by society; all the English can do is try to buy their way out of captivity, or convert the infidel to more humane and rational principles.

The similar story of captivity that is treated as a farce in *Slaves in Algiers* also dramatizes the dichotomy between various religious and national values. The play finds Mrs. Rowson now using America as her main symbol of national virtue. Augustus, the young son of Rebecca, an American woman, announces his intention to help rescue the captives. "Fear, mother," he says, "what should I be afraid of? an't I an American, and I am sure you have often told me, in a right cause, the Americans did not fear any thing" (III.2.49-50). In the final scene of the play, Muley the Dey is so impressed with the integrity of his American friends that he vows to reform his own kingdom, and asks the freed slaves to teach him the way; Constant, one of the captives, advises,

> Open your prison doors; give freedom to your people; sink the name of subject in the endearing epithet of fellow-citizen;—then you will be loved and reverenced—then will you find, in promoting the happiness of others, you have secured your own.
>
> (III.7.71)

The concluding speeches are then delivered by Muley, Henry, and Olivia, an American woman (played by Mrs. Rowson):

> *Muley*: Henceforward, then, I will reject all power but such as my united friends shall think me incapable of abusing. Hassan, you are free—to you my generous conquerors what can I say?

> *Henry*: Nothing, but let your future conduct prove how much you value the welfare of your fellow-creatures—to-morrow, we shall leave your capital, and return to our native land, where liberty has established her court—where the warlike Eagle extends his glittering pinions in the sunshine of prosperity.

> *Olivia*: Long, long, may that prosperity continue—May Freedom spread her benign influence thro' every nation, till the bright Eagle, united with the dove and olive-branch, waves high, the acknowledged standard of the world.
>
> (III.7.71-72)

For added emphasis, the Jew is introduced in both *Test* and *Slaves* as part of the non-Christian, nondemocratic world. In *Test* he is the traditional mercenary, an "extortionate Jew" who conveys the escaping slaves home to England (II, 195). In *Slaves in Algiers* he receives ransom money for the Christian slaves, including Rebecca, an American with whom he falls in love. Ben Hassan participates in an interesting discussion of values with Rebecca (II.2.38); in a soliloquy he states his amazement that Rebecca has not figured out the fact that since he feeds her and has not sold her to the Dey, he has received ransom money for her. As a Jew, he simply cannot fathom the moral standards of the Christian.

Mrs. Rowson's treatment of Catholicism in *Victoria*, *Trials of the Human Heart*, and *Reuben and Rachel* underlines the author's commitment to forms of government, social or religious, which she believes allow the individual rights, freedom, and equality.[3] The Catholic Church is not among these institutions. In the novels it is associated with France, a country that never fares well in Mrs. Rowson's estimation. The practices of convent life are depicted as tyrannical, cruel, and withdrawn from the realities of life. In *Victoria*, Arabella, on a tour of France, speculates about the torture being suffered by the "lives confined" in the convent of St. Omar (II, 3 ff.). Hester Vellum, a good character in *The Inquisitor*, compares convents to prisons (III, 241).

The convent Meriel and Celia attend (in *Trials of the Human Heart*) is located in France, and the heroine does not come away with a good impression of its practice of religion. Declaring to Celia her intention to remain celibate if Rainsforth dies in the Revolutionary War, she insists that her vow is as strong "as if made at the foot of the altar surrounded by all the pomp of monkish superstition" (I, 121). In *Reuben and Rachel*, as noted, the church is the agent of religious oppression and conformity through the efforts of "Bloody Mary." Its intolerance and interference with the freedom of individual choice is also stressed through the refusal of "poor bigoted Beatina," the wife of Columbus, to allow her daughter to marry a Protestant, an act that causes problems for subsequent generations of the explorer's family.

Mrs. Rowson's continuous disapproval of "factions," which she develops in reference to Christianity and extends to the political sphere in her American songs, is also related to her social ideas. Any group that sets itself up as "elect" and "exclusive" violates the author's democratic principles. In *Reuben and Rachel*, Mrs. Rowson satirizes the New England Calvinist who can admit the practical virtue of a fellow Christian and yet, because of doctrine, deny him equal status. When Reuben arrives in America after his father's death, he encounters an innkeeper from whom he first learns about the way Jacob Holmes has calumniated his father. When Reuben remarks that his father is in heaven, the innkeeper suggests that the young man not be too sure:

> "Yea, he was good in the worldly acceptation of the word; he did alms, told no lies, hated no one, paid every man, yea, more than his due; but all this is vanity, filthy rags, unclean vestments. He was not one of the chosen; he was in a lost state."
>
> (II, 266-267)

Mr. Alworth in *Biblical Dialogues* clarifies Mrs. Rowson's position on this matter. One Christian sect must not persecute or oppose others, for to engage in factionalism is to "set ourselves up above our fellow mortals" (II, 386).

Mrs. Rowson denies validity to caste: social, governmental, priestly, and sexual. The societies freest from such distinctions are the Protestant and Anglo-Saxon. Mrs. Rowson drives home this point in her textbook judgments of various groups and nations.

For the most part, the non-Protestant and non-Saxon groups and nations are presented as unsaved, undemocratic, unclean, unproductive, and unhealthy, while England, Scotland, the United States, and other areas that at least attempt to practice Christianity are associated with the opposite characteristics. Although Mrs. Rowson grants some favorable qualities to Mongolia, Siam, Turkey, Arabia, and other "heathen" nations, her language in pointing out their faults is harsh. In *An Abridgment of Universal Geography*, she writes of the Arabians,

> The Arabians are the descendants of Ishmeal, of whose posterity it was foretold, that they should be invincible, "have their hands against every man, and every man's hand against them." They are at present, and have remained from the remotest ages, a convincing proof of the divinity of this prediction. The Arabians in general are such thieves, that travellers and pilgrims, who are led thither through motives of devotion or curiosity, are struck with terror when they approach the deserts.
>
> (p. 132)

Of European Turkey, Mrs. Rowson contends, "The air is salubrious, unless corrupted by the indolence and uncleanliness of the inhabitants . . ." (p. 95).

In contrast, Greenland and Iceland are clean, neat, and religious. In *Abridgment*, Mrs. Rowson praises Switzerland for the industry and intelligence of its people (pp. 75-76). In Norway, "The lowest Norwegian peasant is an artist, a gentleman, and often a poet" (p. 20). Mrs. Rowson cites Scotland's tendency to economy and self-restraint, noting the "few instances of murder, perjury, robbery" (p. 38). England's people are "of all nations the most cleanly. Their marking characteristics are bravery and humanity." Mrs. Rowson lauds the "Englishman of good education" as "the most accomplished gentleman in the world" (p. 43). Her treatment in *Abridgment* of the United States is especially kind to New England and regions that she believed fostered Christianity and democracy. However, with her favorites as well as the areas she criticizes most harshly, she points out the error of entrenched, tyrannical governing hierarchies, religious castes, and the concomitant sexual discrimination.

The government of Siam, Mrs. Rowson declares in *Abridgment*, "is very despotic; even the mandarins prostrate themselves before the king" (p. 120). The author criticizes Poland for being run by a nobility that has "the power of life and death over their tenants and vassals" (p. 72). The only proper function of the higher classes is to ennoble and share with the less fortunate, Mrs. Rowson believes; where privileged classes think only of their own vainglory, the whole society suffers. Turning to the United States, Mrs. Rowson praises Virginia for its "influential men, who were active in effecting the grand revolution in America," but notes that in this state, the advantages of the upper class have not been spread among the "lower order," who are "ignorant and abject; and of a most troublesome, iniquitous turn" (p. 219). North Carolina, where the Episcopal Church is described as in decay, in a similar fashion neglects the education of its children. Mrs. Rowson praises the Carolinians, Charlestonians in particular, but she points out, "if there is any peculiarity in the character of the Carolinians in general, it is only what proceeds from the pernicious influence of slavery, for the absolute authority which they exercise over their slaves, gives them an air of supercilious haughtiness far from agreeable" (p. 228).

Religious elitism is also criticized. As in the novels, the Roman Catholic form of Christianity is associated in the pedagogical works with tyranny and superstition. In *Abridgment*, Mrs. Rowson contrasts undemocratic elements of the Catholic countries with the more creative and free qualities of the Protestant. Spain and France are harshly judged. The former is preeminent in one respect, for having been the home of Cervantes, who is "to be placed at the head of all moral and humourous satirists" (p. 79). Otherwise Spain is marked by "indolence," and while the horrors of the Inquisition are abating, and an edict to reduce the numbers of clergy has been put into effect,

> In 1794 there were computed to be in the kingdom of Spain 54,000 friars, 34,000 nuns, and 20,000 secular clergy; but, says a writer of some eminence, "as little true religion as in any place under heaven."
>
> (p. 82)

France, as usual, receives especially harsh criticism by Mrs. Rowson— especially France during the reign of Napoleon. The author grants the French wit and vivacity, but writes,

A national vanity is their predominant characteristic. It supports them under misfortunes, and impels to actions, to which true courage inspires others.

(p. 55)

Italy, the papal state, is priest-ridden. Although in *Abridgment* Mrs. Rowson praises its accomplishments in the arts, she notes that industry and agriculture are discouraged and "lazy" priests encouraged. She writes, "The baleful effects of superstition and oppression are here evidenced in the highest degree" (p. 91). The legends about the Virgin Mary, examples of superstition, are labeled "ridiculous."

If religious tolerance is practiced, as in the Netherlands, the Catholics deserve the freedom to worship as they choose, but where the church is forced upon the people, Mrs. Rowson demurs. It is the "princely power" of the popes to which she objects, as she states in *Biblical Dialogues* (II, 377). But although the Roman church becomes her central symbol of religious despotism, Mrs. Rowson does not indulge in mere Catholic-baiting. In *Abridgment* she attacks the Greek Orthodox Church for "little differing from popery" because it practices "idolatrous and superstitious customs" such as its "number of fasts" (p. 32). She complains that until Peter the Great arose to reform the Church, "The clergy had formerly great power, which they exercised over the laity in a most despotic manner" (p. 32). The religion of Hindustan is similarly attacked in *Youth's First Step*:

In Hindostan, they have a complete system of superstition; their temples are magnificent; their rites and ceremonies pompous and splendid. Their Brahmins, or priests, are elevated above every other class of men, and claim an origin not only more noble, but sacred. They worship an idol, called Jagernaut, and other inferior idols, with the most horrid and cruel rites.

(p. 176)

Women do not fare well in the societies and groups Mrs. Rowson attacks most vehemently. Among the Turks, for example, women lead constrained, confined lives. Mrs. Rowson's description in *Abridgment* of the capital of Georgia includes this fact among more mundane observations: "the houses built of stone, with flat roofs . . . serve as walks for the women, for the Turkish women seldom or ever go abroad, or are seen by any but their nearest relations" (p. 107). In Egypt "The women . . . are not admitted to the society of the men, not even at table, but remain standing, or seated in a corner of the room while the husband dines . . ." (p. 141).

The baleful effects of Catholicism upon individual females are occasionally pointed out. The Roman Church, Mrs. Rowson argues, keeps the body as well as the mind enfeebled. Mary Astell, the writer on women and one of the exemplary intellectuals in "Female Biography," writes Mrs. Rowson, "was very strict in the observance of her religious duties, and being of the Romish church, is thought to have injured her health by frequent and long abstinence" (A Present, p. 112). The Boston Weekly Magazine, during the period of Mrs. Rowson's probable editorship, contains the lamentable sequel to Mrs. Rowson's story of the accomplishments of a Catholic female, Maria Agnesi. This lady, a professor of mathematics and philosophy at the University of Bologna, according to the article, allows her great gifts to be lost to superstition and mysticism by entering a convent. In this regard she resembles the great Pascal, who similarly misused his intellect:

> The fate of Pascal and Agnesi will remain a melancholy proof, that the most splendid abilities and the highest attainments in literature and science, cannot always defend the mind against the inroads of superstition and fanaticism.
>
> (17 November 1804)

Its few problems notwithstanding, America is, in Mrs. Rowson's view, the stronghold of freedom, and the ultimate symbol of female emancipation. All of her surveys of world history end with the celebration of the new country, in the vein of Reuben and Rachel. In the "Concluding Address for 1808," delivered by a pupil at the school, Mrs. Rowson declares, "in this happy country [America] women enjoy the blessings of liberal instructions, reasonable laws, a pure religion, and all the endearing pleasures of an equal virtuous and social intercourse" (A Present, p. 148).

America, as the symbol of all that opposes tyranny and arbitrary power, must fight any attempts on the part of foreign governments or internal political factions to threaten her independence and freedom. Thus in the patriotic songs, odes, and theater pieces, Mrs. Rowson expresses the same love of freedom from oppressive social systems that she had expressed in the novels and was to develop in the pedagogical works. The fact that her demands extend to greater freedom for women is seen in her employment of symbolic patterns that link the various genres.

The patriotic works continue the themes of the wretchedness of tyranny and slavery. "Faction" is an invidious concept whether practiced in America or by her foes. The exercise of force is condemned and the virtues of belief and commitment to ideals extolled. The song we have from the musical drama, *The American Tar, or the Press Gang Defeated* (1796), entitled "Independent and Free," is a rousing drinking song. The third verse and chorus suggest the song's flavor, and include the specific reference to slavery typical of Mrs. Rowson:

> For commerce whilst the sail we spread
>   To cross the foaming waves boys
> Say who shall dare our rights invade,
>   Who dare to make us slaves boys
> Then let us hand & heart unite
>   Oppression shall before us flee
> Boldly assert each sacred right
>   Be Independant, Brave & Free.

> Then Huzza Huzza Huzza for America
> Ever may we be united & Brave, Independent & Free
> Independent & Free, Independent & Free
> Then Huzza then Huzza for AMERICA
> Brave, independent & Free.[4]

"The Little Sailor Boy," which Nason in his *Memoir* states was written for Mrs. Rowson's brother, William (p. 34), also includes the motif of slavery. Cast in the form of a prayer by "Anna" for "My William," the song ends,

> May no rude foe his course impede,
>   Conduct him safely o'er the waves.
> Oh may he never be compell'd
>   To fight for pow'r or mix with slaves
> May smiling peace his steps attend
>   Each rising hour be crown'd with joy,
> As blest as that when I again,
>   Shall meet my much lov'd Sailor boy.[5]

"Truxton's Victory," a song commemorating the success of Commodore Thomas Truxton and his vessel, *The Constellation*, against the French *L'Insurgente* in February 1799, sounds a similar note of hatred for slavery while it underlines another important point: as America grew to be Mrs. Rowson's main symbol for peace and democracy, France, never very popular with this author, increasingly became her chief symbol of violence and tyranny. In accord with this symbolism, George Washington is Mrs. Rowson's greatest hero, among a gallery including Peter the Great, William Tell, and other figures who delivered a people from tyranny, while Napoleon is her arch villain. The second verse of "Truxton's Victory" is:

Though Gallia through Europe has rushed like a flood,
And deluged the earth with an ocean of blood;
While by faction she's led, while she's governed
    by knaves,
We court not her smiles and we'll ne'er be her slaves.
    Her threats we defy,
    While our standard shall fly,
    Resolved, firm and steady,
    We always are ready
To fight and to conquer; to conquer or die.[6]

At the time these songs were written, the British as well as the French threatened America's ability to trade freely with other countries, and impressment was an issue. France, after the Reign of Terror, was feared by most conservatives as an example of democracy run wild. But Mrs. Rowson's hatred of the nation and its emperor goes far beyond the occasion of the works. To Mrs. Rowson, France under Napoleon is the epitome of a tyrannical, destructive dictatorship, and the emperor himself appears in Mrs. Rowson's pedagogical works as the worst of all tyrants. He embodies all the qualities Mrs. Rowson detested most: irreligion, social ambition, violence, lack of respect for existing order, and male chauvinism.[7] He is mentioned, probably without exception, in the textbooks, and is always described in terms as unflattering as those in the following account of France's contemporary situation:

In that short period [the last twenty years] we behold a kingdom overthrown, a lawful sovereign dethroned, and with his unoffending family massacred. Religion forced to hide her dishonoured head, monstrous opinions disseminated, and every tie of morality or honour trampled underfoot. We see from the ashes of this desolating conflagration a republic arise to all appearance beautiful, firm, and salutary in its effects, to the suffering inhabitants of a ruined kingdom. When, behold an insignificant individual of a more insignificant Italian island, by some bravery, more intrigue, and unparalled good fortune fixed himself at the head of the government, when by the most plausible and artful measures he won the confidence of the people, overturned the republic, usurped the crown, and made himself an absolute monarch. Then this seeming fraternal friend, still farther to blind his infatuated subjects, and to make his own power more absolute, re-established in his kingdom the Romish religion. Yes the man who in the early period of the revolution was almost an atheist, at a later period a Mahometan, now dared to profess himself a christian; while his hands were scarlet with the blood of thousands, systematically slaughtered, and his insatiate ambition grasping at every neighbouring crown, was planning usurpation, rapine and destruction to the nations round him. And while his lips professed to serve the God of peace and mercy, his actions bespoke a monster devoted to the powers of darkness.

("Outline of Universal History,"
A Present, pp. 80-81)

The relationship between Mrs. Rowson's social judgments and the situation of male and female can be seen in the way she links the Napoleonic character to the domestic scene. The emperor is discussed as a husband in several poems in *A Present for Young Ladies*. Lucy's attitude toward him in "Dialogue for Three Young Ladies" is typical of the girls' judgments:

And keep from our shores mighty Woglog away;
For he sets the most dreadful examples in life,
And between you and I, beats and locks up his wife.
Heaven help her, poor soul, she's an empress 'tis true,
But I warrant she's oftentimes pinch'd black and blue.
Her chains, tho' of gold, she may keep for all me,
I'm content to be poor, tho' I may but be free.

(p. 36)

The tyrant is not acceptable in government nor in marriage.

Marriage, like society, should be a democracy. Man can easily become the tyrant, but this is not the best arrangement for either himself or the woman. When all authority exists on one side and total submission on the other, the man loses the love and services of a whole woman, and the woman loses her claim to integrity as well as the ability to grow intellectually. Mrs. Rowson underlines this idea through the constant interplay of themes involving the lives of individual women and the motif of slavery.

The author's interest in slavery is largely in its use as a metaphor. There is little of the realistic in Mrs. Rowson's depiction of captivity, and little genuine understanding of the actual victims of oppression.

While Mrs. Rowson decries the Negro slave trade in Africa, she writes in *Reuben and Rachel* of Reuben's saving a baby from a foundering ship, and giving it for safekeeping to "a kind-hearted Negro wench" (II, 557). In *Youth's First Step in Geography*, she lets slip the thought that the people of the Comora Islands "are negroes, but very humane and hospitable . . ." (p. 160). Sympathy for the downtrodden was a popular attitude in the period, often as a mere exercise in sentiment and sensibility; Mrs. Rowson uses the plight of the slave largely to symbolize the situation of the female.

In *The Test of Honour*, as in the other works, the female slave is given prominence, and her situation as a reduced being, good only for sexual exploitation, is dramatized. The seraglio is a frequent symbol for such a state. In *The Test*, Frederick is given a nice job as a gardener by the Algerian tyrant while the two Christian women are eyed for the harem. Eumenia is threatened with being "sold to the Alcaide, and forced to submit to his horrid solicitations" (II, 193). Semira is nearly forced to turn Mohammedan and become one of the wives of Hali.

A terrible fate for any woman, suggests Mrs. Rowson: to lose her religion, her freedom, and her right to a loving relationship with a man with "a parity of sentiments." Yet that is very nearly what happens to Sarah and other female characters when they marry. Meriel and Sarah are both slaves to "the lordly tyrant man." Both women submit to physical as well as emotional abuse; they are trapped, as much the slave as Semira or Fetnah.

In *Sarah*, Mrs. Rowson underlines this similarity by repeatedly referring to her heroine's "fetters" (p. 69), and "chains" (p. 85). Sarah denounces the male's treatment of the female as "a child, an idiot, or a slave" (p. 114). Later in the story she writes to Ann:

> Want of confidence in a husband, is death to the affection of a wife, and she who is by turns the slave of capricious passion, or the object of contempt or neglect, if she is possessed of the least degree of delicacy and feeling, must suffer a bondage more severe than the slave who is chained to the oar.
>
> (p. 259)

In "Dialogue for Three Young Ladies," Ellen expresses a more ideal view of marriage, and in so doing, employs the language of the songs that celebrate Mrs. Rowson's goals for "Columbia": "Well rather let me/ Be poor—and remain independent and free" (*A Present*, p. 42). Ellen yearns to be "a citizen's wife," and presumably would be glad to "sink the name of subject in the endearing epithet of fellow-citizen." But such an equitable arrangement can only be brought about if men as well as women take their religion seriously. Until then, Mrs. Rowson offers the alternative of patient endurance like that of Meriel and Sarah to girls who marry impetuously and without the mutual respect of the male.

Still, to keep her lessons in religion and "government" alive, Mrs. Rowson offers glimpses of spectacular female resistance to tyranny. There are all those examples in "Female Biography" capped by that of Clelia, a Roman virgin who "scorning captivity . . . swam on horseback across the Tyber" (*A Present*, p. 64). In *Slaves in Algiers* women lead a rebellion.

Fetnah, although she is the daughter of a Jew (himself a keeper of slaves), has learned to love freedom. This love has been fostered by Rebecca, an American who has taught her Christianity. As Fetnah says of the older woman, "She came from that land, where virtue in either sex is the only mark of superiority.—She was an American" (I.1.9). Fetnah sighs,

> So woman when by nature drest
>   In charms devoid of art;
> Can warm the stoic's icy breast,
>   Can triumph o'er each heart.
> Can bid the soul to virtue rise,
>   To glory prompt the brave,
> But sinks oppress'd, and drooping dies,
>   When once she's made a slave.
>
> (I.1.10)

The Morican women see nothing wrong in their abject state as harem creatures; one of them asks Fetnah if she does not love her master, and Fetnah's reply reveals the sexual threat she feels in the Dey's power as well as the fact that this "love" is based upon force rather than attraction:

> No—he is old and ugly, then he wears such tremendous whiskers; and when he makes love, he looks so grave and stately, that I declare, if it was not for fear of his huge scymetar, I shou'd burst out a laughing in his face.
>
> (I.1.6)

Fetnah continues in this vein, replete with phallic symbolism, and reasserts her hatred of her position. When Selima, the Morican, later defends the Dey, Fetnah exclaims:

Oh! to be sure, he is a most amiable creature; I think I see him now, seated on his cushion, a bowl of sherbet by his side, and a long pipe in his mouth. Oh! how charmingly the tobacco must perfume his whiskers—here, Mustapha, says he, "Go, bid the slave Selima come to me"—well it does not signify, that word slave does so stick in my throat—I wonder how any woman of spirit can gulp it down.

(II.2.39)

Fetnah's fear of the Dey's "huge scymetar" and his nasty "pipe" should not lead to the conclusion that Mrs. Rowson rejects sexuality— she does not. She argues, however, that societies, not nature, determine whether women should be treated as participating, rational citizens or as sexual commodities. And she warns her readers in yet another way of the tyranny of sex, the dangers of the one-dimensional, passive personality. As Mrs. Rowson has a young lady declare in "Concluding Address. For 1808,"

It is humiliating to our sex to reflect, that in those countries where the admiration of beautiful women is carried to the highest excess they are slaves, and their moral and intellectual degradation increases in direct proportion to the adoration which is paid to mere external charms; to such a length is this degradation carried, and of so little consequence are they deemed in the scale of intelligent beings, that the voluptuous prophet of Arabia excluded them from light, liberty, and knowledge, and from all the joys of paradise.

(*A Present*, p. 148)

While *Slaves in Algiers* may exhibit the overstatement appropriate to farce, Fetnah's vision of happiness summarizes Mrs. Rowson's view of the relation between religion, society, and sex. Fetnah, alone in a garden, says "I do wish, some dear, sweet, Christian man, would fall in love with me, break open the garden gates, and carry me off" (II.2.31). Her dream is not asexual; her Christian man will "break open the garden gates," but he will not enslave her with new limitations. When Frederic, a Christian and an American (an unbeatable combination), approaches her, Fetnah asks him to take her "where there are no bolts and bars; no mutes and guards; no bowstrings and scymetars—Oh! it must be a dear delightful country, where women do just what they please" (II.2.31-32).

6

Pernicious Poison

He had witnessed her enduring affection, and her noble example of all the passive virtues. Her energy and decision was yet to appear.

(Charlotte's Daughter, 1828)

In chapter 5, we saw how Mrs. Rowson uses slavery as a symbol of the arbitrary subordination of the female as endorsed by various social systems and organizations. Other forces as well keep her in bondage to her traditional, submissive rôle. The passions, for example, are as tyrannical as man and his institutions. Henry in *Slaves in Algiers* says to his Algerian captors as he and the others are taken off to be tortured, "call us not slaves;—you are a slave indeed, to rude ungoverned passion; to pride, to avarice and lawless love . . . the blow that ends our lives, strikes off our chains, and sets our souls at liberty" (III.6.60).

Like any good Christian, the female must exert control over her emotions, and must acquire the harder virtues. She must also know what life is really like, and not be misled by the imagination. She must possess sense as well as sensibility. The contrast between the real and the ideal, previously suggested, becomes a prominent theme through Mrs. Rowson's warnings to exercise a critical attitude toward the images of women encouraged by popular literature. While Mrs. Rowson does not dismiss fiction completely, as do some early American novelists,[1] she repeatedly warns her audience of the dangers of reading fiction improperly, and of adopting bookish attitudes and expectations. She tries to convince the reader of the unreality of the four most popular modes of fiction of her day: the sentimental, the romantic, the novel of sensibility, and the Gothic novel.

A girl who reads only fiction, the wrong kind of fiction, or who takes fiction too seriously will be inadequately prepared for life, argues Mrs. Rowson. Of course, the conventional caveat against novel reading could be used, like the claim to didacticism or truth, as a "gimmick" to dispel suspicion that one's own efforts might undermine community standards. But the danger of fiction was also a serious theme in the works of female novelists who observed women entering upon lives of new possibilities with little solid or practical education. Fanny Burney and Jane Austen developed this theme. Evelina is initiated into a wider world than Berry Hill, and through a combination of trial and error and the precepts of her guardian, learns to live in the broader scene. But what of the girl who has no Reverend Villars in the background to counsel and advise her? The situation of Catherine Morland entering the "complicated" social scene at Bath, armed with a few clichés and lofty-sounding chestnuts from eminent authors—her "education"—is even closer than Evelina's experiences to those Mrs. Rowson tries to depict.

Mrs. Rowson approves and recommends a variety of authors and works. Reading for pleasure as well as for moral improvement is sanctioned and all the Rowson heroines enjoy books. Her creator has poor beleaguered Sarah defend the reading of even ordinary works thus:

> I understand that there is a fine library, [at the home of Marquis H—] but this was locked; however, I found a few novels and poems in one of the bed chambers, and flimsy as the materials which compose the generality of novels are, they have afforded me some hours amusement, and drawn me from myself; a comfort grateful to the unhappy, by whatever means procured.
>
> (p. 199)

Sarah, however, had suffered earlier from unduly high ideals and expectations gained from fiction. She expresses real anguish when, after the inevitable reconciliation with her unloved husband, she writes to Frederic:

> Connubial love! domestic felicity! are ye then realities? Alas, to me, ye have been like fairy tales, credited indeed in youth, but never experienced in any part of life.
>
> (p. 253)

By the time she uses the library of the Marquis H—, she has learned much about life from actual experience and possesses a degree of maturity. Less experienced young women are liable to be taken in by the false views of life created by much fiction, to copy dangerous practices, and to become bored with ordinary life.

Rebecca is such a naive young reader. In The Fille de Chambre, Lady Worthy, upon discovering Rebecca reading Sir Charles Grandison, must warn her that boredom with reality is liable to occur from too much involvement with fiction. Rebecca is quite surprised to find that her books, which she loves because they "awaken my sensibility," are fictions (p. 19).

Meriel experiences much confusion from having overindulged in reading fiction. She writes, "false colouring had raised my expectations and exalted my ideas of love and friendship" (I, 118). She becomes so involved in watching a play that she takes the sorrows of Jane Shore as reality and embarrasses her companions by her loud sobbing. Meriel confuses romantic novels (given her by her friend Dolly Pringle) with reality and copies the practices shown in them. She too trusts what she reads, for her books are labeled "real history, the characters drawn from real life" (I, 42). Infatuated with notions from these books, Meriel indulges in correspondence and a flirtation with young Mr. Pringle, Dolly's brother, for, as she explains, "I found that none of these young ladies mentioned in them ever hesitated at answering their lovers' letters" (I, 47).

In making fun of the novel based upon fact, Mrs. Rowson may seem to satirize her own practices in a disingenuous way. But she would answer that her own books accurately reflect reality while the fiction she rejects offers an untrue picture of the world. Such distortion is the basis upon which Mrs. Rowson satirizes the popular modes of writing in her day.

In *The Inquisitor*, Mrs. Rowson satirizes the neo-Richardsonian sentimental novel and the romantic novel, which is a close relative. The exchange of influence among the various schools of eighteenth-century fiction is so complex that it would be difficult to attribute any particular feature to a single school or tradition. Mrs. Rowson suggests this fact in *The Inquisitor*; the two novels she outlines have much in common. Both contain devices typical of the followers of Richardson, although the second emphasizes the sensational ingredients like dueling and suicide—a tendency often ascribed to the influence of French and German writers such as Rousseau and Goethe. Mrs. Rowson's narrator, who has just witnessed a young female writer defending the importance of sincerity against her bookseller's insistence that she capitulate to public taste, engages in a discussion of fiction with a man sitting in a tree. The latter is writing a sentimental novel; according to his description,

> It is called *Annabella*; or *Suffering Innocence*— my heroine is beautiful, accomplished, and rich; an only child, and surrounded by admirers—she contracts an attachment for a man, her inferior in

point of birth and fortune; but honourable, handsome &c.—She has a female friend, to whom she relates all that passes in her breast— her hopes, fears, meetings, partings, &c.—She is treated hardly by her friends—combats innumerable difficulties in the sentimental way, but at last overcomes them all, and is made the bride of the man of her heart.

(III, 187)

The Inquisitor scoffs at this plan, and suggests that the writer try the same basic plot with added romantic elements. He provides him with this "Sketch of a Modern Novel":

In the first place, your heroine must fall violently in love with an all-accomplished youth at a very early age—keep her passion concealed from her parents or guardians; but bind herself in her own mind to wed no other than this dear, first conqueror of her heart—ill-natured, proud, ambitious fathers, are very necessary to be introduced—kind, affectionate, amiable mothers. The superlative beauty and accomplishments of your heroine, or perhaps the splendour of her fortune, must attract the attention of a man diametrically opposite in person and disposition to her first lover—the father must threaten—the mother entreat—and the lover be very urgent for the completion of his felicity—remember to mix a sufficient quantity of sighs, tears, swoonings, hysterics, and all the moving expressions of heart-rending woe—her filial duty must triumph over inclination; and she must be led like a victim to the altar.—
So much for the first part.
The second volume displays her angelic, her exemplary conduct in the character of a wife—the husband must be jealous, brutal, fond of gaming, keep a mistress, lavish all his fortune on sharpers and lewd women—the wife pious, gentle, obedient and resigned—
Be sure you contrive a duel; and, if convenient, a suicide might not be amiss—lead your heroine through wonderful trials—let her have the fortitude of an anchorite, the patience of an angel—but in the end, send her first husband to the other world, and unite her to the first possessor of her heart—join a few other incidents; such as the history of her bosom friend, and a confidant—Manage your plot in such a manner as to have some surprising discovery made—wind up with two or three marriages, and the superlative felicity of all the *dramatis personae*.
There, Sir, said I, there you have the substance of a narrative

which might be spun out to two or three volumes—there has been many novels introduced to the public built on as slender a foundation as that—The Modern Fine Gentleman, Deserted Bride, Clara and—

(III, 187-189)

Both the projected novels contain popular fictional clichés such as the passively suffering, angelic heroine, cruel parents, unacceptable suitor, and best friend—clichés that Mrs. Rowson continues, fairly gently, to satirize. More serious is the fact that both plots are resolved by a "happy ending" in spite of the obstacles to the heroine's happiness. In *The Inquisitor* and subsequent works, Mrs. Rowson continues to ridicule the clichés of the sentimental novel while satirizing its more serious breaches of verisimilitude. Romantic fiction, though not completely separable from the sentimental, is chastised even more harshly, and the French version, which Mrs. Rowson sees epitomized by the writings of Rousseau, is categorically damned.

Mrs. Rowson often makes fun of the entrenched formula that a fictional heroine must have a best friend to whom she confides all her secrets. Of Annie in *The Inquisitor*, she writes,

Whether love had any share in her thoughts at that moment, I never could get her to confess—but, whether a sentimental young woman, wandering in a solitary walk, and contemplating the works of nature, might not naturally enough wish for a bosom friend to participate in her pleasures, and join in an innocent conversation, I leave to my fair readers to determine—

(III, 168)

This cliché is also satirized in *Charlotte's Daughter*. The secondary heroine, Lady Mary Lumly, is a great reader who expects life to fall into the patterns of fiction. She and another young woman, Theresa, become best friends at their first meeting, encouraged by the popularity of sudden friendships in the sentimental novel. As Mrs. Rowson writes, "they became in the language of romantic misses, 'sworn friends' " (p. 108). Like Miss Thorp in Jane Austen's *Northanger Abbey* (a satire of the sentimental-Gothic blend), the "friend" turns out to be insincere, a development that suggests that friendship, like love, requires time and nurture, and is not wisely indulged "at first sight." Lucy Blakeney, the moral standard in *Charlotte's Daughter*, disclaims romantic illusions. She tries to dissuade Lady Mary from acting foolishly, and says, "I have no idea of romantic attachments and laugh when I hear of love at first sight" (p. 84).

Sarah reveals numerous satirical references to sentimental clichés. In a recital of a trip to Bath, Sarah ridicules the convention of the beautiful and accomplished heroine and her mode of expression (pp. 30-31). She also takes a swipe at the evil-hearted and indefatigable descendants of Lovelace who threaten so many sentimental heroines. Sarah contrasts her situation at the home of her would-be seducer, the Marquis H—, with such a situation in popular fiction:

> I cannot feel easy under a weight of obligation, and I very much suspect that the marquis is at the bottom of all the elegancies so profusely provided in this place. Not that I am so vain or romantically ridiculous, as to imagine he has any sinister designs, or that he means to take the trouble of visiting me in this retirement, and by appearing suddenly before me when I thought him in Ireland, supprise me into an appearance of something very far from indifference. Though I am sensible this would be quite in the novel style, I believe such scenes very seldom take place in real life.
>
> (p. 236)

The great Richardson himself is attacked in "Dialogue for Three Young Ladies" (*A Present For Young Ladies*, pp. 38-45). Three girls discuss the merits of fiction. Lucy is the most credulous about fiction, Ellen is in doubt, and Caroline is wise and critical. These misses have been discussing the likelihood of various fictional plots when the following exchange takes place:

> *Ellen.*
> But cousin, you know 'tis not often we see,
> Girls rais'd from a low to an envied degree,
> And acting with judgment—
>
> *Lucy.*
> now do not say so;
> There was Pamela rais'd but some few years ago,
> From a plain country girl—
>
> *Caroline.*
> to a life full of care.
>
> *Lucy.*
> Made the wife of a Lord—

Caroline.

a lord's follies to bear:
And tamely his libertine humours to suit,
Bear slights and contempt, be obediently mute,

Lucy.

To be sure! when by silent submission they prove
The extent of their confidence, honour, and love.
Then they share in the honours their spouse may acquire.

Ellen.

Now Lucy how foolish; who thinks to aspire
To titles and honour, whose birth is unknown,
Except in the page of a novel alone.

(*A Present,* pp. 40-41)

Romantic love that transcends everyday considerations is brought down to earth with a bump. In *The Inquisitor,* Mrs. Rowson defines love thus:

Real love was born of beauty, nursed by Innocence, and its life prolonged by good sense, affability and prudence—it consists of a strict union of soul and parity of sentiment between two persons of different sexes.

(III, 175)

In the same work, she scoffs at the ideas of a romantic young girl who takes her cue from fiction:

Love! cries the lovely girl, whose imagination is warmed by the perusal of a sentimental novel—love is the cordial drop Heaven has thrown in, to sweeten the bitter draught of life—without love we can only exist—sweet soother of our cares! that can strew roses on the coarsest bed, and make the most homely fair delicious.— Give me love and Strephon, an humble cottage shaded with woodbine; for love will render the retreat delightful!

Charmed with the enchanting scene her busy fancy draws, she imagines happiness exists only in a cottage; and that for the love of her dear Strephon, she could easily, and without regret, forego all the indulgencies of her father's house; all the advantages of wealth, and solace herself with a brown crust and a pitcher of milk. But then her Strephon will always be near her, ever whispering his love, and studying to promote her felicity: fired with these romantic ideas, she takes the first opportunity of quitting her home; and without a moment's deliberation, throws herself upon the honor of a man, who perhaps, had no further regard for her than the hope of sharing her fortune might excite.

(III, 173-174)

This same story is told in *Mentoria*. Belinda Dormer, a "sleeping beauty," falls into an identical trap. Belinda, in love with a young officer, talks "a deal of soft, sentimental nonsense, about a life of uninterrupted felicity with the object of her own choice, though she was to live in the meanest cottage" (I, 43). Belinda marries Horton and eschews the family estate, which is settled upon her father's matrimonial choice for her. Horton turns out to be a philanderer and a fortune-hunter; he leaves Belinda a thirty-year-old widow with children to raise and no estate. Belinda's euphoric attitude, "What was affluence? Nothing when put in competition with love and Horton" (I, 45), parodies the language of the circulating library, which Mrs. Rowson attacks later in *Mentoria* in her essay on "Female Education" (I, 86 ff.).

Exaggerated notions of love and passion as purveyed by romance are contrasted with the more modest feelings of "real" women. Sarah's first kiss, forced upon her by an aggressive male at Bath, provokes the following bit of self-analysis, in which Sarah compares her own emotional reactions to those encountered in books:

> Heaven be praised, my heart is not made of inflammable matter; it is a quiet, rational kind of heart, and has never yet fluttered at the fine speeches of a handsome man, or bounded at the pressure of a hand, sending its vital fluid to kiss the fingers which enfolded mine. Yet, these are sensations I have heard described by others; have read of in romances and novels.

(*Sarah*, p. 34)

When Sarah does fall in love, she is not swept off her feet, and she calmly continues to correspond with her first love, Frederic, even after her marriage. By the end of the book, Sarah loves two men at once, Frederic and the Reverend Haley, whose relationship with Sarah represents what a real union of the sexes should be—a friendship between equals.

Mrs. Rowson reserves her most earnest and vociferous attack on romantic fiction for the work of Rousseau, for she considered such novels as *Eloisa (La Nouvelle Héloise)* to be not only morally corrupting and false in depicting life, but also irreligious. Her story of Annie's moral downfall (*The Inquisitor*) may deserve derision for its simplistic logic; however, it exhibits Mrs. Rowson's feelings dramatically. A Mr. Winlove, who "pretends to laugh at all obligations, moral and religious," enters the bleak life of Annie, a girl born to affluence and educated sentimentally, who has lost her financial security and is trying to survive by working as a milliner's assistant:

> . . . he [Mr. Winlove] preferred the laws of nature; called religion priestcraft; brought innumerable proofs to convince her that her opinion was fallacious, and that she was entirely ignorant of the road to happiness, if she supposed it was to be found by strictly adhering to the musty rules prescribed by the aged and captious, who, unable any longer to enjoy the pleasures of youth, would deprive others of their share.
>
> Take example, dear Annie, said he, from the excellent Eloise, of Rousseau.
>
> She had never read it.
>
> He recommended it very strongly for her perusal.
>
> As she returned home, passing a library, Mr. Winlove purchased the pernicious novel, and gave it to Annie.
>
> She took it home—she read it—her judgment was perverted— she believed in the reality of a platonic passion—she thought she had the virtue of an Eloise, and Mr. Winlove the honour of a St. Preux.
>
> Churchill was the next author that was recommended.
>
> She read—she listened to the soft language of love, and imbibed pernicious poison from every page she read, and every word she heard.
>
> Trusting to her own strength and virtue, she made a private assignation—met him—confessed she loved—and was lost.
>
> But little now remains to be told.
>
> A few months convinced her, that when honour is forfeited, love cannot exist.
>
> Mr. Winlove forsook her.
>
> Her reputation stained—without friends—without peace— despised and insulted by her own sex, pitied by the other, and renounced by her uncle, who had bound her apprentice, she became the associate of the abandoned profligate; and reduced to chuse the dreadful alternative of death or infamy, became a partner in vices which once she would have shuddered but to think on.
>
> (III, 172-173)

French novels, like almost all things French, were anathema to Mrs. Rowson. They appear again as aides to seduction in *Trials of the Human Heart*. The "father" to whom Meriel returns after her years in the convent, and who attempts to make love to her, begins with Meriel's intellectual seduction. The young lady had been satisfied to read Rowe and Harvey, good English authors; the man urges her to take up French novels and romances. Like Annie's seducer, Mr. Howard is a freethinker and tries to convince Meriel to "get the better of these superstitious notions, and learn to think and act for yourself, unbiased by the prejudice of others" (I, 17). Mr. Belger, who enters Meriel's life with similar designs, also urges Meriel to become "superior to the narrow bounds imposed by priest-craft and superstition" (II, 96).

Mrs. Rowson hated freethinkers. Seduction linked with false principles is not an accidental combination. As we have seen, Mrs. Rowson believed the Bible to be divinely revealed history; and, as in *Abridgment*, she assumes the duty as a public personage to "impress upon the minds of youth a love of order and a reverence for religion" (p. iv). As early as 1788 in *The Inquisitor*, then, we see Mrs. Rowson trying to protect her charges against the same forces that she felt threatened them when she wrote *Biblical Dialogues* in 1822: "the cavils of affected philosophy, or the jeering taunts of ridicule." The Mr. Winloves are the George Walkers of the fiction.

When the mind is corrupted, religious faith is lost, and unreal notions may gain ground. To Mrs. Rowson, St. Preux's disdain for convention and the social realities was contemptibly sentimental. Cavalier dismissal of the opinion of society might be all right for a man, but not for young women facing a solid, real world. Leslie Fiedler has noted that Mrs. Rowson and other "bourgeois-sentimental" novelists rejected romantic love and enshrined domestic love. This statement can be substantiated to some degree; however, while Mrs. Rowson would certainly argue that the only "proper" place for sexuality was marriage, this was not because she envisioned marriage as an idyll or the home as a haven, as did many of her successors, but because as long as society held the female in low esteem, the kind of romance Rousseau glorified in *Eloisa* was liable to leave a woman open to disgrace, suffering, and financial as well as more high-flown types of "ruin." She disapproves of platonic love because it throws the woman "off guard."

The cult of sensibility, so deeply involved with the concepts of sentiment and romance, and one of the most pervasive literary fads of Mrs. Rowson's day, is frequently ridiculed for similar reasons. The ideas and characteristics associated with sensibility have occupied many lengthy paragraphs, with critics stressing different aspects of the tradition in their definitions. Richardson, Mackenzie, and Sterne all receive credit for having originated this mode of writing and helping to define the difference between "sentiment" and "sensibility." However, most writers agree that the basic characteristic of the "cult" of sensibility as practiced by the followers of these three authors is that it celebrates feeling for its own sake—pure, spontaneous sympathy for the suffering of others, immediate exquisite reactions of one's own. There is great emphasis on the ability to cry, or "shed the pellucid drop." In *The History of the English Novel*, Ernest Baker writes that in the aspiring writer of feeling "sensibility now becomes, not only the root of all virtue, but virtue itself, the indispensable quality, the hall-mark of the elect."[2]

Within this framework, various scholars stress particular attitudes, characters, and props that they find standard in such writing. J.M.S. Tompkins in *The Popular Novel in England* says that sensibility "enshrined the idea of the progress of the human race," and the notion of "instinctive moral tact."[3] According to Tompkins, its followers are often gifted with "premonitions and supernatural intimations" and unusual sympathetic powers (p. 93). The heroines were likely to be languid, prone to illness, but able to undergo "the grace and dignity of suffering" (p. 104). They were saved for heroic woes, for mental "distraction" rather than mundane problems. Tompkins notes that Burney's Cecilia, for example, "never touches a dish clout" (p. 104).

Herbert Ross Brown's account of the tradition pretty well follows that of Tompkins. In *The Sentimental Novel in America*, Brown distinguishes sensibility from sentiment by noting that sentiment is associated with the "somewhat stuffy domestic circle," whereas sensibility is associated with "a moonlight garden where weeping willows encircle an interesting ruin."[4] He discusses a whole catalogue of standard ingredients and character types such as the friendly tar and the noble savage.

The tradition of sensibility, like the other popular trends, receives continuing criticism in Mrs. Rowson's work. Bell Hartley, Victoria's friend, laughs at the heroine of sensibility by comparing her own commonsense attitude at her wedding to what might be found in a novel:

'Tis so like writing a modern novel to give a description of a wedding. Besides in those kinds of descriptions, the bride faints through excessive delicacy, or weeps and smiles in the same moment; her sweet face is then compared to an April sun breaking through a watry cloud after a shower. But as I was neither so delicate as to faint, nor so foolish as to cry at being united to a man who was my own choice, there will be no room to exercise my scribbling talents.

(*Victoria*, I, 159-160)

Mrs. Rowson, like Jane Austen in *Persuasion*, recommends keeping busy as the antidote to the woes of life, and explicitly criticizes the ineffectuality of the avowed man of feeling in situations requiring practical action. In an episode in *Reuben and Rachel* involving the seventeenth-century settlers of America, Mrs. Rowson writes of a servant overcome by horror and grief when attempting to help his mistress and her children after an Indian raid:

> Extreme sensibility is often not only painful to the possessor, but prejudicial to those whom we may wish to serve. Philip, with a soul exquisitely formed to dictate all the soft offices of humanity, was not so capable of rendering a real service to his distressed mistress, as was the labourer, who, simply comprehending the necessity of immediate relief being obtained, exerted his utmost speed to return to Plymouth. . . .
>
> (I, 153)

Sarah must also learn to rein in her sympathies for others. Anne writes to a friend that Sarah's mind is "a chaos of romantic sensibility" (*Sarah*, p. 12). The adolescent Sarah (at thirteen) exhibits uncritical sensitivity to the suffering of others. Analyzing her young friend, Anne writes,

> Totally unacquainted with the world, she believed it to be such as the books she had read represented; she believed every profession of love or regard made to her, and would give her last farthing to relieve an object of distress, without staying to inquire whether the distress was feigned or real.
>
> (p. 13)

The uncritical heart is satirized in *Charlotte's Daughter* in the character of Mary Lumly, who is ready to pour her money into charity at her first exposure to the poor. Mrs. Rowson describes Mary thus:

> When scarcely past the age of childhood or indeed infancy, she had been allowed to sit beside her mother, while the tale of misfortune, of love or folly, was read aloud by the governess, and being possessed of a quick apprehension, strong sensibility, and a fertile

imagination, she peopled the world, to which she was in effect a stranger, with lords and ladies, distressed beauties, and adoring lovers, to the absolute exclusion of every natural character, every rational idea, and truly moral or christian like feeling. . . .

Her temper was naturally good, but the overweening pride and morbid sensibility, which were the fruits of the imprudent system of her education, rendered her quick to take offence where no offence was meant, and not unfrequently bathed her in tears, without any real cause.

(pp. 36-37)

Lucy, the opposite of Mary, carries out *her* philanthropy with dry-eyed efficiency. She visits the poor "yet was she never heard . . . to sigh profoundly, and look interestingly sentimental" (p. 96).

Two of Mrs. Rowson's poems clearly state her suspicion of the cult of sensibility. In "Women As They Are" (*Miscellaneous Poems*, pp. 105-115), Mrs. Rowson criticizes various methods of raising young girls. In the following portrait, she exhibits her disapproval of the mother who emphasizes feeling at the expense of reason and encourages in her daughter an exclusive and intensive love of fictional sorrow:

"Ah! wo is me," poor LINDAMIRA cries,
The drop pellucid trembling in her eyes;
"Ah! wo is me, I see where'er I turn
Some folly to lament, some wo to mourn."
"Yes," cries mamma, "my lovely girl, I see,
You caught your sensibility from me;
I ne'er could read a fine wrought scene of wo,
But that my sighs would heave, my tears would flow;
And my sweet child does credit to her breeding,
Admires sentiments, and doats on reading."
Poor LINDAMIRA, deep in novels read,
When married, keeps the path she was taught to tread;
And while the novel's page she's eager turning,
The pot boils over, and the meat is burning;
And while she is weeping o'er ideal woes,
Her poor neglected little infant goes
With uncomb'd hair, torn frock, and naked toes.
Her husband disappointed, quits his home,
At clubs to loiter, or with bucks to roam;
While LINDAMIRA still the tale pursues,
And in each heroine, her own sorrow views.

(pp. 111-112)

"The Moonbeam," a poem in manuscript, expresses Mrs. Rowson's love of the real as opposed to the ideal, of the good earth as opposed to the other-worldly scenes associated with the tradition of sensibility:

On a moonbeam let me go,
Sentimental Sylvia cries;
Sick of all I find below
To kindred spirits in the skies.

Borne on fancy's pinions fly
Sylvia, seek some happier sphere;
But one wish granted humbler I
Am quite content to tarry here.[5]

Like the cult of sensibility, interest in the Gothic flourished during Mrs. Rowson's career. By the 1790s the Gothic novel dominated the market for fiction, but Mrs. Rowson repudiated this mode also. In *Reuben and Rachel*, she teases her readers with a few Gothic touches; all the while she undermines and makes fun of the pleasures of terror. Columbia (great granddaughter of Columbus and the heroine of this portion of *Reuben and Rachel*) and her friend Mina are featured in an episode that includes standard features of the Gothic: an old castle, a stormy night, and tales of ghosts. Both girls become frightened at the "melancholy notes" of the wind, although Columbia tries to remain unmoved by Mina's talk of ghosts, and manages to crawl into bed still unconverted to the supernatural. A sudden noise further frightens the girls. Columbia suggests a rational explanation for the disturbance, but is encouraged by Cora, an attendant, to fear the supernatural. The girls spend a restless night, discovering in the morning that all they heard was the sound of a friend arriving at the castle (pp. 74 ff.).

Belief in ghosts and visions is to be expected in the ignorant, in servants and rustics, but not in intelligent, reasonable, Christian young ladies. Tales of the supernatural may be fun, but they encourage superstition. Lucy in "Dialogue for Three Young Ladies" admits her love for such stories; she says, "I love runaway marriages, castles and spectres,/ And libertine lovers, and gen'rous protectors,/ And fighting of duels—" She is interrupted by Ellen, who concludes the dialogue:

Oh! pray dont proceed,
Such novels as that must be wicked indeed.
So let us dear cousins, resolve to read none;
But engross'd by our juvenile studies alone,

Strive to learn all the duties befitting our station,
And our honour's will spring from our friend's approbation.
(A Present, p. 45)

Mrs. Rowson's satirical attitude toward the Gothic could be indulged in with no fear of inconsistency, for she avoided this tradition almost completely. Her dismissal of romance is similarly consistent with her practices. Her ridicule of the traditions of sentiment and sensibility, however, could appear disingenuous—an attempt to "run with the hare and hunt with the hound," that is, "provide all the attractions of sensibility and yet come out on the side of common sense"—as Tompkins in The Popular Novel in England describes the practice of many eighteenth-century novelists (p. 110).

Certainly Mrs. Rowson uses many of the standard ingredients of the neo-Richardsonians. Seduction is a major theme and plot device. Seducers are rung in whenever the action begins to wane or a sense of time passing must be suggested. The number of would-be seducers encountered by the average Rowson protagonist would stagger the imagination of the creator of the sentimental prototype, maybe even that of his followers. However, the character of some of these villains is given believable complexity, a point to be developed later. Further, Mrs. Rowson's standard seducer is as threatening as a germ at a public drinking fountain, and as easily avoided. Except for Montraville and Harry Finchly, such men are no match for Mrs. Rowson's heroines. When Mr. Lacour, Meriel's employer, makes advances, Meriel simply threatens to tell his wife about his liaison with a Mademoiselle Bagatelle (Trials of the Human Heart, II, 66). Mrs. Rowson's satirical treatment of the Lovelacian seducer has been noted. She does not believe in the absolute vice of the seducer and the absolute virtue of the seduced. As she states in Charlotte "no woman can be run away with contrary to her own inclination" (p. 42).[6]

The cliché of the best friend to whom the heroine tells all her problems is retained in Mrs. Rowson's Bell Hartley (Victoria), Amelia Sedley and Celia (Trials of the Human Heart), and Anne in Sarah. Crafty, socially ambitious parents occasionally appear in Mrs. Rowson's fiction. None of the protagonists have cruel parents, however, and the much-used formula that the heroine's instincts and feelings are superior to the advice of parents is decidedly rejected. Obedience to parents, even when the fathers and mothers make wrong decisions, is one of Mrs. Rowson's cardinal preachments. Zayde, a slave in Trials of the Human Heart, refuses release from captivity, for having learned Christianity, she wishes to stay with her mother (IV, 150). Fetnah remains with her father even though he is a Jew and a usurer. In *Biblical Dialogues* obedience is said to be "the greatest proof of love and gratitude that can be given from a child to a parent" (I, 28).

The intense emotionalism of the novels of sentiment, romance, and sensibility occasionally threatens to inundate Mrs. Rowson's pages. Although Ellen in "Dialogue for Three Young Ladies" reminds the others that it was not "so easy to faint and to die" (*A Present*, p. 39), the frequency with which mere sorrow or shock "places a period to the existence" of Rowson characters belies her commonsense attitude.

The sensational elements typical of the romance and the novel of sensibility are occasionally introduced. Shipwrecks abound. Mrs. Rowson also provides her reader with a smidgeon of sex: in a shipwreck scene in *Trials of the Human Heart*, Kingly (at the moment married to another woman) rips off Meriel's blouse to save her life (he makes a rope of it). The theme of incest appears in several novels. However, it is not played up as a beautiful but sinful passion, as it is in William Hill Brown's *The Power of Sympathy*,[7] but is treated as a strictly moral issue. In *Mentoria* a father almost commits incest with his daughter, a fitting punishment for seducing and abandoning her mother. In *Charlotte's Daughter*, the problem of Franklin and Lucy proves how great a sorrow a true Christian (Lucy) can face and overcome.

Duels and suicide, the other two standard sensational ingredients of the fiction of romance and sensibility, appear in Mrs. Rowson's work, but are never glorified. Meriel calls a dueler a "murderer" (III, 124). Suicide is not romanticized as it was by Brown, whose protagonist in *The Power of Sympathy* dies of self-inflicted wounds with a copy of *Werther* by his side. While the heroines of other novelists in the sentimental tradition—for example, several of Charles Brockden Brown's protagonists—are often placed in the position of yielding up their virtue or killing themselves, Mrs. Rowson's heroines are never so situated. She did not consider such a choice realistic enough to be given central treatment in a novel. When Meriel in *Trials of the Human Heart* is threatened with a sexual attack by her pseudo-father, she snatches a pen-knife (favorite weapon of the sentimental writer) and threatens to kill not herself but *him* (I, 73). Suicides always represent spiritual and moral bankruptcy to Mrs. Rowson. In *The Inquisitor*, a lawyer with a guilty conscience kills himself, an act that provides a modicum of excitement. In *Reuben and Rachel*, an Indian maiden, hopelessly in love with a white settler, also commits suicide; but the fact is made clear that while the maiden is lovable, loyal, and intelligent, she *is* a non-Christian and a savage. The difference between her view of self-destruction and the Christian view is clearly set out in a discussion between her and another character in advance of the tragedy (II, 349). Mrs. Rowson keeps the sensational elements within the bounds of her avowed moral purpose and never lets them dominate her work.

Because of the book's popularity and its reputation for evoking tears, critics most often use *Charlotte* to prove Mrs. Rowson a purveyor of sensibility rather than sense. But Mrs. Rowson foresaw the reader's proneness to enjoy the good cry *Charlotte* provides, and ignore its moral purpose. To correct this tendency, she plays the rôle of a third-person author-narrator, who takes a satirical attitude toward her own introduction of tears and suffering. She discusses the moral rhetoric of the novel to avoid being guilty of the excesses she derides in the fiction of others. The following passage is typical:

> "Bless my heart," cries my young, volatile reader, "I shall never have patience to get through these volumes, there are so many ahs! and ohs! so much fainting, tears, and distress, I am sick to death of the subject." My dear, chearful, innocent girl . . . I must request your patience: I am writing a tale of truth. . . . I pray you throw it not aside till you have perused the whole; mayhap you may find something therein to repay you for the trouble.
>
> (p. 106)

The emphasis on anguish and distress in *Charlotte* is not meant to promote a cult of distress or to romanticize the suffering heroine, but to teach the young to avoid Charlotte's (and La Rue's) errors. Mrs. Rowson pointedly stops her story to assure her young readers that her morality is sound; while Charlotte must suffer, La Rue will not continue prosperous as she is at this point in the story, but will face even greater misery than that suffered by Charlotte (pp. 106-107).

According to Mrs. Rowson, sensibility in its proper form was never distinct from or divorced from the use of reason. The ability to feel compassion for others was one of the highest goods in the author's scheme of values; she rejects the stoic and the "icy sons of philosophy," whoever would overburden reason by subordinating feeling among the human faculties. Thus in *Charlotte* the reader is cajoled to use her sensibilities to feel sympathy for Charlotte even though the protagonist's situation might be far removed from her own; but excess, morbid, uncontrolled emotions are dangerous and undesirable. Mrs. Rowson writes of the "deceitfulness" of Charlotte's heart (p. 51), and of her "wounded sensibility" (p. 75). She is a victim not only of male scheming but "a victim to her too great sensibility" (p. 106). Mrs.

Rowson may have been, as Herbert Ross Brown writes in *The Sentimental Novel in America*, "the leader of those who were convinced that 'the heart was the seat of sensibility'" (p. 80), but she clearly believed that that organ was not to be trusted without guidance from the head, for unaided it could be "treacherous," as in the case of poor Charlotte (*Charlotte*, p. 54).

In his study "The Eighteenth-Century American Novel," Robert Kettler notes that Mrs. Rowson's enthusiastic description of Julia Franklin betrays "ambivalence" toward Charlotte. He sees in *Charlotte* the story line, "'See, unaided virtue is at the mercy of the evil world.'"[8] There is some evidence for this interpretation as well as for Kettler's concept of the moral of *Charlotte*:

> ... the ideal, the eidolon, will be destroyed by the very person who seeks it out because it is not substantial enough to bear the vicissitudes of actuality. In America Charlotte gets pregnant and dies; Montraville feels remorse; Julia adjusts to the difficulties and lives on.
>
> (p. 66)

Kettler senses Mrs. Rowson's disapproval of naiveté, but he is mistaken in calling Charlotte an ideal. She is simply a pathetic example of the way of the world with naive and credulous young girls. Mrs. Rowson has a stronger attitude than "ambivalence" toward her protagonist. The character who receives ambiguous treatment is Charlotte's father.

Mrs. Rowson's presentation of Mr. Temple suggests him as the perpetrator of the original sin, by possessing, like his daughter, a treacherous heart. Almost immediately after beginning her story (with the attraction of Montraville to Charlotte) Mrs. Rowson takes the reader into the past to re-create the early youth of Charlotte's father, and his courtship of Charlotte's mother. Mr. Temple is the only "good" character ever allowed to disobey his parents and continue to receive the approbation of the author. Harriet Weatherby, the elder Temple's choice of a wife for his son, is clearly an unsavory woman sure to have led the young man a life of misery if he had obeyed his father. Yet Mrs. Rowson's language in *Charlotte* describing young Temple's intense sensibility and the unworldly attitudes that accompany it are treated with a hint of irony. Observing the "splendid misery" of his sisters who have been betrothed for money, Mr. Temple vows (p. 26), "I will seek Content; and if I find her in a cottage will embrace her with as much cordiality as I should if seated on a throne." Temple has five hundred pounds a year of his own, with which he sets up a pastoral retreat for his family. This idyll is completely violated by events. The young man paints a life of domestic felicity to his Lucy:

> "We will purchase a little cottage, my Lucy . . . and thither with your revered father we will retire; we will forget there are such things as splendour, profusion, and dissipation [but there are]: we will have some cows, and you shall be queen of the dairy; in a morning while I look after my garden you shall take a basket on your arm and sally forth to feed your poultry; and as they flutter round you in token of humble gratitude, your father shall smoke his pipe in a woodbine alcove, and viewing the serenity of your countenance, feel such real pleasure dilate his own heart, as shall make him forget he had ever been unhappy."
>
> (p. 39)

Surely Mrs. Rowson included the sentimental flashback to underline the irony and tragedy of later events. The grandfather who is to smoke his pipe in such contentment is the very person sent to Madame du Pont's school to bring Charlotte home for her birthday party—only to discover her elopement. Mr. Temple is never accused of responsibility for Charlotte's downfall, and he is treated with approval in most scenes of the novel, but there is the suggestion that his intense sensibility, unaccompanied by practical sense, is undesirable. Charlotte's education, at first in a sheltered home and then in a school to which she is sent "at the earnest entreaty of a particular friend" (p. 39), is not well planned by her father. On her "birthday" poor Charlotte is born into a world of sorrow and sin; she commits an act that results in her giving birth, and that ultimately causes her death.

Feeling must be tempered by reason, sensibility with sense. Mrs. Rowson's constant concern with this balance shows that she pays more than conventional "lip-service" to the latter qualities, in spite of her use of some of the stock ingredients associated with the cult of sensibility. In *The Sentimental Novel in America*, Herbert Ross Brown argues that such concern was merely a response to attacks upon the novel, which provoked novelists to assert "the soundness of their own brand of sensibility" (p. 96). But there were "brands" of sensibility among the writers of the late eighteenth century, as Ernest Baker shows in *The History of the English Novel*. Baker cites Henry Mackenzie as an example of a writer closely associated with the tradition of sensibility who became critical of attitudes and states of mind celebrated in its name. Mackenzie questioned, says Baker, the value of refined emotions that do not express themselves in action, which might, on the contrary, lead to "'childish pride of our own superior delicacy, and an unfortunate contempt of the plain worth, the ordinary but useful occupations and ideas of those around us'" (p. 112). Although Mackenzie shows traces of the influence of Rousseau, he dissociates himself from the excesses of the French, especially from the erotic tinge they gave to sentiment and sensibility. Baker calls Mackenzie a "Scottish sentimentalist" (p. 113).

Mrs. Rowson follows the example of Mackenzie in several ways. While she was capable of wringing "the pellucid drop" from her readers in the novels as well as in such poems as "The Orphan Nosegay Girl" and "Maria, a Fiction," while she praised feeling in her poem "Sensibility," she consistently discouraged the cultish side of this phenomenon, eschewed "foreign" interpretations, and derided excesses. If she writes "Hail Sensibility!" in one poem, she also makes reason a subject of song. In "Where Can Peace of Mind be Found, A Duet" she argues,

> Where reason sheds her sober ray
> Where reason faith and virtue stays
> Sweet peace of mind sweet peace of mind. . . .[9]

Mrs. Rowson's satire of the various schools of writing, which is one of the prevalent themes in her work, shows that she consciously remains loyal to her own brand of didactic realistic fiction. She aligns herself with female novelists of similar stripe. The girls in "Dialogue for Three Young Ladies" have this exchange:

Caroline.

And my aunt, though severe, would not be understood
To pass sentence on all, no, where nature speaks out,
And religion is honoured, that novel no doubt
May be read with advantage;

Ellen.

that novel would be
Allowed by my mother a lesson for me.
Such a novel she'd bid me peruse o'er and o'er,
The authors?

Caroline.

are Edgworth, and Burney and More.

By each line they have written, the taste may be formed,
The heart rendered better, its piety warmed,
The judgment corrected—

(A Present, pp. 44-45)

None of the other prevailing modes in literature serves Mrs. Rowson's purpose. She finds that all encourage unrealistic attitudes and expectations in the reader. The Gothic adds emphasis on making the flesh creep and gross improbabilities that do not correspond to her view of life or conform to her projected style of execution and didactic purpose.

Mrs. Rowson genuinely shared the distrust of the imagination that wielded so powerful an influence on early American literature. She affirms many of the premises of the Common Sense philosophers to whom Terence Martin attributes much of this distrust: that there is a real world outside the mind, and that, in a sense, "whatever is, is right."[10] This school of thinkers was conservative and conventional, as Mrs. Rowson was; they distrusted the idealism of Berkeley in philosophy, mysticism in religion, and romanticism in literature. In *An Abridgment of Universal Geography*, Mrs. Rowson enunciates her approval of the general movement in Scottish thought. She notes that while Scotland's theology had formerly been rigidly Calvinistic, it was becoming more gentle, and "the doctrine of the modern Scotch divines is distinguished by good sense and moderation" (p. 38).

The literary references in Mrs. Rowson's work help to create her ideal for women by providing a critique of fashionable feminine types. Mrs. Rowson portrays two kinds of heroines in her fiction, the young lady of intense sensibility who is life's victim, and the robust girl with spirit who fights and endures. The first type is represented only by Victoria and Charlotte, who are sad examples of girls led astray not merely by men but by their own false views of life. They let feeling—in both cases, romantic love—run away with them. They have no practical sense, exert no active force on their situations, and are duped and ultimately driven to despair and death. They adopt the poses of the typical heroine of sensibility, moping about in Ophelia-like garments, singing songs of love and woe, and remaining aloof from reality. All the other protagonists—Mary, Rebecca, Meriel, Rachel, Sarah, and Lucy—are girls in whom sense predominates over sensibility. They may begin life susceptible, sensitive, and naive, but they learn from experience and refuse to fade at "the first rude blast." Their predominant qualities are pluck and resilience. Like Fetnah, they are "spirited ladies." As Robert Kettler points out in "The Eighteenth-Century American Novel," Julia

Franklin possesses the liveliness and confidence that Charlotte lacks. To emphasize this contrast, Mrs. Rowson brings Julia into *Charlotte's Daughter*. She is, of course, the mother of Franklin, Lucy's half-brother. Her bright-eyed vivacity has become true strength. After Montraville's sad death, young Franklin is amazed that his mother survives the tragedies and is willing to let him go off to fight in the army and thus leave her in England without a "protector." Mrs. Rowson explains, "he had not attributed to that lady all the judgment and firmness which belonged to her character. He had witnessed her enduring affection, and her noble example of all the passive virtues. Her energy and decision was yet to appear" (p. 150).

Solid virtues, based upon clear perception of the world as it is, are superior to the refined poses of sentiment and sensibility. In fact, the structure of Mrs. Rowson's novels indicates that she would make her lessons even stronger. The Christian virtues she teaches will not be practiced or tested in artificial situations. She *insists* that her heroines enter the real world; thus she repeats in each novel a basic confrontation: the protagonist, a woman, is ejected from a comforting but rarefied place, either spiritual or real, and is coerced into facing the realities of everyday life. Victoria, Rebecca, and Sarah live in the "bubbles" and air-castles of romantic literature. Mary has a reasonably happy situation that she can pretty well control until a conflict between love and principle arises. Charlotte lives in a fairy-tale world; her home, where she is protected by two adoring parents and a grandfather, is the creation of a dreamer. Meriel has spent her childhood in a convent, and Lucy has lived in the bosom of a safe, protective family. But the façade of safety and protection that surrounds these young women is in each case lost: parents die, the convent must be left behind, wars break out, sex and love enter the garden paradise.

One of Mrs. Rowson's better literary touches appears in *Trials of the Human Heart*. The author has Meriel comment in her opening letter upon the errors of Catholic convent schooling; Meriel says that she and the other girls formed there "an erroneous opinion of the world," which made them consider the world outside "a paradise compared to the solemnity and gloom of our convent" (I, 2). Throughout the correspondence with Celia, while Meriel is struggling with the realities of everyday life, she often yearns for the security, safety, and purity that surround her friend. But this nostalgia is also shown to be sentimental and false. The continuing contrast between the worlds of Celia and Meriel builds toward a genuine irony in Meriel's final words to her confidante, 29 September 1791. Meriel, who has been buffeted about in the everyday world for sixteen years, is now married and reasonably

secure, and she offers her friend Celia protection from the war that
threatens her safety:

> Mrs. Onslow desires remembrances to you. My husband bids me
> say, should the commotions which at present agitate the Gallic
> shore, disturb you in your religious retreat; remember, you have a
> home, to which you can with confidence repair. . . .

(Trials, IV, 172)

7

The Sublunary World

> *Whose model is nature, whose pictures have art,*
> *To shew life so true, that they better the heart.*
> *("Dialogue for Three Young Ladies," A Present, 1811)*

If life does not conform to the illusions fostered by contemporary fiction, then what is it like? Mrs. Rowson has declared in her critical comments that she will present a realistic picture of life in order to teach her lessons most effectively. Her audience must attain some notion of the social realities that she will face—their exact outlines as well as their symbolic import.

The allegorical quality of Mrs. Rowson's work has been touched upon in earlier comments about society as a Vanity Fair. Mrs. Rowson establishes this dimension of the fictional and imaginary world through symbolism, satire, personification, the emblem, and allegorical names and characters. The first two of these elements have been discussed as they pertain to various themes, and thus the allegorical needs only brief mention in assessing Mrs. Rowson's view of the world. The author's use of more modern trends in "realism" may then receive lengthier treatment.

The moral qualities of Mrs. Rowson's world are made concrete and pictorial by the use of personified vices, virtues, and psychological qualities. "Prudence," "Pride," and "Humanity" argue with the Inquisitor over whether he should help an old man he encounters as he travels in his coach (I, 43); "indolence" gives birth to "luxury" in the early colonies (Reuben and Rachel, I, 141). The ubiquitous presence of such figures gives Mrs. Rowson's fictional world, as well as the landscape of her poetry and nonfiction, an old-fashioned static quality.

A love of the emblem by the author as well as her characters contributes to this static world. In Reuben and Rachel, for instance, describing the new American home of the young people, Mrs. Rowson cannot forbear slipping in the idea that the persimmon tree is emblematic of the "pleasures of the world" by being beautiful but bitter (II, 275). Mrs.

Rowson uses the emblem somewhat more skillfully to summarize the quality of various situations, including at times the state of mind of the characters. In *Charlotte*, she pictures Montraville's infatuation with Charlotte, and his decision to pursue the young girl in these terms:

> Arriving at the verge of the town, he dismounted, and sending the servant forward with the horses, proceeded toward the place where in the midst of an extensive pleasure ground stood the mansion which contained the lovely Charlotte Temple. Montraville leaned on a broken gate, and looked earnestly at the house. The wall which surrounded it was high, and perhaps the Argus's who guarded the Hesperian fruit within were more watchful than those famed of old.
>
> . . . .
>
> The evening now was closed, a serene stillness reigned, and the chaste Queen of Night with her silver crescent faintly illumined the hemisphere. The mind of Montraville was hushed into composure by the serenity of the surrounding objects. "I will think on her no more," said he, and turned with an intention to leave the place; but as he turned he saw the gate which lead to the pleasure grounds open, and two women come out, who walked arm in arm across the field.
>
> (p. 24)

Later, when Montraville realizes he prefers Julia to Charlotte, he suffers guilt exacerbated by encountering Julia on a night reminiscent of the one on which he first decided to pursue Charlotte. He identifies the moon (chaste Queen of Night) with the innocent young girl he has seduced (p. 95). The serene life of Charlotte's parents, soon to be blasted, is also presented in the form of an emblematic picture:

> He sought and found a cottage suited to his taste: thither, attended by Love and Hymen, the happy trio retired; where, during many years of uninterrupted felicity, they cast not a wish beyond the little boundaries of their own tenement. Plenty and her handmaid Prudence presided at their board, Hospitality stood at their gate, Peace smiled on each face, Content reigned in each heart, and Love and Health strewed roses on their pillows.
>
> (p. 39)

A love of statuary and monuments as emblems of fate and moral condition marks Mrs. Rowson's pages, as it does those of many of her contemporaries. She often describes her fictional characters' tombstones, as well as the various edifices commemorating virtuous historical personages described in her text books. Victoria's tomb is engraved with

> an olive tree broken down, and a rose withered with this inscription:
>
> By the rude blast of misfortune,
> And the chilling breath of infidelity.
>
> On the top of the monument was a white marble urn, sacred to the memory of Victoria, in large gold letters. On the right stood Innocence weeping:—On the left Meekness, with a placid countenance. At the bottom, Hope supported the urn with one arm, and pointed with the other to Futurity.
>
> (II, 185)

Mrs. Rowson's characters compose similar miniature allegories. Lucy Blakeney in *Charlotte's Daughter*, caught in the rain with young Franklin, calls the clouds "an emblem of misfortune"; Franklin, whose mind is on Lucy, sees them as a "veil thrown over the face of a beautiful woman" (p. 99). In *Charlotte's Daughter* as in *Charlotte*, the emblems are integrated into the narrative, for they reflect the varying states of mind of the two characters, and underline the theme of the book, that even tragedy like incestuous love, which Lucy is entering unawares with Franklin, can be survived by the true Christian.

The allegorical character of Mrs. Rowson's world and its relation to Vanity Fair is underscored by the author's persistent use of allegorical names and characters. One part of the heroines' names often signifies some abstract quality, while the other is taken from the everyday world. Thus Mrs. Rowson presents *Victoria* (ultimate victory of innocence) Baldwin; Mary *Newton* (new tone); Charlotte *Temple* (the body as the temple of the soul); Rebecca *Littleton* (little tone); and Mentoria, or Helena Askam ("Ask her" would have lacked subtlety). A gallery of semi-allegorical *dramatis personae* possessing some degree of individuality, who are nevertheless associated by their names with their leading vice, virtue, or situation, surround the protagonists. There is

Lady Maskwell, the hypocrite and pseudo-aristocrat, in *Victoria*; La Rue, a "woman of the streets," who learns to regret the sorrow she causes Charlotte, and whose punishment is depicted in the final scene of *Charlotte*; and Montraville (Mon travail), who carries his sorrow to his death in *Charlotte's Daughter*. Belcour in *Charlotte* and Mrs. Bellmour, the lady who "vamps" Mr. Howard in *Trials of the Human Heart*, illustrate a further habit of Mrs. Rowson's with nomenclature: to use as a name a French phrase suggesting the opposite of the character's true personality. For all these tendencies Mrs. Rowson had plenty of examples in the late-eighteenth-century drama and novel.

Her habit of peopling her books with legions of almost completely flat "types" representing abstract qualities, professions, or points of view reminds the reader of Bunyan as well as later playwrights and novelists who tended to soften the device. Mrs. Rowson's works teem with "Friendlys" and "Worthys" who are never developed as individual personalities. The attorney in *Reuben and Rachel* is unblushingly called Mr. Allibi, while a creditor in *Trials of the Human Heart* is Mr. Leeson (Lease on). Mr. Woudbe in *The Inquisitor* is a *poseur* whom the narrator would have "supposed a man of fashion; yet I knew him to be a mechanic" (II, 149).

To complement her use of allegory, Mrs. Rowson develops certain techniques associated with more modern forms of realism.[1] She takes her central situations and characters from the everyday world, and she individualizes many of the elements of the fiction according to the principles of "formal realism" as described by Ian Watt in his study of the eighteenth-century novel.[2] These techniques aid the moralist in her attempt to give her ideas understandable, concrete form, and also to project the desired air of authenticity. But Mrs. Rowson also tries to reflect the quality of ordinary life as part of her program of education. As we have seen, she rejected the ideals of romanticism, and accepted a commonsense view of the reality of everyday life. The world may be a Vanity Fair and only a temporary resting place for Christian, but it is not just a state of mind. This world as well as the next must be faced, and the young woman must develop a practical view of the problems, worldly as well as spiritual, that must be met.

In the interests of such teachings, as well as to fulfill her other goals, Mrs. Rowson adopts the methods of treatment associated with literary realism. She sets her narratives in a solid, individualized time and place, and stresses the everyday quality of this world. She presents many of her settings, situations, and characters with the detail, pungency, and vividness typical of the realist. She chooses problems and choices for her characters that she thinks represent those they might actually face, and tries to present them without sentimentalizing or stressing the macabre or heroic.

Mrs. Rowson's characters never inhabit "an imaginary land" of "cypress and rue" as Charles F. Richardson describes the setting of *Charlotte*.[3] The protagonists learn their lessons in ordinary places like the shires of England, in London, Soho, Bath, Brighton, New England, and Philadelphia. Their activities take place in the present. Mrs. Rowson avoids the mists of past and future—even in *Reuben and Rachel*, her one departure from the eighteenth and early nineteenth centuries, she does not romanticize the past but tries to show its connection and similarity to the everyday present. The immediate backdrop in Mrs. Rowson's fiction is likely to be a park bench or a shop, rather than the vaguely located places of the romance, such as the remote estate ambiguously financed by inherited wealth and run by characters devoted to scholarly pursuits. For Mrs. Rowson not only establishes her narratives in place and time, but exhibits the true novelist's concern for what J.M.S. Tompkins calls "ways and means."[4]

Each of the fictional protagonists is given a specific birthplace: Lancashire for Mary, Chichester for Charlotte, Lincolnshire for Rebecca, London for Sarah, and Hampshire for Lucy Blakeney. When we first meet Lucy, she is in a cottage "about five miles from Southampton on the coast of Hampshire" (p. 21). The author attempts to portray the various backgrounds with some degree of accuracy; for example, the local characters are engaged in appropriate, everyday activities. Mr. Stephens in *Test* is shown going to "an electioneering party." Before their adventures are completed, the heroines visit a variety of places, always clearly identified and specific. Charlotte goes to New York during the Revolutionary War, Rebecca is shown in the household of her aristocratic London employers; later, she lives in a New England village during the Revolution. Before she becomes the bride of George Worthy, she has visited a shop, tried to sell a piece of jewelry, and been thrown into debtor's prison. Far from representing a vague world of "cypress and rue," *Trials of the Human Heart* is firmly set in the contemporary world of mercantile eighteenth-century London. Meriel and her mother spend a brief time in Fleet prison and then occupy a "cheap lodging, on the Surrey side of Blackfriars bridge" (II, 22).

To make her fictional world reflect the real, Mrs. Rowson creates interest in how things are done. She always specifies the incomes and occupations of her characters, keeps track of their luggage and their clothes, and gives all the characters, except the aristocrats, everyday jobs. Charlotte's Montraville is in the army, Mr. Littleton is a veteran trying to live on a pension, Meriel's Rainsforth is in the navy, Sarah's husband, after losing his money, works at a counting house, as does Meriel's brother. Those who cannot turn an honest dollar are in debtor's prison along with Charlotte's grandfather, Rooksby, Clara, Mr. Howard, Darnley, and others.

In *Northanger Abbey*, Jane Austen makes fun of the casual attitude of the sentimental Gothic novel toward ordinary matters such as the running of a house and the problem of money. Mrs. Rowson does not share the attitude of that tradition. She never takes work or money for granted. The landlady must be paid, the boat captain tipped. The characters must eat, drink, and be clothed. In *Sarah* Mrs. Rowson devotes attention to the heroine's struggles with the mundane cares of domesticity, and the other fictions are fully peopled with servants, merchants, and the bulk of society who fill the everyday world. The stomach as well as the soul is considered; hunger is one of the problems frequently met by the protagonists. It is rendered with realistic specificity in *The Fille de Chambre*. Mrs. Rowson notes that the party bound for America "had not even a candle to light the binnacle, which contains the compass, and the whole of their allowance now amounted to one biscuit and half a pint of water per day each person" (p. 112). The unromantic, everyday nature of the body's demands is underlined in *Sarah* by the heroine, who writes to Anne of her experience with it,

> . . . my limbs were fatigued, my feet sore, my spirits depressed, and my stomach faint; for the bread and milk taken at the cottage in the morning, was all the sustenance I had that day received. Harrassed and desponding as my mind was, I am not heroine enough to say I forgot my bodily sufferings in the more poignant mental misery. I wept, my dear Anne, for very hunger and weariness, and every other feeling was for the time absorbed in the reflection that I had no where to repose my head, no wherewithal to satisfy my appetite.
>
> (p. 211)

Mrs. Rowson tries to give her scenes an air of reality by providing specific detail of sights and sounds. The voyages in *The Fille de Chambre* are vivid, with the provisions becoming a palpable element. The description of the landing at Boston is worth quoting at length:

> The port of Boston is situated in such a manner, that, after having made land, six or seven hours good sailing will take a vessel into safe harbor, so that our weary voyagers began to think of landing that evening, however late it might be when they arrived; but as the night came on, the wind increased, accompanied by snow and sleet; the cold at the same time being intense, it froze as it fell, and in a very short period the ropes about the ship were so incased with ice, that they became immovable; the darkness increased, and to

add to their distress, they lost sight of the light house at the entrance of the harbour. . . .

. . . .

About ten o'clock all their fears were realized, and a sudden shock convinced them they had struck on some rocks. The ensuing scene from that time till seven the next morning is better imagined than described, for till that time they had no prospect of relief, but continued beating on the rocks, the waves washing over them, and expecting momentary dissolution. As the day-light advanced they discovered the island from which the reef ran, to be inhabited. Several muskets were immediately discharged, and signals hung out, and about eight o'clock they discovered people coming to their assistance. It was impossible to bring a boat near the vessel, but the tide beginning to leave her, the men waded into the water, and placed a ladder against her side, down which the immediate fear of death gave Miss Abthorpe and Rebecca courage to descend; but what were the feelings of Mr. Seward, when he found the impossibility of his little daughter's going down, so dangerous was it rendered by the ice that enveloped the steps of the ladder, and from whence, if she fell, she must have been dashed to pieces or lost among the rocks. . . .

(pp. 115-117)

Rebecca's first sight of the New England winter scene is also convincing. Mrs. Rowson writes, "A new world now opened on Rebecca, who . . . beheld with astonishment how every object was bound in the frigid chains of winter. The harbour, which she could see from the house on the island, was one continued sheet of ice" (p. 117).

The war in the background of Rebecca's story is brought into focus by having an American soldier left dying in the Abthorpes's New England house. One of this soldier's companions swears, "D—n him . . . he is in our way; if he don't die quickly we will kill him" (p. 122). Rebecca and the Abthorpes must bury the corpse quickly because of the heat.

In *Trials of the Human Heart*, Mrs. Rowson continues to try to depict the look and feel of things. Her inclusion of the details of the material and color of Meriel's gown, and the procedure followed during Meriel's experience in the brothel, helps make the episode convincing. Meriel writes to Celia:

. . . she [the madame] made me drink some tea, and then taking me up stairs, insisted on my dressing myself in a brown lutestring nightgown, with a cap and linen suitable. We then went into an elegant parlour, and in a few moments Mr. Welldon [Meriel's client] was announced. . . .

(II, 33)

At supper, Mr. Welldon is "insinuating," and when the old woman leaves, Meriel bursts into tears and catches at her hand. The scene continues with the old woman chiding Meriel for her tears, though Mr. Welldon may "think her the more agreeable for them" (II, 34).

Mrs. Rowson's catalogue of the contents of the trunk that Mr. Welldon fills for Meriel may be an example of the "crude realism" endemic to the neo-Richardsonian novel, but this is the kind of practice followed by many "realists." Further, Mrs. Rowson's description may also be said to contain some significance to the story, for Mr. Welldon's presents include drawing and writing materials as well as "grey lutestring" and "dark chintz" (II, 44). This fact shows that he respects Meriel's intellect in addition to sympathizing with her financial plight.

Mrs. Rowson's description of the new flat and the new life Sarah and Darnley must face when they have lost their money is an advance over the technique in *Trials*. It achieves an air of verisimilitude, adds a touch to the characters, and gives Sarah's problems the down-to-earth quality Mrs. Rowson seeks to portray:

Two small rooms, up two pair of stairs, at a Stay-Makers in Greek-street, Soho, with a privilege of cooking our dinner in the kitchen, belonging to the family, is become the residence of your friend. I have no servant; Darnley cannot afford to keep one; and I think you would laugh, could you take a peep at me in a morning, and see me bustling about, getting breakfast, sweeping the rooms, &c. &c. I am awkward enough, Heaven knows; and as to cooking, I make but a poor hand at it indeed. Darnley, who loves good eating as well as any man I know, fumes and frets; well, he really has cause—but I intend to try my best, and learn all the profound mysteries of roasting, boiling, stewing, frying and broiling; then the compounding of puddings, pies, and rich sauces. I beg your pardon; I forgot we shall have but little to cook, and therefore, a very slight degree of knowledge in the culinary art, will suffice.

(p. 106)

In *Charlotte's Daughter* the solidity of the world inhabited by Reverend Matthews and his wards is suggested through the use of detailed set pieces such as the description of Lucy's birthday feast. This scene is brought to life with "good sirloins of beef," "plumb puddings," and "wine sangaree," as well as with details of the behavior of local types (pp. 122-123).

The creation of memorable characters was not Mrs. Rowson's forte as a writer of fiction; however, she attempts to give many of her *dramatis personae* a degree of verisimilitude. Although their activities may be ultimately traceable to the seven deadly sins or the Christian virtues, they are by and large of a human scale, neither impossibly brave and noble nor implacably evil. Their immediate motives are influenced by the world in which they live; they are as often driven by the need for financial security and respectability as by the "power of sympathy," undying love, or diabolical hatred.

The scheming and social-climbing personality of Lady Maskwell in *Victoria* is to some degree explained by the woman's deprived background. The antagonist in *The Test of Honour* is no satanic villain, but Frederick's obdurate parent, who operates from concern for his son's well-being and from a genuine misogyny, which he abandons when proven wrong. The portrayal of the characters in *Charlotte* also shows Mrs. Rowson trying to suggest a realistic degree of complexity. Sympathy for Montraville is elicited by the narrowness of the choices he is given and by his feeling the economic "squeeze." And he is given some good qualities. Mrs. Rowson describes Charlotte's seducer as "generous in his disposition" and "liberal in his opinions" (p. 50), but easily swayed, and thus betrayed by bad company. La Rue and Belcour, the bad company to which Montraville is subjected, are closer to being stock villains. However, while La Rue is self-seeking, money-grubbing, and cruel, the strong feminist notes in *Charlotte* suggest that she is not exclusively to blame for her behavior and character; society is guilty of the same sins. La Rue's enticement of Charlotte is part malevolence, part commerce, but her attachment to Belcour and then marriage to Colonel Crayton are the stratagems of a desperate female in the world where, as Montraville's father says, girls must be provided for while boys may "exert their talents" (p. 52); a world where Mr. Temple observes his sisters married, or "legally prostituted to old decrepit men" (p. 26). Even with Belcour Mrs. Rowson attempts a hint of complexity; she writes, "Something like humanity was awakened in Belcour's breast by this pathetic speech [one of Charlotte's] . . ." (p. 103). Corydon, La Rue's paramour, is also given a soft spot (pp. 118-119), so that all virtue is not ranked on one side against abject vice on the other.

The Littletons of *The Fille de Chambre* represent Mrs. Rowson's attempt to provide her heroines with believably fallible parents rather than the cruel, scheming stereotypes imputed to the sentimental novel. Rebecca's parents resemble the Bennets of *Pride and Prejudice*. The mother is characterized as a person with "sentiments that are narrow and illiberal," and "that kind of worldly knowledge which rendered her suspicious of the integrity of every human being" (p. 9); she is still young and attractive, silly, and in spite of her suspiciousness, sentimental. She clings to romantic notions such as a disapproval of second marriages. Mr. Littleton is "honest, possessed of valour, good sense, and a liberal education" (p. 9). He and Rebecca side against Mrs. Littleton, and there is an interesting note of mother-daughter competition. Mrs. Rowson explains,

> This juvenile appearance of her mother was a great misfortune to Rebecca, for Mrs. Littleton was ever more pleased with being told she looked like her eldest sister, than in being complimented with being the mother of so lovely a young woman; indeed, she considered every compliment paid to her daughter as derogating something from her own merit. She considered her more as a rival than a child. . . .
>
> (p. 10)

Lady Ossiter, the unfeeling daughter of Lady Mary Worthy, comes alive in the lengthy scene in which she fusses over her mourning clothes just before her mother's funeral. She chatters to Rebecca about the virtues of various fabrics and then says to the heartbroken girl,

> "Do you think I should go without powder? You look monstrous well without powder; but then you have light hair, and your black dress, though so very plain, is becoming. Who are you in mourning for, child?"
>
> (p. 49)

Meriel is Mrs. Rowson's liveliest heroine. She is romantic, and this fact is sustained throughout *Trials of the Human Heart* (while this quality never plays much part in the life of Rebecca after its initial introduction). Even though Meriel learns that novels and plays are not real, and is taken advantage of by nearly everyone around her, she admits she remains a bit of a dreamer. She calls herself a "castle builder" whose ideas are "bubbles." Oak-hall, the family seat of Rooksby, Meriel's husband, inspires Meriel's imagination with its "romantic" atmosphere and antiquity (III, 4). The ambiance, along with

Meriel's fondness for Rooksby's mother, perhaps tips the balance in Rooksby's favor. Meriel is made of flesh and blood; she experiences pleasureable physical contact with a married man, Mr. Kingly. She writes Celia,

> He pressed my hands to his bosom: my head sunk upon his shoulder and my tears flowed without restraint. Oh, my Celia! let the prude, the rigidly virtuous blame me: the affection of my heart at that moment triumphed!
>
> (IV, 26)

In another episode, Meriel feels attraction for Mr. Belger, an "infidel" who provokes her to religious doubts; she writes Celia that she can control her actions but not her feelings.

Mrs. Rowson invests Meriel with more human feelings than she allows Mary and Rebecca. Meriel often admits to Celia that she is proud, and her actions bear out this admission. The pain with which Meriel swallows her pride to deliver merchandise to the home of a former social inferior is made believable by Mrs. Rowson. Meriel does what she must in order to earn her fee, but she refuses to be patronized with a piece of cake and a glass of wine to be shared with the servants (II, 54). Her reaction is similar when her brother offers her money, but not respect (IV, 119). Mrs. Rowson has tried to create a personality of human proportions.

Meriel is not irresistible to men. Rooksby prefers Clara, and accepts Meriel only because Clara is unobtainable. Rainsforth-Kingly finds happiness with another women when he and Meriel are separated. Meriel ages far beyond the seventeen years of the romantic heroine. Her story spans sixteen years, and before she and her beloved are united, she is in her thirties. Again, Mrs. Rowson attempts to show her characters in a truer light than that of the sentimental novel. By the time they marry, Meriel and Kingly have both had other spouses and are not in their first youth.

Among the secondary characters in *Trials of the Human Heart*, Meriel's brother stands out as an example of Mrs. Rowson's attempt to sustain believable minor figures. In the beginning he is portrayed as a thirteen-year-old tormentor: Meriel writes, "if I deliver my sentiments on any subject that excites my sensibility or veneration, then sister is going to turn a sentimental actress, or a methodist preacher . . ." (I, 116). In their interview later, when Meriel refuses his money, the brother says to Meriel that "you are as good a preacher as ever" (IV, 119).

In Hamden Auberry of *Reuben and Rachel*, Mrs. Rowson comes

closest to creating a believable leading man. Hamden is an aristocrat educated by his aunt, Lady Anne, and encouraged by his early training to revere wealth and social prominence. Hamden suffers doubts about Rachel that nearly prevent his marriage to her. When he sees her with lower-class companions during her days of poverty in London, he wonders about her virtue; at one point he ruminates over his indecision:

> Hamden was silent; a certain something struck cold upon his heart. No wonder; it was the cold, hard drop that turns whatever it falls upon to stone. Poverty has a most unaccountable petrifying quality; many a heart has it rendered impenetrable as adamant; many a bosom has it incased in marble, or enveloped in ice, so firmly congealed, that only the sun of prosperity, riding in full meridian, could soften or relax it.

> . . . .

> Would I be willing to relinquish all hope of future affluence, honour, title, and devote my life to obscurity and Rachel Dudley? I fear not. I should repine at the advantages I had relinquished, and embitter her life by my own fruitless regret.
>
> (II, 259)

Although Mrs. Rowson did not develop completely believable male partners for her heroines, she never created in them the outlandish physical and mental supermen nor the pure, emasculated figures of comparable writers. Mrs. Rowson's heroes are somewhat nebulous, but not inhuman as, for instance, Ishmael is in the books of E.D.E.N. Southworth.[5] Mrs. Rowson's men are average fellows, physically stronger than the female, who engage in "manly" activities such as careers in the army and navy.

In *Sarah*, Mrs. Rowson creates a heroine with flaws that are not simply excesses of virtue as Meriel's come close to being. Sarah is easily flattered, having been accustomed to attention from her father's friends. Her reaction to her loveless marriage, to revert to the "spoiled child" side of her self, puts a realistic touch to her character. Her wise older friend, and epistolary confidante, Anne, writes of her,

> Sarah, indulged from infancy in elegant habiliments, though her own taste prevents her dressing fine, is thoughtlessly extravagant; elegant laces, rich satins, with gloves, caps, shoes, &c. suitable, are

not procured for a trifling sum in the course of a year; and Sarah is, perhaps, not so careful of her clothes, or attentive to the expenditures of her house keeping as she ought to be; her heart is naturally liberal; she has no idea of being imposed on by her servants, and when sometimes a slight suspicion will cross her mind, that her provisions are wasted, or her clothes wilfully lost, any plausible excuse will quiet her, and from a native love of peace, she will cease to inquire concerning her domestic concerns, or appear satisfied, when in fact, she is not convinced; she exerts but little authority in the management of her family: dressing, making and receiving visits, late hours at night, and, consequently, late mornings, have, in appearance, totally altered the character of the late interesting Sarah.

She gives dinners and suppers in very high style, and is herself the very soul of the parties she draws around her. . . .

(pp. 62-63)

In addition to these faults, Sarah gambles.

In *Sarah*, Mrs. Rowson continues to aim at verisimilitude in portraying seducers; here they are not unusually licentious or depraved, but flawed men who take advantage of the way of the world. Mr. O'Donnell elopes with Mrs. Bellamy's daughter in the hope of making a financially sound marriage. No monster, he helps Sarah later in the story. The Marquis H— is not motivated by sexual revenge like Lovelace and his descendants, but is attracted to Sarah and mistakes her position because he sees her associating with kept women. When Sarah's position is clarified, he makes no attempt to kidnap or coerce her, but withdraws from pursuit—and even offers disinterested financial assistance. He writes a very gentlemanly letter.

In addition to keeping her characters within a believable scale, Mrs. Rowson is occasionally able to realize her characters through the use of psychological detail. In *Victoria*, the heroine is seen moving slowly toward melancholia as Mrs. Rowson describes her behavior and her dreams and poems. The vividness with which Charlotte's postpartum psychosis is presented enlivens Charlotte as a character. In spite of the Shakespearean overtones of the passages in which this experience is described, Mrs. Rowson must be given credit for using lifelike detail not found in the typical "mad scene" and for making the reader experience the disturbance of the heroine:

Charlotte had now been three days with her humane preservers, but she was totally insensible of every thing: she raved incessantly for Montraville and her father: she was not conscious of being a mother, nor took the least notice of her child except to ask whose it was, and why it was not carried to its parents.

"Oh," said she one day, starting up on hearing the infant cry, "why, why will you keep that child here; I am sure you would not if you knew how hard it was for a mother to be parted from her infant: it is like tearing the cords of life asunder. Oh could you see the horrid sight which I now behold—there—there stands my dear mother, her poor bosom bleeding at every vein, her gentle, affectionate heart torn in a thousand pieces, and all for the loss of a ruined, ungrateful child. Save me—save me—from her frown. I dare not—indeed I dare not speak to her."

(p. 119)

One of Mrs. Rowson's best touches in *Sarah* is Sarah's description of her own wedding day. She writes Anne that just as she and Mr. Darnley knelt at the altar, "my nose gushed out with blood; my handkerchief and clothes were suffused with the crimson torrent" (p. 6). Herbert Ross Brown treats this incident as an illustration of the extreme emotionalism of sentimental heroines; but examined in the context of the story, that of a young woman entering a hateful marriage, it can be recognized as an effective, realistic detail that helps the reader envision the wedding scene, and provides a rich symbol of Sarah's psychological state. The nosebleed combines the notions of illness caused by acting against one's own judgment, the soiling and making ludicrous of a supposedly holy ceremony—an act that foreshadows the quality of the Darnley marriage—and the sexual fears that in Sarah's day included visions of wedding-night blood.

Many of the types that abound in Mrs. Rowson's world are rendered with convincing detail even while they retain a semi-allegorical status. Abigail Prune (Mrs. Penure), one of Rebecca's employers, is so stingy that she cannot bear to throw anything away, and she expects Rebecca to create fashionable hats for her out of her collection of "every ribband she ever had in her possession" (p. 168). Mrs. Penure disapproves of Rebecca or anyone else "wasting" time reading. She herself reads only the "Bible, and the Housekeeper's Account." She states, "I was always studying to make the most of my time and how to save or earn a penny" (p. 168). Mrs. Rowson's description of Abigail includes pungent, not pretty, detail that helps solidify the character Rebecca must cope with. Abigail, who had "seen forty seasons revolve," sees herself in the mirror and observes.

... a shape ... so exactly straight, that it was impossible to perceive the least difference between the bottom and the top, and instead of that roundness, which constitutes elegance in the form of a woman, her waist was as perfectly flat as though she had been pressed between two boards.

(p. 166)

Abigail's appearance also includes teeth "of jetty hue" and coloring which "might have rivalled the tints of the most beautiful orange lilly" (pp. 166-167).

A disagreeable headmistress with whom Sarah must cope is given similar treatment. Anne writes of Sarah's potential employer at an interview,

Here we were interrupted by the rustlidg [sic] of silk, and Madam *la Govenante* entered in all the consequence of rich padusoy, lace ruffles, and an enormous head, where gauze, wire, pompoons, and ribbon, strove for pre-eminence.

(p. 19)

When the interview between Mrs. Harrop and Sarah does not go smoothly, the headmistress' confusion is rendered vividly by the comparison, "The broad face of Mrs. Harrop now resembled the tints of a full blown pioni" (p. 20).

Mrs. Rowson varies the patterns of her characters' speech as a clue to their moral status, and also to portray life convincingly. The heroines and other admirable characters tend to use "literary" English with only an occasional colloquial touch. False, negative characters often use repetitious, faddish jargon, the young men occasionally break into slang, and a variety of socially determined speech variations help create a recognizable world.

Mr. Stephens in *The Test of Honour* employs a colorful style that rings true; his vulgar imagery and expletives show his rudeness and his obtuseness. When he sees his son depressed, he says,

"Why Frederick, my boy ... you look as low-spirited as an old maid who has lost her favourite monkey; come, prithee lad, cheer up; I have got such news for you as will make your heart dance again; I wanted to tell you last night, but you was in such a devilish hurry to go to bed; ecod it has made me almost young again. Why you don't look pleased now; you don't seem happy."

(I, 73)

Lady Ossiter, in *The Fille de Chambre* speaks in a false, brittle manner. She drops French phrases into her chatter, and frequently uses the word "monstrous" to mean "very" or "quite." When Lord Ossiter announces that he will forgo an evening of entertainment and retire early (he really plans to seduce Rebecca), Lady Ossiter, who is on her way to meet her own lover, wisecracks, "why, sure you are going to take pattern by the sober cit." (p. 75). The friendly sailor who mixes naval jargon into his conversation may be a stock character in early fiction; still Mrs. Rowson's use of this figure in *The Fille de Chambre* effectively adds a touch of verbal variety to her novel, as well as solidity to the shipboard acquaintances.

Of course, those techniques with language and dialogue are rudimentary. But they show the direction of Mrs. Rowson's aspirations. In *Trials* Mrs. Rowson continues to develop her language toward greater naturalness. Meriel's style is somewhat more flexible and everyday than Rebecca's. She writes to Celia of her early married happiness with Rooksby that, "if he is as gallant and tender twelve months hence, I may perhaps, stand a good chance for claiming the *flitch of bacon*" (III, 55).

The speech patterns of the characters in *Trials* are varied, as are the situations and milieus Meriel encounters. Meriel's aunt produces the kind of old saw typically offered by female relatives to young girls who must postpone marriage and other desired goals. As Rainsforth goes into the navy, she comments that "absence and salt water are in general a cure for love" (I, 131). The sober sensibility of Mrs. Kingly, the woman who marries Meriel's true love, is contrasted—through juxtaposed letters—with the young-girl worldly wisdom of Amelia Sidney, Meriel's best friend. Mrs. Kingly refuses to advise Meriel to marry Rooksby, but she writes that she would be happy "to see you raised to a station you was formed to adorn" (III, 25). Amelia urges Meriel to accept Rooskby so she can "have the pleasure of pointing out your elegant equipage" (III, 27); as she later asks "who ever heard of misery in a coach and six?" (III, 51). Silly Dolly Pringle, who early in Meriel's life tempts her into novel-reading and assignations, goes about saying "La, Miss," as a preface to almost every statement.

The various religious and ethnic types in *Reuben and Rachel* speak according to at least book versions of their individual speech styles. The Quakers are given a touch of life through this technique. Tabitha, for example, when she hears of Rachel's friendship with Hamden, remonstrates,

". . . thou didst not send word that a stranger would walk with thee; that thou wouldest lean on his arm, and suffer him to kiss thy hand, in a manner not becoming a maiden who wisheth to preserve her reputation. And this stranger was clothed in scarlet and gold, and eats the bread that is purchased by murdering his fellow-creatures. Verily, I say, my spirit waxeth wroth when I think the daughter of Cassiah Penn turneth from the worship of her father's house, and runneth after strange gods, and delighteth to dwell in the tents of idolaters."

(II, 221)

Stedfast Trueman's description of the demise of Jacob Holmes reflects the judgmental streak that the Quaker shared with the Puritan, and the interest both had in the gory details of a seemingly deserved misfortune:

"Verily he sleepeth with his fathers," said Trueman. "He was greatly hurt about three months since, by a fall from his horse; the bruise was internal, brought on a spitting of blood, which baffled all medical aid, and he went off suddenly, when he supposed himself mending ... More is the pity; the rod of affliction, that warns us of approaching dissolution, is a salutary and necessary judgment, that as we bow under the correcting hand, we may implore that mercy which is never withheld from the penitent sinner."

(II, 352)

The Indians in *Reuben and Rachel* speak the language of Longfellow's savages, spicing their dialogue with nature imagery and references to the Great Spirit. Mrs. Rowson may have gotten her notions of Indian speech and behavior from various histories and narratives, but then, firsthand observation and authentic portraiture of the Indian has never been an attribute of American art.[6]

The language of *Sarah* is livelier and more in the realistic mode than that in any of the other novels. Sarah's own speech is not as genteel as that of earlier Rowson heroines. Sarah has a sharp tongue and she is prone to be satirical about herself and others. Describing her job with the Bellamys, she writes to Anne of her "double capacity of humble toad eater to grandmamma, and madam *governante* to little darling" (p. 115). She describes her situation further with verve and irony:

But I beg your pardon Anne, that after having got you safe to Dublin, I have hurried you back, to make you pass a stormy night at sea, with a dangerous coast on your lee; but as you have escaped shipwreck, you may even come quietly again to Dublin; and setting down by my elbow, in a little room up two pair of stairs, which is but superior to a closet, in a very small degree; the furniture of which consists of a half tester-bed, a deal table, a small iron grate, that will hold a handful of fire, and two rush bottom chairs; now, is not the apartment most elegant? Come sit down, and be quiet, and I will tell you all about madam Bellamy, and her fair daughter madam O'Donnel, and her sweet pretty, peevish, petulant, perverse grand-daughter, Miss Caroline O'Donnel.

The old dame does not want ideas in her head, nor language to express those ideas; but she is one of the most changeable, capricious beings, that nature ever formed. Her manners have been formed upon the scale of high life; and she certainly has, in early days, sacrificed to the graces; for even now, she can converse with condescending affability, every word accompanied by a fassinating smile; she can be cheerful even to volability; persuasion will hang upon her tongue, and the genius of taste, wit, and elegance preside in her apartment. But see her two hours after, you will not know her for the same women; her brow will lour, her large black eyes will flash malignity, the demon of spite and slander take possession of her tongue; and her language will be such, as almost the lowest female would blush to utter.

(pp. 117-118)

Sarah's irony is also exercised upon Darnley's mistress; describing Mrs. Romain's separation from the financially depleted George, she writes to Anne,

So, my dear Anne, by degrees I discovered that the tender, fond, *fainting* Jessey, to pass the wearisome hours while Darnley was in confinement, had taken a trip to the continent with Lord G —. The ostensible reason alleged was to place her son in some foreign seminary for education; and if she could travel in a chariot and four, with a footman, groom, and servant, out of livery attending, it was certainly a prudent saving of her own money, and a much more agreeable mode of making the journey, than either in a hired chaise or a stage coach.

(p. 104)

When her obtuse husband asks Sarah if she did not think Mrs. Romaine acted "in a most extraordinary manner," Sarah reports to Anne that she replied, "I see nothing extraordinary in it . . . she wanted an excursion of pleasure, and a good opportunity to make one offering, with a rich and handsome young nobleman for a companion, she could not resist the temptation" (p. 104). Sarah's vocabulary includes contemporary, everyday terms and references that lend reality to her speech. After Mr. Darnley's first financial collapse, Sarah writes Anne that if she is incoherent, "You will not think that strange, when I tell you, I am actually writing in a spunging house" (p. 91).

A discussion of morals between Sarah and Mrs. Bellamy, who encourages her own daughter to be the mistress of a married man, is made interesting and given a note of authenticity by Mrs. Bellamy's language. Some examples of her comments as reported by Sarah follow:

"You seem lost in the *profundity* of *cogibundity*," said Mrs. Bellamy, laughing, and laying her hand on my arm, "and pray what may be the subject of your meditation?"

. . . .

"I would gratify it [Sarah's curiosity], but that I suppose your *primitive purity* would take alarm; you would draw up your head, and contract your little consequential brow."

. . . .

"O, the heart is always thought invulnerable, until it is absolutely lost; but pray, my frigid friend, if youth, beauty, and riches, have no power on that impenetrable bosom, what may the requisites be, necessary to awaken it from the torpor of stupidity?"

(pp. 126-127)

Mrs. Bellamy questions Sarah about the treatment she has received from Darnley, and Sarah insists that she cannot "connect myself with any man while Mr. Darnley lives" (p. 128). Asked again her requisites for a man she might really love, Sarah responds with her ideals, and Mrs. Bellamy attempts to puncture them by saying, "Oh! hold, for heaven's sake! a pretty formal, old fashioned piece of clock-work you have put together; do you ever expect to meet with such a nonpariel?" Later, she adds, "You are a strange being, Mrs. Darnley; but suppose this *black swan* should appear, what would become of your fine resolutions then?" (p. 129). Mrs. Bellamy's description of Lady Linden, the woman whose husband her daughter sees, provides a further sampling of her vocabulary; the Lady is "an unmeaning cream-faced thing," "an inanimate statue" with a "swinging fortune" (p. 124).

The authenticity of the country setting in *Charlotte's Daughter* is brought out by the talk of the cottagers and other local folk. "Oh yes, sir, and we gets all the physic and such stuff from the Potticary without paying," an old woman assures Reverend Matthews (p. 49). At the country inn where Sir Stephen takes Lady Mary, a female servant replies to questions concerning the whereabouts of Mary's seducer:

> "but Dora when she was cleaning the parlour where their honours played cards last night, sawed this bit of paper, but what it's about we can't tell, for neither she nor I can read joining hand."
>
> (p. 116)

Mrs. Rowson subjects her heroines to everyday problems as well as to romantic trials like seduction and shipwreck. Poverty is the central problem the uneducated, dependent, unprotected female must face, and nearly every Rowson heroine is subject to its rigors. Mrs. Rowson is not alone in using this ploy as part of her protagonists' experiences, but she manages to convince the reader that she knew something about the actual woes of bankruptcy. She does not romanticize nor sentimentalize poverty as many writers did. Catherine Sedgwick, for example, in *The Poor Rich Man, and the Rich Poor Man*,[7] extends the idea that material wealth may be inferior to spiritual riches to the argument that poverty is literally better than wealth. There is the fun of "making do" (Sedgwick, p. 31) and better opportunities to know God. Mrs. Rowson wanted her audience to take a harder view. Inordinate love of money is a sin, but being poor is never painted as fun, and a firm grasp of finance is shown to be good sense.

Mrs. Rowson's subject is realistic. The author realized as well as Virginia Woolf that the problems of the female in the man's world are not all spiritual,[8] and, like Mrs. Woolf, advocated keeping an eye on one's purse as well as one's apron strings. In her presentation of the financial ups and downs of her heroines, Mrs. Rowson stresses the sordidness and horror of poverty as well as the meanness and mediocrity.

From her first novel, Mrs. Rowson was preoccupied with the real problems of making one's way in the world. She introduces the story of Mary Philimore into *Victoria*. Mary is a precursor of Rowson heroines to follow. Unlike Victoria who has a concerned mother and sister to attend her, Mary is alone. Her guardians have wasted her inheritance, and she must repair to "cheap lodgings" and look for work. The practical obstacles to this search are noted; Mary writes, "I put an advertisement in the news-paper, and went after places, but the want of a character always stood in my way" (I, 122).

The ugliness and unromantic quality of Charlotte's situation is brought out in the scene in which Charlotte asks for charity from the farm wife from whom Montraville had rented a house. The woman replies angrily to Charlotte's request to stay on without paying:

"Charity . . . charity indeed: why, Mistress charity begins at home, and I have seven children at home, *honest, lawful* children, and it is my duty to keep them; and do you think I will give away my property to a nasty impudent hussey to maintain her and her bastard; an I was saying to my husband the other day what will this world come to; honest women are nothing now adays, while the harlotings are set up for fine ladies, and look upon us no more nor the dirt they walk upon: but let me tell you, my fine spoken Ma'am, I must have my money; so seeing as how you can't pay it, why you must troop, and leave all your fine gimcraks and fal der ralls behind you. I don't ask for no more nor my right, and nobody shall dare for to go for to hinder me of it."

(pp. 110-111)

Mrs. Rowson also tries to make Charlotte's melodramatic trip through the storm realistically frightening by noting the women along the roadside who wash the clothes of the Revolutionary soldiers. This is the next step down for Charlotte.

Meriel's experiences blend the sordid and dramatic trials of poverty with the everyday inconvenience and humiliation of being poor. Her trip to the brothel and a near-fatal illness exemplify the first kind of adventure. The second is shown in her attempt to make a living and in her dealings with other poor souls also striving for survival. Meriel finds that earning a living as a milliner involves wounding her pride and integrity. She writes Celia,

. . . I cannot flatter, I cannot tell a woman whom age, and other natural defects, have rendered extremely plain, that a full dress cap with artificial flowers small handkerchief, and all the gay trappings that belong to the smiling season of eighteen, will become her face and figure: and yet this is a very necessary ingredient in the composition of a milliner.

(*Trials of the Human Heart*, II, 58)

Meriel is very shocked when her heroic act in saving her landlady's children does not curtail the woman's mercenary demands. And she learns further facts of life in a mercantile world when she is forced to sell her belongings. She writes to Celia when she does not get the anticipated price for her furnishings, that she is learning "the vast difference between buying and selling." She describes her interview with the buyer as follows:

> But when the man had looked them over, and taken an inventory, he offered me only thirty five guineas for the whole, in which was included my piano forte. I urged how much more they had cost me, and how little they had been used. He answered that was nothing to him; he could afford to give no more; there were some things would be of no use to him; they would lay a dead stock upon his hands, and if I did not choose to take that, it was all very well, he had rather leave them than have them.
>
> (II, 102)

The aforementioned landlady is not above taking Meriel's clothes, and the "laceman" gives short payment for the trim. Meriel notes, "the edgings were produced, when to my utter astonishment, the laceman declared he would not take them without an allowance of one third of what I paid for them only a few months before" (II, 103).

Sarah's experiences with poverty are even more realistic. She has never learned to manage money, and this improvidence is one of the chief sources of friction between her and Mr. Darnley. We have seen Sarah struggling with the "mysteries" of roasting and stewing, and Anne discovers her friend "In a very confined lodging, actually employed in ironing her husband's shirts" (p. 112). Sarah writes to Frederic of the mediocrity of her situation:

> . . . Darnley has employment in the warehouse of a manufacturing company, to receive orders, and note them in a day book; for this he receives a stipend of sixty pounds per annum. We occupy a small house, more like a cottage than any thing else, about half a mile from the town; our whole establishment consists of one girl to do the drudgery, my little Charles, Mr. Darnley, and myself.
>
> (p. 253)

The heroine who "never touches a dish clout" is too rarefied for Mrs. Rowson.

A well-informed female will be skeptical of the ways of the world. Like Mary in Test of Honour, she will learn to ask for a receipt when she pays a bill—even an unjust one. Held up for money by an unscrupulous ship captain in cahoots with her cousin Geoffrey, Mary says,

"Dismiss those wretches [jailers], and I will discharge the demand, tho' I am certain it is an unjust one. But hold! I will pay you before these men; and then you cannot pretend to deny the receiving the money."

(II, 97-98)

Mrs. Rowson adds, "She rang for pen, ink, and paper; put down the money, and desired a receipt in full of all demands" (II, 98).

Mrs. Rowson does not accept the morality[9] of the eighteenth-century mercantile world, but she does accept its reality. And she suggests that her readers know that world's difficulties. She never launches fictional couples on matrimony unprovided for. Rebecca's George says that "abundance of riches cannot secure happiness!" Mrs. Rowson could not agree more; but although she allows George to refuse the lucrative job offered him by Rebecca's uncle, she provides him with the means to support a family. In the final scene of *The Fille de Chambre*, George explains, "We will retire into Berkshire, to the estate you so generously settled on my family . . ." (p. 205). Incidentally, at this point in the novel, Rebecca also has two thousand pounds.

There is no compromising by Mrs. Rowson with the Mr. B's of the world. Although Sarah is tempted to trade her virtue for the security the Marquis H— offers her, she overcomes the urge. Mrs. Rowson is no Worldly Wiseman, nor does she teach "prudential morality" or that "virtue is the best policy," as several critics have suggested.[10] Her standards are absolute; she only says that a sensible grasp of social realities, including financial matters, is desirable. A doctor friend of Meriel's improves his practice as he is helped by Meriel to upgrade his appearance, and Meriel writes,

you cannot think how the doctor is rising in reputation, since his appearance is so mended. He is now often seen coming out of the doors of the wealthy, which I hope presages he will one day become wealthy himself.

(*Trials*, III, 105)

The Mary Lumlys of the world must learn to make sensible financial as well as sentimental arrangements. Even the incompatible marriage of Sarah and Darnley might have been made more bearable by better financial arrangements. Anne writes to Elenor of the Darnleys' frequent quarrels over money, and expresses the author's opinion about such friction:

"And here I must digress to remark, that in my opinion, the state of total dependence in which women in general are, must tend to weaken that affection, that confidence, which should subsist between married persons. I cannot imagine but the domestic happiness would be greatly increased, were wives released from that solicitude and anxiety which every woman of sensibility must feel, who is obliged to apply to her husband for every shilling she expends. . . ."

(p. 244)

Mrs. Rowson tries to show her audience some of the actual outlines of everyday life. She wants them to live in the world as she sees it and never lets them forget that that world presents practical as well as spiritual problems. One of these problems is the fact that the good life costs money. In her patriotic songs and poems Mrs. Rowson takes up the popular interest in American "commerce" with special zeal. To her, a healthy economic base is necessary for a genuine and thriving American art, just as it is for a well-rounded individual. Even her poetic idyl, "Choice" (*Miscellaneous Poems*), reflects this attitude. Mrs. Rowson begins her picture of the ideal life:

> I ask no more than just to be
> From vice and folly wholly free;
> To have a competent estate
> Neither too small, nor yet too great;
> Something of rent and taxes clear,
> About five hundred pounds a year.

(p. 137)

8

The Preceptress

> Pray, Miss, don't detain me, I'm going to school,
> And our governess long has established a rule:
> She who for three months the most neatly is dressed,
> Comes the soonest to school, says her lesson the best,
> Shall receive from her hand the reward of a book,
> And what's more, a kind word, an affectionate look.
> ("Dialogue–Mary and Lucretia,"
> A Present for Young Ladies, 1811)

Mrs. Rowson's most successful creation was her persona, the "author" of the works who is never offstage for long but always hovering nearby with chalk and pointer, reward and punishment. She can clarify the moral direction of a story and cajole and direct her reader to the right point of view. She becomes a friend and model for the reader. Mrs. Rowson is her own best heroine, whose situation and responses well illustrate her feminist views.[1]

This persona is ubiquitous.[1] None of Mrs. Rowson's works is without some reference to the personality of the writer. The dimensions of this personality are established largely through the prefaces and are developed through the narrators and speaking voice of the various works; they are extensions of Mrs. Rowson's real personality insofar as the latter is known. The author often points out the autobiographical nature of details and episodes in the fiction and refers to her activities outside her books, but these references are very selective. Mrs. Rowson always presents herself as the penwoman and teacher, the English woman transplanted to America. The "author" attains a unity and singleness of purpose hardly possessed by the actual author. She seems more real and is more memorable than many of the dramatic characters. Robert Haswell's letter to Susanna, quoted in chapter 1, shows how central Mrs. Rowson's literary alter ego was to her work by its emphasis on the love the young girls of Boston have for the author, rather than on their love of her works.

To some degree Mrs. Rowson's literary self matures as Susanna Rowson grows older, and reflects the author's actual career, but the basic qualities of the preface and narrative speaker are consistent, like Mrs. Rowson's goals. In an early work such as *The Test of Honour*, Mrs. Rowson presents herself as the youthful "female scribe" and shows the defiance of youth by daring her reader to question her motives in writing:

> To alledge my reason for commencing author, would only be to gratify the curiosity of impertinent, ignorant people: the well-bred, sensible reader (if any such should honour this book with a perusal) will never trouble themselves with inquiring into a motive insignificant in itself, and of no consequence to them.
>
> (p. vi)

Over the years, the author becomes more friendly and intimate with her audience. She is willing to share her personal concerns and motivations. In the preface to *Biblical Dialogues*, she explains how her own religious problems led her into writing the treatise and freely includes references to her family situation. Biographical details that reflect the situation of the author begin to appear in the Rowson works with *Victoria* and grow until the author becomes a fully-fleshed personality.

Although the epistolary and dramatic forms Mrs. Rowson employed in half her fiction do not conveniently lend themselves to development of an authorial personality, Mrs. Rowson manages to remain visible. She is never outside her works, "paring her nails." *Victoria* lacks a preface in which to develop a persona and is written in letters; still, Mrs. Rowson manages to suggest the identity of the narrative voice and the actual author by mentioning her real-life patroness, the Duchess of Devonshire, as an example of female virtue. As in her other epistolary fiction, the device of letters breaks down, due either to the author's lack of skill or her design to remain front and center. The third-person voice intervenes to explain events.

In only one work, Mrs. Rowson adopts a mask or persona that is a distortion of the actual author, and this departure from her usual method is explained as a matter of decorum. A masculine narrator-protagonist is used in *The Inquisitor* because "a man may be with propriety brought forward in many scenes, where it would be the height of improbability to introduce a woman" (pp. vii-viii). But only the sex of the narrator is assumed; the voice of the Inquisitor is in no way different from Mrs. Rowson's standard narrative voice. The interpretation of events and the moral comments are familiar. And Mrs. Rowson, the female writer, is clearly behind the masculine figure; in the preface, she has a male interlocutor ask her why she has used such a device. In the story of Mariana, Mrs. Rowson weaves most of the events of her own life, her experiences as an early resident of both Britain and America, into that of the fictional characters (II, 139).

A Trip to Parnassus continues the building of the Rowson persona by means of the preface and the presentation of a poet-narrator consistent with the authorial voice of the preface. *A Trip* and *The Test of Honour* are the only two Rowson works that do not bear the author's name on the title page; both, however, clearly identify the author as a female and establish attitudes that Mrs. Rowson develops in later works.

Charlotte represents Mrs. Rowson's best use of the commenting, third-person narrator; in this novel many of the qualities of the Rowson speaking voice are blended, and the moralizing is more artfully related to the events of the story than that in *Mentoria* or William Hill Brown's *The Power of Sympathy*. The elaborate prefatory defense of the novel as both true and uplifting, and the buildup of the author as a scrupulous, dedicated guide, focus attention upon the narrator-author. *Mentoria's* preface achieves similar goals, and although the book is basically epistolary in method, the text is frequently interrupted for direct author comment.

Mrs. Rowson's literary self acquires individuality in *The Fille de Chambre*. The preface of 1794 has the author, as noted earlier, engaging in a lengthy debate over artistic procedure. The story is narrated in the omniscient third person, and lest the reader forget that Mrs. Rowson the well-known writer is the source of the story, the author breaks into the narrative on several occasions with autobiographical comments. Of the sailor who shares his food with Rebecca and the Abthorpes, Mrs. Rowson writes,

> Exalted humanity, noble, disinterested sailor, may you ever experience from your fellow creatures the same benevolence that expands and elevates your own heart. May your days be many and your prosperity equal to your deserts.
>
> (p. 115)

The passage is footnoted, "This apostrophe is the genuine emotion of gratitude, the author having in a situation similar to the one described here, experienced relief bestowed in the same disinterested manner" (p. 115).

In the second American edition (1814) of *The Fille de Chambre,*
Mrs. Rowson drops the prefatory interview with Mr. Puffendorf, and in
an "Introductory Chapter," provides a fuller account of the factual
background of her novel. Like *Charlotte,* which she now pinpoints as
having been told to her by "the lady, whom I introduce under the name
of Beauchamp," *The Fille de Chambre* claims to be based to a large
degree upon real events. Both result from the author's "reflective turn
of mind," which prompted her "to comment on passing events, and
think seriously on circumstances that are treated as ordinary and
uninteresting by the generality of the world" (p. iii). Mrs. Rowson goes
on to refer to the "great vicissitudes of fortune . . . on both sides of the
Atlantic" that she has experienced (p. iv); she sorts out the fictional and
the actual in her novel, and paints a scene in which she revisits the
locale of the actual events in New England.

More than one impulse may have motivated Mrs. Rowson to include
such biographical material in the two editions of *The Fille.* Footnotes
appear in Richardson, Rousseau, and other eighteenth-century
novelists, to explain and authenticate. Mrs. Rowson's letters show a
sensitivity to criticism of her status in America as a British woman,
which is also evidenced in the prefatory reply in *Trials of the Human
Heart* to William Cobbett's attack on her patriotism.[2] The result of her
use of biographical material, however, is to keep her literary personality in the forefront of her works. Mrs. Rowson's tales of the past always
emphasize her situation as an alien, which is likely to arouse sympathy
in her readers, and her rôle as author, which reminds them of what she
has provided them in entertainment and instruction. The penwoman is
stressed. The actress, the wife, the businesswoman—they have no part
in the literary self Mrs. Rowson is creating.

Mrs. Rowson manages to thrust herself as author even into her play,
Slaves in Algiers. In the printed version her chance comes in the
preface. Again, she is the female writer, disadvantaged by lack of
education. She confides to her audience that she has written in haste
and that there are alterations in the piece since the first performance;
she tells of her indebtedness to Cervantes for parts of her plot. Nor is
Mrs. Rowson in her preferred rôle to be kept out of the performance of
the play. At the conclusion of the dramatic action, she steps out of the
character of Olivia, and appears as author to address the audience
directly. She demands,

> Well, Ladies tell me—how d'ye like my play?
> "The creature has some sense," methinks you say;
> "She says that we should have supreme dominion,
> "And in good truth, we're all of her opinion."

Like the drama, *Trials of the Human Heart*, as Mrs. Rowson's most sustained attempt at the epistolary novel, presents the ubiquitous author with a challenge. The letters that make up this novel possess somewhat more probability and unity of form than Mrs. Rowson had achieved in *Victoria* or *Mentoria*. The characters usually remember that they are writing specific information to a specific correspondent. In only a few instances does the author threaten to break directly through the fictional world to address the reader, as in the following aside, which resembles Mrs. Rowson's digressive style rather than Meriel's everyday form of address. Meriel writes, as she describes her experience in the brothel,

> Oh! ye rigidly virtuous of my own sex, turn not from me with horror and contempt, consider my agonizing distress, glance with an eye of compassion over the dreadful resolution, and let a tear of pity blot the offence from your memories.
>
> (*Trials*, II, 32)

The epistolary novel is a frustrating form for an author who loves to moralize and comment directly. But Mrs. Rowson does not let *Trials of the Human Heart* loose upon the world without clearly stamping it with her own personality. In its lengthy preface, the author responds indignantly to William Cobbett's attack on her work and her patriotism. She calls him a "loathsome reptile" who has "crawled over" her work (pp. xiii-xiv). She then proceeds to answer his charges against her patriotism by providing him—and the reader—with "a slight sketch of my private history, with which, I rather imagine, the *creature* alluded to, is entirely unacquainted" (p. xv). Mrs. Rowson expands upon the "vicissitudes" she has experienced; she tells the reader of her father's imprisonment in America and of the help given by various Americans during the bleakest moments of the family's sojourn here. This is a selective, nostalgic account of the actual relationship of the author to America. She reveals nothing of her return to America with the theater company, only that she came back "in a very different situation" (p. xix). She ignores Cobbett's comments upon her feminist views and his criticism of America for fostering such sentiments.

Reuben and Rachel finds Mrs. Rowson in transition between her rôles as teaching-writer and writing-teacher. Her tone in the preface is increasingly chatty and personal. She assumes that everyone knows the character of the author and is interested in her concerns. Thus she confides not only her professional problems to her reader, but also the "ill-health" that has prevented her from publishing *Reuben and Rachel* at the designated time. She expresses her usual horror at the prospect of corrupting the minds of her readers and tells her audience of her decision to spend most of her future time on formal education. She narrates the novel in the third person, while making strong use of letters and narrators within the tale. She occasionally interrupts the narrative to address the reader directly with problems of art and morality.

The preface to *Sarah* provides even more personal comment and continues to develop the literary personality of the author. Mrs. Rowson hints at experiences of her own that ally her with Sarah and her audience. They have convinced her that life holds both good, "roses scattered in a wilderness," and evil, "many a thorn, and many a flint, that have lacerated my feelings to the very quick" (p. ii).

The prefaces and narrative voice of the pedagogical works assure the public that the author is the familiar Mrs. Rowson. Now the established teacher with a school of her own, Mrs. Rowson offers her subject in *An Abridgment of Universal Geography* as one of her own favorite areas of research; she notes, "I had myself ever found Geography an interesting and amusing study" (p. iii). She alludes to her teaching duties and methods of presentation. Similarly, *A Spelling Dictionary* is offered as a result of Mrs. Rowson's personal experience with teaching the young. None of Mrs. Rowson's efforts is ever represented as coming from an impersonal, objective source.

A Present for Young Ladies finds the author deep in her rôle as educator. Although many of the pieces in the collection are dialogues, or poems and addresses written to suit the age and outlook of the young ladies who recited them, the preceptress always hovers near. She appears in the poem "The Bee, A Fable," the tale of an industrious bee who survives winter while his improvident relatives languish, which is represented as having been spoken by Mrs. Rowson's niece, Mary Haswell:

Yes, there's a moral; hear it if you please;
This is the hive, and we're the little bees,
Our governess is the adviser sage
Who fits us for the world's delusive stage,
By pointing out the weeds among the flowers,
By teaching us to use our mental powers;
To shun the former, and with nicest care
Cull from the latter all that's sweet and fair,
Extract their honey, keep their color bright
To deck the chaplet for a winter's night.

(p. 15)

Mrs. Rowson rounds off the occasion of *A Present* by referring once more to herself. The speaker in "Concluding Address, 1810" says of the ideas she has expounded,

> Our Preceptress has been urgent to impress this subject deeply on all our minds, I speak but her dictates, but my heart gives assent to her reasoning, and hopes aided by the direction of my revered and pious relation [a clergyman], never to disgrace the education I have received.
>
> Mrs. Rowson would fain express her grateful sensations, for the support and encouragement she has received during fourteen years, in which she has been engaged in the instruction of youth; but where gratitude is felt in the heart, words are but a poor vehicle to convey its meaning. She has hitherto endeavoured to prove hers by an assiduous attention to our improvement, to our health, to our manners and morals; she will henceforth evince it (though on a smaller scale) by the most conscientious discharge of her duty in the cultivation of those tender plants which may hereafter be intrusted to her care. She bids her friends most tenderly farewell—She will no more meet you on this annual day but the memory of your kindness will rest upon her heart, the warm sense of gratitude with which that heart glows can be chilled only by the hand of death.
>
> (p. 156)

Exercises in History and *Biblical Dialogues* find the Rowson persona fully developed; her self-confidence is greater, her tone more intimate and confiding than ever. In the preface to the first work, Mrs. Rowson tells us her age, chats about her years of teaching, and again looks forward to her own imminent death (p. iii).

The preface to *Biblical Dialogues* shows Mrs. Rowson continuing her chats with her reader and, by referring to her own struggles with the subject of the book, affirming and enhancing her literary self. She confides her personal struggles to teach, as well as earlier struggles to learn:

> To trace all moral and religious truth up to its divine source, it is necessary that children should not only be taught to read, but to understand the BIBLE. To teach them to read it was an easy task, but to make them understand it, associate ideas, to connect the events related, the persons mentioned, the places where those events happened, and where those persons lived, with the same events,

persons and places mentioned in Profane History, was an herculean labour. I perfectly remembered the time, when to my own uninformed mind the world of the Bible, and the world of which I felt myself an inhabitant, were two distinct worlds; as I advanced in life, a naturally inquiring disposition, assisted by some learned and judicious friends, and an insatiable love of reading, began to open my understanding; and though I then could not comprehend the highly figurative language of the Prophets, or more sublime parts of the inspired writings, yet I began to perceive the connexion between the Old and New Testaments, and in a slight degree between Sacred and Profane History; and as I happily had a step-mother (a New-England lady) who, whenever I did wrong, made me judge of the rectitude of the action by referring me to the commandments delivered from Sinai, or our Lord's sermon on the mount, I was early accustomed to make the Bible my study and guide.

(pp. iii-v)

The persona of Mrs. Rowson's miscellaneous works exhibits many of the outstanding traits of the author-teacher of the fiction and textbooks. A few of Mrs. Rowson's poems are in the form of dramatic monologues, for example, "The Independent Farmer," and one or two songs, like "America, Commerce, and Freedom," use a masculine "We"— otherwise the author's miscellaneous works reveal a point of view consistent with that of the novels and texts. Mrs. Rowson does not provide a preface for her poetry, but the signature implies the character of the speaker when not otherwise indicated; the speaker is often specifically feminine as in "Rights of Woman," always firm of opinion, and eminently capable of moral judgment—the same mentor appearing in the other works. If the poet and lyricist is not offering advice to "A Young Lady, Who Requested the Author to Write Something On Her" (an act reminiscent of Mrs. Rowson's one-word critiques of pupils at the Academy),[3] she is extending it to her new young country—advising it on the creation of American art ("Commemorative of the Genius of Shakespeare"), on war ("Truxton's Victory"), and on politics ("Eulogy, George Washington").

Besides her ubiquity, the Rowson persona exhibits other characteristics of tone and stance that remain constant and that add the final touches to the author as the young woman's friend and model. In this and the foregoing chapters, many qualities of the speaker's tone have been established. The author-mentor is feminine, highly moral, compassionate, a woman rich in both intellectual and life experience. She is by turns sweet, satirical, preachy, indignant, and accepting. Her attitude toward her readers and toward herself encourages her pupils to enter into new activities and to adopt a rounded and complete self-image.

Mrs. Rowson seems to like her audience. She has fun at the expense of her readers. She depicts them as human and fallible, not as stiff priggish little misses or monsters who need reform. She is on their side, although never on their level. In *The Test of Honour* Mrs. Rowson offers a misleading chapter title, "A Physician Found in the Island"—the doctor turns out to be a goat whose milk saves Mary from the illness she contracts while a castaway. In the fiction, Mrs. Rowson gives the audience the elements of suspense and drama that she supposes they thirst for—with good-humored acknowledgment of their desire for entertainment. Her aims include amusement as well as instruction, for her pedagogical theory endorses the idea that students learn best when they enjoy their lessons. Her texts often include interesting anecdotes and detail. She is always concerned about keeping her readers interested.

In *Charlotte* Mrs. Rowson teasingly promises her readers strong scenes, a treat that she never provides, but that supposedly keeps them reading:

> . . . perhaps your gay hearts would rather follow the fortunate Mrs. Crayton through the scenes of pleasure and dissipation in which she was engaged, than listen to the complaints and miseries of Charlotte. I will for once oblige you; I will for once follow her to midnight revels, balls, and scenes of gaiety, for in such was she constantly engaged.
>
> (p. 107)

Charlotte's Daughter also shows Mrs. Rowson's tolerance of her young audience's interest in persons of their own age. She concludes a lengthy analysis of Reverend Matthews's background and financial situation with the concession that because it may not entertain her readers she "will bring forward the young ladies" (p. 35).

The author is never a harsh critic of error, as long as it remains error and not willful corruption as in the case of La Rue. Although she makes fun of and warns against giving in to romantic impulse, she reserves her strongest scorn for those who cannot forgive. The latter are usually depicted as adult rather than young women. These women are no different, Mrs. Rowson asserts, from her other readers who love a juicy episode. Mrs. Rowson is especially sarcastic in *The Inquisitor* as she satirizes the prudery and hypocrisy of people who are shocked at Annie's story and cannot allow the girl a second chance:

> You shall have it [Annie's story] directly, good ladies—I know you love a little private history.
>
> Mercy on me! cried Miss Autumn, what sort of a story are we to have now? the history of a filthy creature, who lived with another woman's husband, and then turned street-walker?
>
> Even so, dear Madame; and if your immaculate modesty will be too much shocked at the recital in public, double down the page, take it up in your chamber, and read it when you are alone; it will save you the trouble of a blush—
>
> And do you think, Mr. Inquisitor, that your works will be proper for the perusal of youth?
>
> I hope so, Madam; Heaven forbid that I should ever write a page, whose tendency might make me blush to own it, or in my latest hour, wish to blot it out—my narrative is calculated to inspire at once pity and horror—
>
> Pity! good Lord—I never heard the like—pity for an abandoned hussey, who merits the most flagrant punishment?
>
> You'll pardon me, Madam, if I differ from you in opinion—I would have every woman to feel a proper horror and detestation of the crimes this unhappy girl has committed; but, at the same time, pity the weakness that led into them, and the miseries the commission of them has entailed upon her.
>
> I have no patience, Sir; I insist upon it, that the breach of chastity in woman deserves the most rigorous punishment.
>
> Unfeeling woman! if thou art really virtuous thyself, boast not thy superiority over thy afflicted, fallen sisters; but retire to thy closet, and thank thy Creator, that *he gave thee not a form that might lead thee into temptations*, or endued thee with fortitude to withstand them—
>
> But now for Annie's story.—
>
> (II, 162-163, italics mine)

In *Charlotte* Mrs. Rowson begs the self-righteous matron who may read the book to be compassionate, for "how many secret faults lie hid in the recesses of our hearts, which we should blush to have brought into open day" (p. 76).

Mrs. Rowson understands and to some degree condones youth's love of pleasure. In the interview between Tabitha and Rachel in *Reuben and Rachel*, she defends harmless amusement. She writes of Rachel's indulgence in too much pleasure in London:

Forbear, ye rigid, ye experienced matrons, to blame our heroine; it is the particular blessing of youth to be enabled to enjoy the present moment, forgetful of the past, nor fearing the future. Then censure not those who eagerly gather the roses, unmindful of the briars that surround them, or who, delighted with their beauty and fragrance, forget, in the enjoyment of their sweets, the pain they suffered in gathering them.

(II, 242)

Occasional glints of humor and self-deprecation keep the mentor from becoming aloof and severe. In *A Trip to Parnassus*, Mrs. Rowson writes some pretty good lines at the expense of various bloated reputations among contemporary actors. Mrs. Stephen Kemble is advised,

"But child . . . your HUSBAND is here,
"We'd advise him no more on the stage to appear.
"His manner's so aukward, his form so uncouth,
"His voice so discordant, to tell you the truth,
"Whene'er on the stage he pretends to advance,
"He reminds us of *Bears* when they're learning to dance."

(p. 19)

But while Mrs. Rowson can be sharp in criticizing the artistic merit of others, she does not pretend to great achievement of her own. The last laugh in *A Trip* is on the narrator; when she offers herself for Apollo's judgment, the god disappears in a flash of lightning and the poet awakes from her dream (p. 26).

Mrs. Rowson remains close to her audience by confiding her artistic as well as her personal problems to the reader. In *Mentoria*, for example, she interrupts the letters to defend her condensation of the material with the argument that "the publication of the whole would render this work too extensive" (II, 72). *Reuben and Rachel* contains a lengthy invocation of Mrs. Rowson's muses that concludes with an apology to the "gentle reader" for "giving you the history of my own feelings" (II, 265).

In the final chapters of *The Fille de Chambre* and *Charlotte's Daughter*, Mrs. Rowson announces her intention to leave the reunions and love scenes to the reader's imagination, a technique employed by Jane Austen in creating her persona. This procedure allows the author to emphasize her own rôle, and it also underlines the Rowson belief in the difference between reality and the imagination. While realistic and partially based upon fact, the stories are made-up; the author never intends to deceive.

Mrs. Rowson writes as a woman involved in the hurly-burly of life, not tucked away in a genteel parlor. As we have seen, she claims the rôle of teacher from the first, and increasingly presents herself as someone who has experienced great trials, and survived both physically and morally. Her comments as narrator often contain notes of cynicism that show her worldly wisdom. We have seen some of these in the discussion of poverty. A further example from *Trials of the Human Heart* underlines this tendency. Meriel acknowledges

> the thorough knowledge I have of the human heart led me to reflect, that when a person has unexpectedly risen to opulence from obscurity, his feelings grow callous he forgets and totally neglects those branches of his family who . . . have not been equally the favourites of fortune. . . .
>
> (IV, 115)

The author often inserts these comments casually, as in her description in *Charlotte's Daughter* of the arrival of the young ladies at Brighton; the girls' "simple style of dress, unobtrusive beauty, and the general report that they were all three heiresses" bring them numerous suitors (p. 67).

Mrs. Rowson is never impersonal or uninvolved. In *Charlotte* she expostulates,

> Gracious heaven! when I think on the miseries that must rend the heart of a doating parent when he sees the darling of his age at first seduced from his protection . . . my bosom glows with honest indignation, and I wish for power to extirpate those monsters of seduction from the earth.
>
> (p. 42)

She is equally fervent as she turns directly to the audience in *The Fille de Chambre* and describes the joy of Rebecca's party when they are rescued from starvation on the passage to America (p. 115).

One of the most important aspects of Mrs. Rowson's persona is her attitude toward herself as a woman in the professions. From the first, she represents herself as hamstrung by the attitudes of society and the limited education she has received because of her sex. She is usually good-natured toward male critics and men in the occupations she practices, except in the case of William Cobbett, whose attack was unusually provocative. She represents herself as proud, and superior to many trends on the current literary scene.

Mrs. Rowson's prefatory remarks in *Mentoria* and *Slaves in Algiers* (previously quoted), and her frequent defense of her work as artless and natural, show her need to assert the right to a literary career in the face of society's probable disapproval and her incomplete education. In *The Test of Honour* she defends herself against her critics:

> SINCE Novel writing and reading is become the chief employment of the female world, why should not I take up my pen, and endeavour to entertain the public, as well as many others of my sex? My talent is but small, and, perhaps, some kind friend may tell me. I had better have hid it in a napkin, than expose its slender texture to the scrutinizing eye of criticism: perhaps also, some of my own sex, who have neither a passion for scribbling themselves, or reading the productions of others, may tell me, I had better employ my time at my needle. My good matronly housewifely ladies, I thank you for the hint; but if I only use my pen for amusement; if I never neglect more material concerns, to follow that amusement; why may I not indulge a propensity, so innocent in itself, and which I will take care shall never be productive of any harm to others?
>
> (pp. i-ii)
>
> (Rowson)

In the preface to *Mentoria* it is the male critic whom she imagines will challenge her. But Mrs. Rowson refutes his putative objections to her work in a humorous way; her "a-well-day for me" and picture of the man with "spectacles on nose, and pouch by's side" (p. iii) has a light tone. Not that Mrs. Rowson did not fight little wars with the male as reader and critic. In *Charlotte*, the only reference to a male reader makes him an outsider likely to raise questions of probability (p. 113), just as the Alworth boys of *Biblical Dialogues* were prone to do in their probing of the Bible.

Mrs. Rowson's attitude toward men, however, is never bitter and hardly "emasculating." Man is not the enemy. The attitudes of women are equally defeating to the aspiring writer—as the stories demonstrate, and the authorial voice underlines. Mrs. Rowson accepts her men colleagues as she hoped they would accept her, with respect; she often credits various male scholars as sources for her pedagogical work even as she emulates the styles of various masters.

Mrs. Rowson presents herself as a writer fully aware of shabby marketplace practices, but superior to them. The literary taste of the book-buyer is a serious drawback to an author's career. As Mrs. Rowson noted in *The Inquisitor*, religion and philosophy do not sell very well; only "love" sells. Making fun of an idle young man called "The

Lounger," Mrs. Rowson has this useless member of society admit, "I never read anything except it be a ballad, or the last dying speech of people that were hanged" (*The Inquisitor*, I, 61). *A Trip to Parnassus* is offered as an alternative to the type of theater critique popular in the 1780s. Referring to Anthony Pasquin, whose *Children of Thespis* included scathing attacks on the personalities of theater people, Mrs. Rowson writes in her "Advertisement" that she "has carefully avoided the steps of the Gentleman of the Temple, who not satisfied with speaking of them, merely in a public light, has wantonly exposed or traduced their private character."

Most important of all Mrs. Rowson's characteristics is her refusal to adopt a tone of diffidence about her work at a time when so many female authors feared to be identified. Pseudonyms or such author designations as "by a lady" or "Anonymous" were very popular. English women now lauded as enthusiastic feminists who employed such self-protection include "Jane Anger," author of a 1589 defense of women, Anne Finch, the seventeenth-century poet (1661-1720), and Lady Mary Wortley Montagu (1689-1762).[4] This tendency persists into the nineteenth century with Jane Austen, the Brontës, and George Eliot. Mrs. Rowson's American predecessors, Anne Bradstreet and Judith Sargent Murray, also avoided publicity. Bradstreet's brother-in-law took *The Tenth Muse* (as he named her collection of poetry) to a publisher without Anne's knowledge.[5] Judith Sargent Murray identified herself as the author of "The Gleaner" eassays only when they were collected in book form; during their run in the *Massachusetts Magazine* they were signed "Mr. Virgillius" in order to avoid "the indifference, not to say contempt, with which female products are regarded."[6]

Because "presumptuous" female authors were not tolerated, many contemporary women prefaced their novels with tales of decrepit parents to support or their own illness and poverty, in order to win sympathy from the critics.[7] Mrs. Rowson never indulged in such stratagems; in fact, in *The Inquisitor*, she satirizes the practice of seeking pity. The interview between the young female author and the printer contains this passage:

And how do you mean to get subscribers?
—By shewing my proposals, and simply requesting them to encourage my undertaking.

Oh! God bless me, he replied, still looking askance, for he never changed his position, or raised his eyes from the ground, except it was to look at his elbow, and contemplate his thread-bare sleeve—

It will never do to go that way to work—you must have a tale of distress to tell, or you will never procure one subscriber—
I am not very much distressed, said she; and if I was, why should I blazen it to the world?

(I, 54)

Mrs. Rowson occasionally remarks upon her slim talents, but she refuses to shrink from challenge. She expresses no fear of fame as did Fanny Burney, whose horror at having produced a best seller resembled that of a woman who has delivered a monster.[8] She tries every genre, while Hannah More, her English contemporary, sorted various literary modes into those suitable to the male and those appropriate to the female,[9] and her American predecessor, Mercy Warren (sister of her old friend and mentor, James Otis) worried that writing satire was unfeminine.[10] Mrs. Rowson unabashedly compares her efforts to those of prominent men long before Sally Wood, in the preface to *Julia* ("by a Lady of Massachusetts," 1800), contended that her natural female limits confined her to writing novels because she was not capable of history and poetry.[11]

Mrs. Wood accepted the "confined and limited bonds" of the female. In her novel *Dorval* (1801), she states that "Woman's noblest station is retreat."[12] It is hard to imagine Susanna Rowson making such a statement. Mrs. Rowson tries to bring the female out of what Simone de Beauvoir calls her "cave of immanence,"[13] that is, her condition of dependence and passivity, which Mrs. Rowson neatly symbolizes by the grotto in which Fetnah refuses to remain. Through the creation of a persona, as well as through her strenuous concentration upon the problems of women, she tries to create models for her audience that will encourage them to active, full lives.

In spite of these efforts, Mrs. Rowson's feminism has been seen in a variety of conflicting lights. Terence Martin judges Mrs. Rowson's views relevant only to the eighteenth century and not to modern feminism.[14] Yet in dealing with attitudes rather than specific rights, Mrs. Rowson may have been more "modern" than those who concentrated on gaining the vote, only to find that suffrage is not necessarily accompanied by professional opportunities and freedom from stereotypes.

Though written in an old-fashioned style, Mrs. Rowson's works show that she considered most of the issues dealt with by the women writers who followed her in nineteenth- and twentieth-century America, and that her solutions parallel many of those advocated in both eras.

The resolutions drawn up at Seneca Falls include a plank defending public speaking for women.[15] Lucy Stone, an active abolitionist and suffragette, and the first female in Massachusetts to earn a college degree, writes about the low esteem and poor pay awarded women in the few professions they could enter.[16] Lucretia Mott complains of women's loss of rights in marriage,[17] as do Stone and Elizabeth Cady Stanton.[18] Susan B. Anthony provides a sophisticated analysis of the poverty of untrained, uneducated women in the cities.[19] The dearth of rôle models was a problem for these writers.[20] Margaret Fuller's recommendation for professional freedom, " 'Let them [women] be sea captains if they will,' "[21] recalls Mrs. Rowson's statement that success in "any profession whatever" should not be "incompatible with virtue." Both Fuller and Harriet Martineau analyze the notion of masculine and feminine temperament, and like Susanna Rowson, devise an androgynous personality model.[22] The Grimké sisters and others write of the parallel between the situation of the slave and that of the female, and use the Negro as a symbol of woman's status.[23]

Mrs. Rowson's feminist views have as many parallels in the twentieth century. Books discussing the professional inequities abound, as do manuals on how to achieve financial independence in marriage. From Virginia Woolf[24] to Betty Friedan,[25] women writers discuss the relationship between "means" and the opportunity to exercise feminine talents, and this topic is increasingly publicized.[26] Like Susanna Rowson, Friedan, Matina Horner,[27] Naomi Weisstein,[28] and others, urge women to train themselves for employment and try to isolate the continuing attitudes and forces that keep them from professional advancement. Kate Millett notes the degrading images of women in men's fiction, and treats Henry Miller with the same contempt that Mrs. Rowson felt for Rousseau.[29]

Today's feminist concern with rôle models for women recalls Mrs. Rowson's effort to raise female self-esteem by providing childhood reading specifically tailored for girls. *Reuben and Rachel* is a precursor of the recent attempts to rewrite the "Dick and Jane" series, while "Female Biography" anticipates efforts like the present study, and the many current re-creations of the careers of women who deserve recognition.

The debate over sex and temperament continues, with the tendency to put women on a pedestal, because they are supposedly morally superior to men, finding new form in such studies as Ashley Montagu's *The Natural Superiority of Women*[30] and Elizabeth Gould Davis's *The First Sex*[31]—studies that claim for women higher powers of adaptation and precedence in evolution. Like Rowson and Fuller, many recent writers advocate an androgynous personality in which neither the traditionally "masculine" nor "feminine" is dominant.[32] Simone de Beauvoir[33] and Margaret Mead[34] produce volumes on sex and temperament. Naomi Weisstein uses a familiar metaphor in her article "Woman as Nigger."[35]

Before and after the struggle for the vote, women find themselves debating the same questions that Mrs. Rowson considered. Superficial changes in acceptable behavior, such as smoking in public, wearing pants and short hair, even sexual freedom, obscure the static quality of discussions of women and the persistence of the attitudes and problems that cause sexual friction. This lack of movement is highlighted by Mrs. Rowson's career.

The question of how much influence Mrs. Rowson had on the feminism of the writers who followed her is a difficult one. The fact that Susanna Rowson's books were very popular with the type of middle-class women who began the struggle for women's rights has been well established. Elizabeth Cady Stanton's writings show that she was encouraged by the works of various writers of Mrs. Rowson's ilk. The feminist movement proceeded in the spirited, but conservative vein Mrs. Rowson favored. The reformers' arguments were based upon conventional and biblical morality,[36] while their personalities showed more of Susanna Rowson's spunk than the timidity of other popular women writers. Rowson's Meriels, Rebeccas, and Julias may have found their way into the social reformers just as their literary descendants became the adventurous "American girl."

Mrs. Rowson's school orations and her support of elocution may have been a positive force in later advances for women. Constance Rourke sees a connection between Rowson and Margaret Fuller. She writes in *The Roots of American Culture*: "what was fearlessly Mrs. Rowson's own was the training of young women in the art of public speech"; Margaret Fuller's "Conversations," an innovation similar to the consciousness-raising sessions of the present, "fell in with the practice of public dialogues."[37]

Mrs. Rowson was without question the prototype of the numerous women writers of the nineteenth century in America. Individual motifs and patterns that appear in later writers can be found first utilized in her works. Just as important, she showed these women that they might succeed outside the home. Helen Papashvily points out a specific example of Mrs. Rowson's influence upon the career of a later writer: Mrs. Catherine Palmer Putnam, a pupil of Mrs. Rowson's, convinced her son, the publisher G.P. Putnam, to bring out Susan Warner's novel *Wide Wide World*, which, like *Charlotte*, was a great popular success and helped women retain a place in the writing arts.[38]

The fact that Mrs. Rowson has been remembered more for the sentimental notes in her fiction than for her positive goals for women deserves brief attention. The aesthetic weaknesses in Mrs. Rowson's style may have contributed to this situation, but this seems inadequate to explain the degree of misinterpretation of her works.

We might blame this misreading on the efforts of the aggressive book salesman Parson Weems, who kept pushing Mrs. Rowson's publisher for more and more copies of *Charlotte* and got that novel into the hands of the readers at the expense of other equally readable Rowson novels.[39] Of course, Weems was merely exploiting the book buyers' insatiable thirst for pathos; but his success substantiates Mrs. Rowson's view of the book market and her contention that only "love" sells.

Rowson's own prospective converts occasionally refused to see the import of her teaching—a common phenomenon of social movements where style is sacrificed to a call for action. Earnestness is easily ridiculed, and the irreverent young, as well as the more subtle, resist indoctrination even when it is for their own good. Miss Myra Montgomery, a pupil of Mrs Rowson's, writes of the 1808 exhibition at the Rowson school at which portions of "Female Biography" were read:

> Miss Lambert appeared to great advantage, while defending the character of our injured sex by reading Mrs. Rowson's poem on women & atho [sic] she did not obtain the prize from her Preceptress, yet she established her reputation with the audience as being unquestionably the best speaker.—In the Biographical Class, the doctrine of the equality of women with the other sex was resumed & although by sedulously ransacking ancient & modern history Mrs. Rowson could not find a sufficient number of honourable examples of female excellence to reach 3 times round the class; yet, we made a pretty formidable show by informing the assembly how several virago queens & blustering heroines had, by killing themselves or others condemned "themselves to everlasting fame" & more particularly I told them how two females had such an overpowering, yet, natural desire to expose secrets & betray confidence, that they could discover no method of holding their tongues but, by *man*fully biting them off—[40]

Mrs. Rowson's reluctance to turn her work over to male critics was prophetic. The men who have held Mrs. Rowson's reputation in their hands have not been well tuned to the author's aspirations. Even Elias Nason, Mrs. Rowson's enthusiastic critic and biographer, thoroughly misunderstood her aims. In the *Memoir*, he quotes various persons who knew Mrs. Rowson, and unwittingly uses her arch-villain Napoleon as the male standard by which to judge her goals for the female:

> The artistic hand of Mrs. Rowson made good mothers. One of them [a former pupil] writes to me: "Six ladies who were at school with me, I am still acquainted with. They have all made good wives and mothers; have reared large families; some of their sons have become distinguished men, and thus these ladies have fulfilled the destiny which Napoleon considered a woman's highest glory!"[41]

Mrs. Rowson's unusual career illustrates not only the static quality of discussions of the "woman problem," but the degree of resistance and misinterpretation attendant upon a strong belief in the equality of the sexes. Her consideration of the many feminist issues, when matched with those of later writers, demonstrates how early, how often, and how clearly women have answered the supposedly difficult question, "what do women really want?" with the reply, "self-determination and professional fair play."

Mrs. Rowson found one contemporary male reader sympathetic to her views on women, and he leaves us a picture of her as the forceful personality she was. John Swanwick, a merchant and congressman of Philadelphia, defended her from William Cobbett's attack in *A Kick for a Bite* (1795). In his reply to Cobbett, *A Rub from Snub*, Swanwick offers "a word of comfort to Mrs. Rowson," in which he finds her "a bright ornament to female science."[42] Mrs. Rowson might have caviled at the adjective, but she was no doubt pleased at Swanwick's question to Cobbett: "Can you prove that a male education would not qualify a woman for all the duties of a man?" (p. 76). Swanwick assures Mrs. Rowson that he will combat Cobbett for her, and suggests to the latter, who was known in his writings as "Peter Porcupine," that he is getting off easy:

> You ought to be more cautious and circumspect in discharging your quills, or at least never venture too far from your hole; because, should you provoke the vengeance of Rowson, you would stand no more chance than insects beneath a discharge of thunder bolts. Whippets that seize the heels of horses often get their brains kicked out, and men walking bare-footed over hot ashes, are apt to get their toes burnt.
>
> (pp. 79-80)

Notes

Abbreviations

American Sisterhood
    The American Sisterhood: Writings of the Feminist Movement from Colonial
    Times to the Present. Ed. Wendy Martin. New York: Harper & Row Publishers,
    1972
Benson, Women in Eighteenth-Century America
    Benson, Mary Sumner, Women in Eighteenth-Century America: A Study of Opin-
    ion and Social Usage. New York: Columbia University Press, 1935.
BWM
    Boston Weekly Magazine
CHAL
    The Cambridge History of American Literature. Colonial and Revolutionary Litera-
    ture; Early National Literature, vol. 1. Ed. William Peterfield Trent, John Erskine,
    Stuart P. Sherman, Carl Van Doren. New York: G.P. Putnam's Sons, 1917
DNB
    The Dictionary of National Biography. Ed. Sir Leslie Stephen and Sir Sidney Lee.
    London: Oxford University Press, 1921-1922
Halsey, "Introduction"
    Halsey, Francis W. "Historical and Biographical Introduction," Charlotte Temple:
    A Tale of Truth. New York: Funk and Wagnalls Company, 1905
MacCarthy, Female Pen
    MacCarthy, B.G. The Female Pen. 2 vols. New York: William Salloch, 1948
Martin, "Emergence of the Novel"
    Martin, Terence. "The Emergence of the Novel in America. A Study in the Cultural
    History of an Art Form." Ph.D. diss., Ohio State University, 1954
Nason, Memoir
    Nason, Elias. A Memoir of Mrs. Susanna Rowson, with Elegant and Illustrative
    Extracts From her Writings in Prose and Poetry. Albany, N.Y.: Joel Munsell, 1870
Neal, Essay
    Neal, James. An Essay on the Education and Genius of the Female Sex. To Which is
    Added, An Account, of the Commencement of the Young Ladies' Academy of
    Philadelphia, Held the 18th of December, 1794. Philadelphia: Jacob Johnson &
    Co., 1795
Rossi, Feminist Papers
    Rossi, Alice S., ed. The Feminist Papers: From Adams to de Beauvoir, 1973, reprint
    ed., New York: Bantam Books, 1974
Rowson Collection
    Rowson Collection, Barrett Library, University of Virginia. Charlottesville
Tompkins, The Popular Novel in England
    Tompkins, J.M.S. The Popular Novel in England, 1770-1800. London: Constable &
    Co., 1932

Vail
    Vail, R.W.G. "Susanna Haswell Rowson, The Author of Charlotte Temple: A Bibliographical Study," *Proceedings of the American Antiquarian Society*, 42 (1932), pp. 47-160
Wright
    Wright, Lyle. *American Fiction 1774-1850, A Contribution Towards a Bibliography*. New rev. ed. San Marino, Calif.: Huntington Library, 1960

Chapter 1

1. William Charvat suggests this idea. He points to Mrs. Rowson's keen awareness of the market and her early contribution; Charvat writes, "as the producer of nine works of fiction, four of which she wrote after emigrating, she deserves consideration as the first American professional writer of fiction" (*The Profession of Authorship in America, 1800-1870*, ed. Matthew J. Bruccoli [Columbus: Ohio State University Press, 1968], p. 20). R.W.G. Vail, who has written a thorough bibliographical study of Rowson, concurs, using as his criterion the fact that the author wrote for money. If financial expectation is the standard for judging professionalism, Mrs. Rowson certainly qualifies. According to her biographers, Mrs. Rowson was very hard pressed financially throughout most of her life, especially when she first began writing fiction. William Rowson was never a great success at any of his endeavors, and the Rowsons did not have leisure for amateur activities. According to Charvat, Mrs. Rowson did not profit from the popularity of *Charlotte* because she did not hold the American copyright (p. 21). But she was always aware of the need to promote her work. References in *Victoria* (1786), her first novel, to her English patron, the Duchess of Devonshire, are embarrassingly obsequious. *Trials of the Human Heart* is dedicated to the subscriber who ordered the most copies of the book; and Mrs. Rowson obtained copyrights in her own name to several of her later efforts.

More important than these considerations is the attitude of the author toward her work. Mrs. Rowson's prefaces show her desire to be taken seriously by the public and critics. In all cases but two she signed her own name to her work and insisted upon the importance of her endeavors. The pedagogical works were undertaken as aids to teaching—an activity that Mrs. Rowson boldly calls her "profession" during her school years. The volume and character of her efforts are simply not that of the amateur or leisure-time penwoman.

The Cambridge History of American Literature (CHAL) takes the standard position on this matter; it favors Charles Brockden Brown (Carl Van Doren, "Fiction I: Brown, Cooper," p. 287). Terence Martin calls Mrs. Rowson "a highly articulate amateur"; he cites one of her statements that writing might be a suitable way to pass leisure time, while he neglects her many more frequent comments on the seriousness of the undertaking, and her awareness that she at all times addresses a definite audience ("Emergence of the Novel," p. 77).

2. *The Oven Birds: American Women on Womanhood, 1820-1920* (Garden City, N.Y.: Doubleday & Company, Anchor Books, 1972), p. 5.

3. Vail, p. 51. These biographical notes and the few that follow, which are accepted by Vail and Mrs. Rowson's earlier biographers, follow a well-beaten path. Vail bases

much of his information on Samuel L. Knapp, *Memoir of Mrs. Rowson*, first published in the Boston *Gazette*, 1828, and reprinted in *Charlotte's Daughter* (Boston: Richardson & Lord, 1828); Nason; Halsey, "Introduction."

4. Georgiana Cavendish (1757-1806), eldest daughter of John, first earl of Spencer (*DNB*). The Duchess was sought after socially, a friend of many celebrated writers, including Walpole and Johnson, and was a writer herself.

5. *Poems on Various Subjects* (London: G.G.J. and J. Robinson, 1788). "No copy known," according to Vail (1932). A recent search of some forty libraries suggests that Vail's description still holds. With this and subsequent bibliographical notes, see bibliography for further details.

6. *The Test of Honour* (London: John Abraham, 1789). This work is not signed by Rowson. The author is listed as "A young lady." Internal evidence creates no questions as to its authorship. Vail cites Knapp's attribution of *The Test* to Mrs. Rowson.

7. Besides the evidence Vail cites, there are many other references to Mr. Rowson's being overshadowed by Susanna. John Bernard, a contemporary actor in some of the same theaters in which the Rowsons performed, writes that Mr. Rowson was "eclipsed" by his wife (*Retrospections of America, 1797-1811*, ed. Laurence Hutton and Brander Matthews [New York: Harper and Brothers, 1887], p. 365).

8. The rumor of Mr. Rowson's fondness for drink has had wide currency. Mabel Osgood Wright, a modern descendant of Mrs. Rowson's, who at one time contemplated writing a biography of her ancestor, put the case more forcefully than any of the published writers; she called William "decidedly a deadbeat," and wondered how the correct Mrs. Rowson concealed his drinking from her students at the academy (letter to R.W.G. Vail, 19 August 1932, correspondence file of the American Antiquarian Society, Worcester, Massachusetts). Among the Elias Nason manuscript notes for his *Memoir* (Rowson Collection, no. 7379b) is this fillip:

Lines to Mrs. R. repeated by the author in the Old Book Store School St., Nov. 9 1871: Miss Martha Welch Jackson aged 85:

Why is it Rowson in your face
The lily only has its place,
Or is it that the absent rose
Has gone to paint your husbands nose—

Miss Jackson was obviously a contemporary of the Rowsons. Whether this poem had wide popularity or was privately enjoyed by the author is open to speculation. It has the ring of a pupil's song about his teacher, but reference to Nason's list of Mrs. Rowson's pupils reveals no Martha Jackson. The surname does occur.

Also· in the Nason workbook is an item in an undated, unnamed newspaper in response to a question as to whether Susanna Rowson was related to a George Murdock. It describes William Rowson thus: "A very red nose will be remembered as a distinguishing feature of his countenance."

As Vail points out, whatever William's weaknesses were, he and Susanna remained married for thirty-eight years, and Susanna wrote a playful and affectionate poem to him on the occasion of their twenty-fifth wedding anniversary (p. 51). Although many writers have repeated the opinion of one of Mrs. Rowson's students that the boorish husband of her novel *Sarah* was based on her own spouse, the Rowsons shared interests in music and theater. Drawings of Mr. Rowson show him to resemble W.C. Fields, and stories about him suggest that he was probably good company and of much help to Mrs. Rowson in running the academy. Vail quotes from contemporary references to his business chores (p. 51). Mary E. Sargent recounts a possibly revealing anecdote: sometime during the school's location in Medford, when the church choir was absent,

Mr. Rowson and a General John Montgomery took over the singing ("Susanna Rowson," *The Medford Historical Register* [April 1904], p. 39).

9. *Slaves in Algiers; or a Struggle for Freedom: A Play Interspersed with Songs* (Philadelphia: Wrigley and Berriman, 1794). *Slaves* and *The Volunteers* were "comic operas" according to the definition of Julian Mates in *The American Musical Stage Before 1800* (New Brunswick, N.J.: Rutgers University Press, 1962). The productions of such pieces were quite lively; in fact, the stage during Rowson's era was notable for elaborate costumes and scenery and for the combination of dance, music, and spoken dialogue. Also see Oscar George Sonneck, *Early Opera in America* (New York, London, and Boston: G. Shirmer, 1915).

10. *The Female Patriot; or, Nature's Rights* (Philadelphia: 1794). Vail provides evidence of performance of this piece. Whether it was printed is not established.

11. *The Volunteers; a Musical Entertainment* (Philadelphia: printed for the Author and sold at the Music Shops, [1795?]). Music composed by Alexander Reinagle. Historians of American theater agree on the location and date of the first performance: "New Theatre, Philadelphia, January 21, 1795" (Vail, p. 158). Songs from the work are available, but the libretto is not.

12. *Americans in England, or, Lessons for Daughters* (Boston: 1796). Again, opinions differ as to whether this work was printed. Vail's "no copy known" appears to hold.

13. *The American Tar, or the Press Gang Defeated*. Music by R. Taylor. Performed New Theatre, Philadelphia, 17 June 1796; opinions differ as to existence of this piece in print.

14. George O. Seilhamer, *History of the American Theatre: New Foundations* (Philadelphia: Globe Printing House, 1891), vol. 3, p. 343.

15. Oscar Fay Adams, "Susanna Haswell Rowson," *Christian Register* (17 March 1913), p. 296. According to one source quoted by Mary Sargent, Mrs. Rowson's career as an actress was a drawback to her acceptance as a teacher; another source mentions Rowson's connection with the Duchess of Devonshire, which suggests that the latter's patronage helped establish a proper image. See Mary E. Sargent, "Susanna Rowson," *The Medford Historical Register* (7 April 1904), p. 39.

16. Mrs. Rowson's connection with the *New England Galaxy*, which was begun in 1817, has been established by the editor of the magazine, Joseph Tinker Buckingham. In his *Personal Memoirs and Recollections of Editorial Life . . .* , vol. 1 (Boston: Ticknor, Reed & Fields, 1852), he writes: "Mrs. Susanna Rowson was an acceptable and highly-valued correspondent of the Galaxy. Her contributions were chiefly of a religious and devotional character and usually signed with her initials, 'S.R.' " (p. 83). Mrs. Rowson's first biographer, Knapp, wrote that "She also conducted the *Boston Weekly Magazine*, and contributed largely to the success of that periodical by her ability as an editor and writer" ("A Memoir of the Author," in *Charlotte's Daughter* [Boston: Richardson & Lord, 1828], p. 10). In an 1828 review of *Charlotte's Daughter* (*Essex Gazette*, Haverhill, Mass., 17 May 1828), Whittier mentions Mrs. Rowson as "the conductor" of the *Boston Weekly Magazine* (*Whittier on Writers and Writing: The Uncollected Critical Writings of John Greenleaf Whittier*, ed. Edwin H. Cady, Harry H. Clark [Syracuse, N.Y.: Syracuse University Press, 1950], p. 18). Subsequent writers have repeated the idea that Mrs. Rowson edited the periodical. A well-documented biography is needed to trace the extent of Mrs. Rowson's work, for the editors' names do not appear on the publication. Neither Knapp nor Nason offers detail concerning this work. Further, a note from one of the publishers of the *Boston Weekly Magazine* (Samuel Gilbert) to Nason, in reply to a request for information on this matter, states,

She used to write under the signature of the Gossip I think—but she [?] no control of the paper—& I am not *possitive* now, whether we pd her anything for her services.

This missive is labeled "from Mr. Gilbert ed—BWM—aged 82 Jan 10 1859," and is found in the Nason notes (Rowson Collection).

The "Gossip" is a series of articles that ran in many of the issues of the *BWM*. It includes reflections upon a wide range of topics, but concentrates on personal and moral problems. It bears evidence of Mrs. Rowson's hand, from the subject matter to specific turn of phrase. As Nason notes, however, it may have been the product of more than one writer. He concerns himself about the column's "puffing" Mrs. Rowson's work. More intriguing is the fact that several Rowson books are criticized rather strongly in the issue of 22 January 1803:

> There are some Novels also from the pen of a lady whom I know not how to term with propriety either European or American, (Mrs. *Rowson*) which might be read with advantage, especially by females; but even her works are not without danger-ous tendency, and perhaps of all her numerous productions there be not more than three which could by an impartial Censor be recommended. *Reuben and Rachel*, an historical romance is the best; *Charlotte*, and the *Inquisitor*, have a considerable degree of merit.

Mrs. Rowson often pointed out the dangers of fiction, but never her own. Furthermore, she had been attacked before on the subject of her nationality, and had responded with righteous indignation. On 1 July 1802, by virtue of her husband William's naturaliza-tion, Mrs. Rowson became an American citizen. Surely, as editor or part editor of a paper, Mrs. Rowson would not have allowed references like the above in print. This and other items, as well as the lack of information on Mrs. Rowson's connection with the *BWM*, make use of material from it tentative.

17. *Hearts of Oak* (Boston[?]: 1810-1811). This play's existence and Mrs. Rowson's authorship are based upon a brief item in John Bernard's *Retrospections of America, 1797-1811* (ed. Laurence Hutton and Brander Matthews [New York: Harper and Brothers, 1887]) concerning the 1810-1811 Boston season. Vail says "probably never printed" (p. 137).

18. William Cobbett [Peter Porcupine, pseud.], *A Kick for a Bite; or, Review upon Review; with a Critical Essay, on the Works of Mrs. S. Rowson, in a Letter to the Editor, or Editors, of The American Monthly Review* (Philadelphia: Thomas Bradford, 1795), p. 24.

19. Rowson Collection, no. 7379b, Robert Haswell to Susanna Rowson (19 May 1796).

20. *Charlotte: A Tale of Truth*, in *Three Early American Novels*, ed. William S. Kable (Columbus, Ohio: Charles E. Merrill Publishing Co., 1970), p. 21. All subsequent quotations from *Charlotte* will be from Kable's edition, which is based on the 1791 edition.

21. *The Popular Book: A History of America's Literary Taste* (1950; reprint ed., Berkeley: University of California Press, 1963), p. 63. Mathew Carey, The American publisher of *Charlotte*, wrote in 1812 to Mrs. Rowson that the sales of her book "exceed those of any of the most celebrated novels that ever appeared in England. I think the number disposed of must far exceed 50,000 copies; & the sale still continues . . ." (quoted by Earl L. Bradsher, in *Mathew Carey. Editor, Author and Publisher. A Study in American Literary Development* [New York: Columbia University Press, 1912], p. 50).

As further illustration of *Charlotte*'s popularity, Vail notes that the book has been published in twelve American states and four foreign countries, England, France, Germany, and Ecuador (p. 65). In addition, a dramatized version of the story appeared in 1899: Harriet Pixley Plumb, *Charlotte Temple, A Historical Drama*, Three Acts, With Prologue (Chicago and London: Publishers Printing Co., T. Fisher Unwin), [1899]). This play is even more pathetic than the original. The occasionally acerbic tone of the narrator is missing. At Charlotte's deathbed, La Rue, the villainess, begs her husband's forgiveness, and is denied it. Charlotte and Montraville are reunited and Montraville is forgiven just before the heroine dies.

22. *Golden Multitudes: The Story of Best Sellers in the United States* (New York: Macmillan Co., 1947), p. 39.

23. This legend is discussed most fully in Halsey, "Introduction," pp. xlix ff. Halsey cites an early version by "John Tripod" (John Bacon Barnitz), which claims that the sexton of Trinity Church, a Tommy Collister, in 1800 showed "Lucy" her mother's grave. Lucy supposedly ordered a slab on pillars erected bearing the inscription "SACRED TO THE MEMORY OF CHARLOTTE STANLEY/Aged 19 years," along with the insignia of the house of Derby. This was, according to the same story, stolen, but replaced with a slab bearing the name Charlotte Temple. The connection between Charlotte and the house of Derby is given further attention in Mrs. [C.W.H.] Dall's *The Romance of the Association; or, One Last Glimpse of Charlotte Temple and Eliza Wharton. A Curiosity of Literature and Life* (Cambridge, Mass.: Press of John Wilson and Son, 1875). Numerous newspaper accounts of this story keep the legend alive during the nineteenth century. Halsey notes that Nason (*Memoir*, 1870) does not question the legend and that the Rowson family believed *Charlotte* to be based on life. He notes that there has never been a denial by the family of Montrésor. Halsey offers substantiation for Bacon's source, Tommy Collister: the church records show such a person appointed assistant sexton in 1788, appointed sexton in 1790, and serving until 1816 (Halsey, "Introduction," p. lvii). Halsey also cites a letter from Wm. H. Crommelin to William Kelby (New York Historical Society, 8 July 1876) to the effect that the inscription plate *was* stolen from the Charlotte Temple grave in 1845 (not 1800 as Bacon had said), that it was recovered and then lost. Crommelin had "Charlotte Temple" cut into the stone slab. Apparently he did not say what the inscription on the original plate was. The whole matter of *Charlotte* as a *roman à clef* continues to intrigue and baffle investigators. Philip Young's recent research, which will be included in a forthcoming book on women of the Revolutionary period, turns up no Charlotte Stanley in newspaper entries of persons buried in Trinity Churchyard. Young argues that Montrésor was in America at the time he supposedly seduced Charlotte Stanley, and could not have left her to marry another woman, as Montraville does in *Charlotte*, because he was already married.

24. Philadelphia: Barclay & Co., 1865.

25. "Washington Household Account Books, 1793-1797," *Pennsylvania Magazine of History and Biography* 30 (Philadelphia: 1906), pp. 176, 179. Among "Sundries" for 21 April 1794 is "D°/p'd by Mrs. Washington's order in part for subscription to a publication by Mrs. Rowson . . . 2.00." For 12 May 1794: "Contg't Sxy's. p'd for a book called Charlotte (by Mrs. Rowson) for Mrs. Washingon . . . 67."

26. *A Trip to Parnassus* (1788), a long critical poem, received some praise; Susanna Rowson was called "not the least successful of Suckling's imitators" and "a much better versifier" than her model by the *Monthly Review* (Vail, p. 146). All of the novels were granted some good points, most often elevated morality. As the *Critical Review* said of *Victoria*, "she who would support the cause of piety and virtue cannot err" (Vail, p. 148). American critics also approved. Of her works in general the editor of the *New England Galaxy* wrote,

Mrs. Rowson, author of Charlotte Temple and numerous other works, much read

and admired, is a writer of no ordinary mind. To advance knowledge, excite virtue and cherish philanthropy, have been her objects and her aim. With powers to make herself distinguished, she has been content to be useful. If she has lost any portion of that world of fame which was within her reach, it has not been by reclining in idleness, or running after the golden apples; but in tarrying to cultivate the delicate flowers and savory herbs in the garden of youthful intellect, in teaching.that the highest knowledge is goodness and the purest fame is virtue. Her pen has never been employed but to give elevation to sentiment, chastity to feeling, dignity to argument, and to make religion lovely and alluring to the young and gay. Her muse of vigorous wing and purest flame has been satisfied in decking the cradle of affection or the bier of friendship, in wreathing the garland for the tomb of the patriot and pouring her sweetest incense on the altar of devotion. Truly it may be said of her that she has written 'No line which dying she could wish to blot.' (*New England Galaxy*, 6 February 1818, quoted in Nason, *Memoir*, p. 161.)
James Neal in 1795 ranks Mrs. Rowson with Mrs. Chapone, Mrs. Inchbald, Mercy Warren and others as "genuine daughters of the Muses" (*An Essay on the Education and Genius of the Female Sex. To Which is Added, An Account, of the Commencement of the Young Ladies' Academy of Philadelphia, Held the 18th of December, 1794, Under the Direction of Mr. John Poor, A. M. Principal* [Philadelphia: Jacob Johnson & Co., 1795], p. 5).

27. Tompkins, *The Popular Novel in England*, p. 140. And see note immediately above.

28. Brief mention of Mrs. Rowson is found in Charles F. Richardson's survey of American literature (*American Literature 1607-1885*, vol. 2 [New York: G. P. Putnam's Sons, 1889], p. 286).

29. "Rubbish," is the twentieth-century estimate Charles Angoff makes of Mrs. Rowson's poetry (*A Literary History of the American People*. new ed., vol. 2 [New York: Tudor Publishing Co., 1935], p. 202). Angoff's epithet represents one vein of modern criticism of Susanna Rowson's work. CHAL agrees that the poetry is of little merit (Samuel Marion Tucker, "The Beginnings of Verse," p. 179). G. Harrison Orians lumps Mrs. Rowson with the field of eighteenth-century American novelists, all of whom he considers "without professional skill and originality" (*A Short History of American Literature. Analyzed by Decades* [New York: F.S. Crofts & Co., 1940], p. 46). Alexander Cowie says that *Trials of the Human Heart* could "hardly have edified conservative readers of the day" (*The Rise of the American Novel* [New York: American Book Co., 1948], p. 15). William Charvat considers Charlotte a "misery novel," "early soap opera," which found popularity because of skillful promotion (*Literary Publishing in America, 1790-1850* [Philadelphia: University of Pennsylvania Press, 1959], p. 62).

But Mrs. Rowson has not fallen completely into unsympathetic hands. Several scholars in the present century have been enthusiastic. Arthur Hobson Quinn grants Susanna Rowson "real significance," "compelling interest," and "power of description" and contends that she was "a vivid portrayer of the virtuous woman adventuress" (*American Fiction: An Historical and Critical Survey* [New York: D. Appleton & Company, 1936], p. 17). Constance Rourke shares Quinn's admiration for Mrs. Rowson's heroines; she writes enthusiastically of the verve with which Mrs. Rowson lived and wrote (*The Roots of American Culture, and Other Essays* [New York: Harcourt, Brace and Co., 1942]).

Lillie Deming Loshe and Terence Martin separate Mrs. Rowson from the field of early

American novelists. According to Loshe, Mrs. Rowson's world must be distinguished from "the more politely imaginative world of her 'female' contemporaries" (*The Early American Novel* [New York: Columbia University Press, 1907], p. 13). Terence Martin grants Mrs. Rowson the status of a genuine "novelist": he argues that Mrs. Rowson's aims were so thoroughly didactic in a didactic age, that she could relax somewhat more than her contemporaries, could use digressions, her "Bless my soul!" asides to the reader, with ease and command and thus was able to exercise her imagination without falling into the excesses of such contemporaries as the author of the improbable *History of Constantius and Pulchera* ("Emergence of the Novel," p. 234).

Several other modern studies praise Mrs. Rowson. She is still credited with the ability to handle pathos. *Literary History of the United States*, comparing *Charlotte Temple* to the other two most frequently read novels of its period, *The Power of Sympathy* (1789) by William Hill Brown, and *The Coquette* (1797) by Hannah Foster, calls it the "most touching as a story" (Robert Spiller et al., vol. 1, 3d rev. ed. [New York: Macmillan, 1963], p. 178). Although the story is "old-fashioned in its rhetoric," it is written "with a sincerity and power that can be felt even today" (p. 177). Alexander Cowie in *The Rise of the American Novel* notes Mrs. Rowson's possession of "that understanding of human nature which is essential to a novelist" (p. 17); still, he says that Mrs. Rowson's works in general "deserve the oblivion" (p. 15).

30. *The Sentimental Novel in America, 1789-1860* (Durham, N.C.: Duke University Press, 1940).

31. *The Early American Novel* (Columbus: Ohio State University Press, 1971), pp. 22-23, 40.

32. *All the Happy Endings: A Study of the Domestic Novel in America, the Women Who Wrote It, the Women Who Read It, in the Nineteenth Century* (New York: Harper & Brothers Publishers, 1956), p. xvii.

33. *Love and Death in the American Novel*, new rev. ed. (New York: Dell Publishing Co., 1969), pp. 72, 74.

34. *The Roots of American Culture* (New York: Harcourt, Brace and Co., 1942). Constance Rourke approvingly calls Mrs. Rowson a "feminist," and a "reformer" (p. 79), and finds that these tendencies enliven the poetry, the plays, and the fiction. In reference to the novels, Rourke writes,

> Mrs. Rowson looked upon the male sex with a skeptical eye. In her *Victoria*, the heroine loses her mind as a result of male scheming; indeed her delicate, distraught heroines almost invariably suffered deeply through masculine faults, failures or downright deviltry.
>
> (p. 79)

I agree with Rourke's description of Mrs. Rowson, but not with her conclusions about the male as the cause of the women's problems.

Chapter 2

1. *A Trip to Parnassus; or, the Judgment of Apollo on Dramatic Authors and Performers* (London: John Abraham, 1788).

2. Terence Martin argues this point in "Emergence of the Novel," chapter 6.

3. *The Coquette, or, The History of Eliza Wharton. A Novel Founded on Fact*, in *The Power of Sympathy and The Coquette*, ed. William S. Osborne (New Haven, Conn.: College and University Press, 1970).

4. Tompkins, *The Popular Novel in England*, p. 4; Ian Watt, *The Rise of the Novel: Studies in Defoe, Richardson and Fielding* (1957; reprint ed., Berkeley: University of California Press, 1967), p. 33.

5. *Victoria* (London: J.P. Cooke, 1786).

6. The first edition of *The Inquisitor; or, Invisible Rambler* (3 vols.) was published in London by G.G.J. and J. Robinson, 1788. References to *The Inquisitor* will be based upon the second American edition, which is available in microprint (Philadelphia: Mathew Carey, 1794).

7. *The Test of Honour* (London: John Abraham, 1789). See chapter 1, note 6, regarding the authenticity of *The Test*.

8. The original edition of *Mentoria* was published by William Lane at the Minerva Press, probably in 1791. This and further references to *Mentoria* will be based upon the more easily available first American edition (Philadelphia: Robert Campbell, 1794).

9. The first edition of *Charlotte* was published in London by William Lane, Minerva Press, in 1791. See chapter 1, note 20, regarding *Charlotte*, later *Charlotte Temple*. All page references are from *Charlotte: a Tale of Truth* in *Three Early American Novels*, ed. William S. Kable (Columbus, Ohio: Charles E. Merrill Publishing Co., 1970).

10. The first edition of *The Fille de Chambre* was published in London by William Lane at the Minerva Press in 1792. Only one volume of this edition has been located; references to the work are based upon the first American edition (Baltimore: J.P. Rice, 1794).

11. *Trials of the Human Heart* (Philadelphia: Wrigley & Berriman, 1795).

12. Meriel's beloved, Rainsforth, changes his surname to Kingly when he marries. Thus he may be called by either or both names.

13. *Reuben and Rachel; or, Tales of Old Times* (Boston: Manning & Loring, 1798).

14. *Sarah* (Boston: Charles Williams, 1813); originally published as *Sincerity* in *BWM* (4 June 1803-30 June 1804).

15. *A Sequel to Charlotte Temple* (Boston: Richardson & Lord, 1828).

16. *An Abridgment of Universal Geography, Together with Sketches of History. Designed for the Use of Schools and Academies in the United States* (Boston: John West, 1805[?]).

17. *A Spelling Dictionary, divided into Short Lessons, For the Easier Committing to Memory By Children and Young Persons; and Calculated to Assist Youth in Comprehending what they Read. Selected From Johnson's Dictionary, For the Use of Her Pupils. By Susanna Rowson* (Boston: John West, 1807).

18. *A Present for Young Ladies; Containing Poems, Dialogues, Addresses, &c. &c. &c. as Recited by the Pupils of Mrs. Rowson's Academy, at the Annual Exhibitions* (Boston: John West & Co., 1811).

19. *Youth's First Step in Geography, being a Series of Exercises making the Tour of the Habitable Globe. For the Use of Schools* (Boston: Wells and Lilly, 1818).

20. *Exercises in History, Chronology, and Biography, in Question and Answer. For the Use of Schools. Comprising, Ancient History, Greece, Rome, &c. Modern History, England, France, Spain, Portugal, &c. The Discovery of America. Rise, Progress and Final Independence of the United States* (Boston: Richardson and Lord, 1822).

21. *Biblical Dialogues Between a Father and His Family: Comprising Sacred History, From the Creation to the Death of Our Saviour Christ. The Lives of the Apostles, and the Promulgation of the Gospel; with a Sketch of the History of the Church Down to the*

Reformation. The Whole Carried on in Conjunction with Profane History, 2 vols. (Boston: Richardson and Lord, 1822).

22. See, for example: Anne Firor Scott, Women in American Life. Selected Readings (New York: Houghton Mifflin Co., 1970); Rossi, Feminist Papers.

23. "The Prologue," "In Honor of That High and Mighty Princess Queen Elizabeth of Happy Memory," The Works of Anne Bradstreet, ed. Jeannine Hensley, Adrienne Rich (Cambridge, Mass.: Harvard University Press, 1967).

24. Vena Bernadette Field, Constantia: A Study of the Life and Works of Judith Sargent Murray 1751-1820, University of Maine Studies, 2d ser., no. 17 (Orono: University of Maine Press, 1931), p. 68.

Chapter 3

1. Benson, Women in Eighteenth-Century America, p. 99.

2. Tompkins, The Popular Novel in England, passim, and see page 163 for the term "legal prostitution" in reference to marriage as used by Mrs. Griffith, later discussed in the present chapter. Also see MacCarthy, Female Pen, vol. 1, pp. 260-261, for attitudes and expressions in Sarah Fielding's David Simple (1744) that—as will become clear—parallel similar elements in some of Susanna Rowson's works. Fielding's heroine has free-wheeling views on love and marriage, refuses to be an unpaid "upper servant."

3. William Wasserstrom, Heiress of All the Ages: Sex and Sentiment in the Genteel Tradition (Minneapolis: University of Minnesota Press, 1959), p. 5.

4. Neal, Essay, p. 2.

5. Frank L. Mott, A History of American Magazines: 1741-1850 (New York: D. Appleton & Company, 1930), p. 65.

6. A modern edition that includes all parts of Brown's dialogue is Alcuin: A Dialogue, ed. Lee R. Edwards (New York: Grossman Publishers, 1971).

7. Mary Benson summarizes the ideas of Mrs. Murray as expressed in the latter's collection, The Gleaner, published in Boston, 1798. Mrs. Murray approved of "the revolution of thought in recent years which made it possible for them [women] to devote time to studies other than the needle. . . . [She] drew a glowing picture of this new and more enlightened era in female history, which was to manifest itself in the intellectual development of women free from romantic ideas of marriage and ready to act as enlightened and thoughtful mothers. She believed that women might become as independent as Mary Wollstonecraft had wished, if they were taught to earn their own living and to regard matrimony only as a probable contingency. Education for economic independence would enable women to make choices in marriage with much greater freedom" (Benson, Women in Eighteenth-Century America, pp. 176-177). Mrs. Rowson agrees with all these ideas.

8. Sally Sayward Barrell Keating Wood, Dorval; or the Speculator (Portsmouth, N.H.: Nutting & Whitelock, 1801). Published anonymously.

9. Dorothy Yost Deegan, The Stereotype of the Single Woman in American Novels: A Social Study with Implications for the Education of Women (New York: King's Crown Press, Columbia University, 1951), pp. 131-132.

10. A 1960 case in which a wife filed suit for damages against a defendant who had incapacitated her husband by injuring him in an auto accident, and thus deprived her of his services, impelled a modern judge to describe the earlier legal position of women with a perceptiveness difficult to paraphrase:

Such being the mother's "rights" with respect to her children it follows, with the relentless logic of the common law, that her rights respecting her property and her person are no more generous. She was his chattel. What was hers was his. The wife says Bracton, "has nothing which is not her husband's." They were one, and, as one opinion put it, he was that one. All of her personal property, money, goods and chattels of every description, became his upon marriage. Since she was "under the power of her husband," it followed that she had "no will of her own" and having no will of her own could not enter into a contract. Of course, he was entitled to her services in the home as he would be to those of any servant in his employ. Should he lose them through the acts of another that other must respond in damages. But should the husband be injured, and she thus lose his protection and solace, might she equally with him, maintain a like suit for her loss? In light of what has been said the question is nonsensical. To have a lawsuit we must have to start with, someone capable of suing another. She, however, could not bring any action in her own name, for she was a legal nonentity. But this was not all. What if she were so injured by another as to be incapable of performing her wifely duties? Has the husband suffered a legally recognizable loss, so that he might cause that other to respond in damages? The answer is clear from the common law, as is the theory upon which it was based. He had. It was an actionable trespass for one to interfere with the services of another's servant. This menial in the house, this chattel, responding to the term "wife," also rendered services. It would follow, and it did follow, that the husband had a right of action for injury to her, grounded upon the theory that she was his servant. But could she sue for the loss of services of the master? Clearly not. J. Smith in Montgomery v. Stephen, 359 Mich. 33, 101 N.W. 2d 227 (1960).

11. *Monthly Magazine and American Review* 3 (September 1800), no. 3.

12. Katherine Anthony, *First Lady of the Revolution: The Life of Mercy Otis Warren* (Garden City, N.Y.: Doubleday & Company, 1958), p. 95. John Adams is quoted as replying to Abigail's request that the husband not be allowed to continue absolute master of his wife:

I begin to think the Ministry as deep as they are wicked. After stirring up Tories . . . bigots, Canadians, Indians. . . . At last they have stimulated the [women] to demand new privileges and threaten to rebel.

13. *Economic Feminism in American Literature Prior to 1848*, University of Maine Studies, 2d ser., no. 2 (Orono: University of Maine Press, 1925).

14. Fanny Wright (1795-1852), general reformer and utopian, wrote and worked late in Mrs. Rowson's career. She lectured at societies in her name, and helped get the Married Women's Property Law enacted (ibid., p. 54; Rossi, *Feminist Papers*, pp. 86 ff.).

15. *Pennsylvania Magazine of History and Biography* 68, no. 3 (July 1944), pp. 243-268.

16. Rowson Collection, 7379a, n.d.

17. "To Anna: An Address to a Young Lady Leaving School" (n.d. 7379a. Rowson Collection). This poem, slightly altered, appears in the preface to *Mentoria* and in *Victoria* ("To Sophie," pp. 87 ff.).

18. "He is Not Worth the Trouble," J. Hewitt, composer (Boston: J. Hewitt, [ca. 1813]); see bibliography for discussion of dating.

19. Adams is praised in "Ode, on the Birth Day of John Adams, Esquire" (1799), in *Miscellaneous Poems* (pp. 32-39), as well as in the "Eulogy to George Washington, Esquire" (pp. 44-54). Washington appears in many selections.

20. *Love and Death in the American Novel*, new rev. ed. (New York: Dell Publishing Co., 1969), pp. 74-75.

21. *All The Happy Endings: A Study of the Domestic Novel in America* (New York: Harper & Brothers Publishers, 1956), p. xvii.

22. Samuel L. Knapp, "A Memoir of the Author," in *Charlotte's Daughter* (Boston: Richardson & Lord, 1828).

23. Neal, *Essay*, p. 20.

24. *A Vindication of the Rights of Woman, with Strictures on Political and Moral Subjects*, ed. Charles W. Hagelman, Jr. (New York: W.W. Norton & Company, Norton Library, 1967), p. 222.

25. Margaret Wyman, "The Rise of the Fallen Woman," *American Quarterly* 3 (1951), p. 161. Wyman sees Mrs. Rowson's support for the erring female, and her pique at the "unfeeling world which rejects such women." On this same subject, Wendy Martin (using only *Charlotte* as a basis for judgment) takes the more familiar view that Mrs. Rowson's treatment of the seduced is punitive and illiberal ("Seduced and Abandoned in the New World, 1970: The Fallen Women in American Fiction," in *American Sisterhood*, pp. 257-273).

26. Elizabeth Boyd, *The Happy-Unfortunate or the Female-Page*, ed. William Graves. Garland Series, Foundations of the Novel (New York: Garland Publishing, 1972).

Chapter 4

1. Ernest Jackson Hall, in "The Satirical Element in The American Novel" (Ph.D. diss., University of Pennsylvania, 1922), points out the vein of social criticism in the early popular fiction. He writes of *Charlotte* that it "satirizes the conditions that make seduction possible" (p. 9).

2. *The Popular Novel in England*, p. 9. Herbert Ross Brown in *The Sentimental Novel in America 1789-1860* (Durham, N.C.: Duke University Press, 1940) applies this theory to Mrs. Rowson. Like others, he sees in her a predilection for the reformed rake, a tendency that would show belief in the basic goodness of mankind; but while Mrs. Rowson believed in the power of repentence and redemption, she never allowed a heroine to unite with a former rake, and she dramatized the foolishness of too much trust in the capacity of habitual wrongdoers to reform their daily lives. Charlotte's downfall, for example, is partially the fault of an interfering do-gooder who, knowing that Miss La Rue's background is sordid and discreditable, insists upon giving her a second chance. Mrs. Rowson writes,

> Among the teachers at Madame Du Pont's school was Mademoiselle La Rue, who added to a pleasing person and insinuating address, a liberal education and the manners of a gentlewoman. She was recommended to the school by a lady whose humanity overstepped the bounds of discretion: for though she knew Miss La Rue had eloped from a convent with a young officer, and on coming to England had lived with several different men in open defiance of all moral and religious duties, yet finding her reduced to the most abject want, and believing the penitance which she professed to be sincere, she took her into her own family, and from thence recommended her to Madame Du Pont, as thinking the situation more suitable for a woman of her abilities.
>
> (*Charlotte*, p. 40)

3. *Love and Death in the American Novel*, new rev. ed. (New York: Dell Publishing Co., 1969), p. 63.

4. *The Oven Birds: American Women on Womanhood, 1820-1920*, ed. Gail Parker (Garden City, N.Y.: Doubleday & Company, Anchor Books, 1972), p. 13.

5. For two examples of the American Puritan attitude toward women who step out of their place, see Anne Firor Scott, *Women in American Life. Selected Readings* (New York: Houghton Mifflin Co., 1970). Mrs. Scott reprints John Winthrop's famous contention that a Mrs. Hopkins, one of his contemporaries, had developed a "sad infirmity of mind" as the result of too much reading and writing (p. 12). Mrs. Scott also includes excerpts from the trial of Anne Hutchinson, among them an interrogator's statement that "you [Hutchinson] have stepped out of your place, you have rather been a husband than a wife, and a preacher than a hearer, and a magistrate than a subject, and so you have thought to carry all things in church and commonwealth as you would, and have not been humbled for this . . ." (p. 15).

6. *The Boarding School; or, Lessons of a Preceptress to her Pupils; consisting of Information, Instruction, and Advice, Calculated to Improve the Manners, and form the Character of YOUNG LADIES*. By a Lady of Massachusetts (Boston: I. Thomas and E.J. Andrews, 1798), p. 28.

7. Judith Sargent Murray, "On the Equality of the Sexes," in Rossi, *Feminist Papers*, p. 21.

8. Samuel Sewall, "Talitha Cumi," *Sewall Letter Book, Coll. Mass. Hist. Soc.*, ser. 6, vols. 1-2 (1886-1888).

9. Rossi, "Introduction: Social Roots of the Woman's Movement in America," *Feminist Papers*, pp. 257-258.

10. Quoted by Nancy Hale, *New England Discovery: A Personal View* (New York: Coward McCann, 1963), p. 34.

11. In Neal, *Essay*, p. 30.

Chapter 5

1. Note that Mrs. Rowson's American heroes are Adams and Washington, but never Jefferson.

2. America appears in Mrs. Rowson's earliest work. One of the characters in *Victoria* describes Major Belmour as having "crossed the Atlantic, to assist in bringing poor wavering America to her duty" (I, 72). Several other references also show Mrs. Rowson attached to Britain as her symbol of freedom. Arabella Hartley feels patriotism for England when (on a tour of France) she observes a national emblem on a citadel (II, 8). *The Inquisitor* with its eulogy of love (see chapter 3 above) is obviously addressed to a British audience; the idea that this feeling "ornaments the highest station, and adds new lustre even to the British diadem" begins a tribute to the king and queen (III, 176). *Mentoria*, addressed to Mrs. Rowson's "dear country-women," shows the author still loyal to Britain. America is mentioned in connection with Horton, a thoroughly bad character who has gone to the New World to seek his fortune (I, 42), while *Mentoria's* father is described as a "brave soldier" who was killed at Quebec (I, 15). In *Charlotte* the Revolutionary War and America are associated with rebellion. One disobedient child (Charlotte) elopes to another (America) and by means of a young man engaged to support the rights of Britain.

The *Fille de Chambre* serves as a transition to Mrs. Rowson's jingoistic American phase. Mrs. Rowson decries the horrors of war in such expressions as "fraternal love gave place to jealousy, dissension, and blind party zeal. The son raised his unhallowed arm against his parent, brothers drenched their weapons in each other's blood, and all was horror and confusion" (p. 120). She also shows the cruelty of the Americans to the Abthorpes in the stress of the conflict. On the other hand, she praises the people of New England in a passage Robert Heilman calls "unique in a series of descriptions calumniating dour Puritanism" (*America in English Fiction, 1760-1800: The Influences of the American Revolution* [Baton Rouge: Louisiana State University Press, 1937], p. 270). Mrs. Rowson writes,

> Ere this, the inhabitants of New-England, by their hospitality and primitive simplicity of manners, revived in the mind of our heroine the golden age, so celebrated by poets. Here were no locks or bolts required, for each one, content with his own cot, coveted not the possessions of his neighbor; here should a stranger make his appearance in their little village, though unknown by all, every one was eager to shew him the most civility, inviting him to their houses, and treating him with every delicacy the simplicity of their manner of living afforded.
>
> (p. 120)

3. Of course, Mrs. Rowson is not alone in her anti-Catholicism, and to some degree her position reflects the feeling that was rampant in both the colonies and England; but it is nevertheless fair to find her feminist bias in the kind of criticism she makes of the Church.

4. "Independent and Free," music by R. Taylor (Philadelphia: Carr's Repository, [1796]). See bibliography for further information.

5. "The Little Sailor Boy," music by B. Carr (Philadelphia: Carr's Musical Repository, [1798]).

6. "Truxton's Victory" [Boston: Thomas & Andrews, 1799?].

7. Mrs. Rowson does not mention Napoleon's explicit statements downgrading women; whether she read them or sensed what they would be like is not clear. Let the following stand as an example of the emperor's many pronouncements about the female:

> Nature intended women to be our slaves . . . they are our property; we are not theirs. They belong to us, just as a tree that bears fruit belongs to a gardener. What a mad idea to demand equality for women! . . . Women are nothing but machines for producing children.

Quoted in *Sisterhood is Powerful: An Anthology of Writings from the Women's Liberation Movement*, ed. Robin Morgan [New York: Vintage Books, 1970], p. 34).

Chapter 6

1. Cf. Mrs. Rowson's attitude on this subject to that of typical contemporaries. Hannah Foster categorically states that reading novels "leads to impure desires" (*The Boarding School* . . . [Boston: I. Thomas and E.J. Andrews, 1798]). Leonora Sansay, another writer supposedly influenced by Mrs. Rowson, offers a dramatic tale of a girl gone wrong through destructive reading (*Laura*. By a Lady of Philadelphia [Philadelphia: Bradford & Inskeep, 1809]). Mrs. Rowson takes a more moderate stand than these writers. She recommends authors of fiction who deserve reading, and her taste is more catholic than that of Mrs. Foster, who dismisses Sterne with the statement, "Wit, blended with indelicacy, never meets my approbation" (*The Boarding School*, p. 204).

2. Ernest A. Baker, *The History of the English Novel: The Novel of Sentiment and the Gothic Romance* (London: H.F.&G. Witherby, 1934), vol. 5, p. 16.

3. *The Popular Novel in England*, pp. 92, 94.

4. *The Sentimental Novel in America, 1789-1860* (Durham, N.C.: Duke University Press, 1940), p. 74.

5. Rowson Collection, 7379a, n.d.

6. Seduction, as has been noted, could carry a large weight of meaning. Mrs. Rowson's use of this popular motif in many instances is peculiarly sexless. At times she uses seduction as a metaphor for the loss of integrity or simply the loss of a socially valuable commodity. Women "get screwed" by society when they lack money and social standing, and are at the same time denied education and the opportunity to work. But "it is past the days of romance" says Mrs. Rowson in *Charlotte* (p. 42) when the male carries the female off against her will. Mrs. Rowson casts a cold eye on the glamour of rape. Her heroines are never permitted the luxury of evading a moral choice, as Lucinda in *The Mountain Mourner* does. Lucinda cries through the entire novel in which she appears, and finally reveals the dramatic news thus:

"Oh!" said she, "I still remember his cruel and triumphant words—that 'resistance would no longer avail me!' "

Mrs. P.P. Manvill, *Lucinda; or the Mountain Mourner. Being Recent Facts, in a series of Letters, from Mrs. Manvill, in the State of New York, to her sister in Pennsylvania*, 2d ed. [Ballston Spa, N.Y.: William Child, 1810], p. 140.

7. William Hill Brown, *The Power of Sympathy, or The Triumph of Nature. Founded on Fact*, in *The Power of Sympathy and The Coquette*, ed. William S. Osborne, Masterworks of Literature Series (New Haven, Conn.: College and University Press, 1970). Brown's novel was first published in 1789.

8. Robert Ronald Kettler, "The Eighteenth-Century American Novel: The Beginning of a Fictional Tradition" (Ph.D. diss., Purdue University, 1968), p. 65.

9. "Where Can Peace of Mind be Found," Composer, John Bray (Boston: G. Graupner, [1821]).

10. Terence Martin, *The Instructed Vision; Scottish Common Sense Philosophy and the Origins of American Fiction*, Indiana University Humanities Series no. 48 (Bloomington: Indiana University Press, 1961).

Chapter 7

1. The realistic side of Mrs. Rowson's fiction has been noted by both Lillie Deming Loshe (*The Early American Novel* [New York: Columbia University Press, 1907], p. 13); and by Fred Pattee (*The First Century of American Literature, 1770-1870* [New York: D. Appleton-Century Company, 1935], p. 90). Loshe writes, "In her choice of horrors, and the representation of theme, Mrs. Rowson is essentially a realist, whose trick of giving vividness by touches of homely detail was probably learned from Richardson, who got it from Defoe. The description of the room furnished for Meriel by her benefactor . . . resembles one of Pamela's conscientious catalogues. This crude realism of situation, without any corresponding truth of character, has given Mrs. Rowson a high place among successful exploiters of domestic melodrama, and it separates her didactic sensationalism from the more politely imaginative world of her 'female' contemporaries."

2. Ian Watt, *The Rise of The Novel: Studies in Defoe, Richardson and Fielding* (1957; reprint ed., Berkeley: University of California Press, 1967).

3. Charles F. Richardson, *American Literature, 1607-1885* (New York: G.P. Putnam's Sons, 1889), vol. 2, p. 285.

4. *The Popular Novel in England*, p. 136.

5. See for example *Self-Raised, or From the Depths* (New York: Grosset & Dunlap Publishers, 1864).

6. Cf. Mark Twain, "Literary Offenses of Fenimore Cooper" (1897), reprinted in *The Portable Mark Twain*, ed. Bernard de Voto (New York: Viking Press, 1946), pp. 541-557, and current complaints of writers and others concerning literary and film treatment.

7. Catherine Maria Sedgwick, *The Poor Rich Man, and the Rich Poor Man* (New York: Harper & Brothers, 1836). The epigraph reads, "There is that maketh himself rich, yet hath nothing; there is that maketh himself poor yet hath great riches."

8. *A Room of One's Own* (1929; reprint ed. New York: Harcourt, Brace & World, 1957).

9. Arthur Hobson Quinn argues in his study *American Fiction: An Historical and Critical Survey* (New York: Appleton-Century-Crofts, 1936): "The most severe criticism of her [Mrs. Rowson's] work lies in its implicit acceptance of a cold-blooded eighteenth-century morality, British in essence, which permitted a man of wealth to purchase any virtue he desired and accepted as inevitable the hard lot of any woman without friends or money, whom a single mistake might destroy" (p. 19). Mr. Quinn is, as this study has pointed out, mistaken in his assessment of Mrs. Rowson; she protested against this system vehemently.

10. J.M.S. Tompkins uses the term "prudential type of morality" to describe the moral standard of the sentimental novel (*The Popular Novel in England*, p. 136), and this topic is given significant attention in other similar studies.

Chapter 8

1. See Terence Martin, "Emergence of the Novel," for a suggestion of this point.

2. When Mrs. Rowson was accused by William Cobbett of lacking sincerity in her praise of America, she replied in the preface to *Trials* that she felt as though "having a tender lover, and an affectionate brother who are equally beloved, [she] sees them engaged in a quarrel with, and fight, each other . . ." (p. xvii). A letter to Anthony Haswell, Susanna's cousin (21 May 1796), enclosing a copy of *Trials*, expresses a similar feeling. Mrs. Rowson complains that her works have become a subject for "scribblers to exercise [their] wits upon . . . all truly because I am an English woman." She adds, "I yet have an accountable affection for America and all that appertains thereunto. . . . Why, my dear cousin, do they imagine english people devoid of gratitude or sensibility, and think them bound to forget friendships former, or benefits because, forsooth, the two nations do not agree in political concerns." Transcript of a Letter, Rowson Collection, 7379b, 21 May 1796.

3. "Six School Reports," Rowson Collection, 7379a, n.d.

4. *By a Woman Writt: Literature From Six Centuries By and About Women*, ed. Joan Goulianos (Baltimore: Penguin Books, 1973), pp. 23, 71, 121.

5. Adrienne Rich, Foreword to *The Works of Anne Bradstreet*, ed. Jeannine Hensley, Adrienne Rich (Cambridge, Mass.: Harvard University Press, 1967), p. xxvi.

6. Vena Bernadette Field, *Constantia: A Study of the Life and Works of Judith Sargent Murray 1751-1820*, University of Maine Studies, 2d ser., no. 17 (Orono: University of Maine Press, 1931), p. 69.

7. MacCarthy, *Female Pen*, vol. 2, p. 40. Also see Dorothy Blakey, *The Minerva Press 1790-1820* (London: Oxford University Press, 1939), p. 50; and Tompkins, *The Popular Novel in England*, p. 140, for discussions of the anonymity and apologetic tone adopted by female novelists.

8. MacCarthy, *Female Pen*, p. 41.

9. Hannah More, *Works: Strictures on the Modern System of Female Education–Sacred Dramas* (New York: Harper & Brothers Publishers, 1855), vol. 6, p. 146. It is difficult to imagine Susanna Rowson making the gesture Miss More did: refusing membership in the Royal Society of Literature (1820) because "membership was an impropriety for women" (Mary Gwladys Jones, *Hannah More* [Cambridge: Cambridge University Press, 1952], p. 265).

10. Katherine Anthony, *First Lady of the Revolution: The Life of Mercy Otis Warren* (Garden City, N.Y.: Doubleday & Company, 1958), p. 95.

11. Sally Sayward Barrell Keating Wood, *Julia and the Illuminated Baron. A Novel. Founded on Recent Facts . . . By a Lady of Massachusetts* (Portsmouth, N.H.: United States Oracle Press, 1800), p. v.

12. *Dorval; or the Speculator. A Novel. Founded on Recent Facts. By a Lady . . .* (Portsmouth, N.H.: Nutting & Whitelock, 1801), p. iv.

13. *The Second Sex*, trans. and ed. H.M. Parshley (1953; reprint ed., New York: Bantam Books, 1961), *passim*.

14. Martin, "Emergence of the Novel," p. 225.

15. "Seneca Falls Convention, Declaration of Sentiments and Resolutions, 1848," *American Sisterhood*, p. 46.

16. "Speech Before the National Women's Rights Convention of 1855," *American Sisterhood*, pp. 49-50.

17. "Discourse on Women, 1849," *American Sisterhood*, pp. 53 ff.

18. Lucy Stone and Henry B. Blackwell, "Marriage Contract, 1855," *American Sisterhood*, pp. 51-52: Elizabeth Cady Stanton, "Letter on Marriage and Divorce, 1855," *American Sisterhood*, pp. 79-81.

19. "Social Purity, 1875," *American Sisterhood*, pp. 90-92.

20. Gail Parker, *The Oven Birds: American Women on Womanhood 1820-1920* (Garden City, N.Y.: Doubleday & Company, 1972), p. 4, and *passim*.

21. Rossi, "The Making of a Cosmopolitan Humanist: Margaret Fuller," *Feminist Papers*, p. 150.

22. Fuller's treatment of this issue is found in *American Sisterhood*, pp. 205-207. Harriet Martineau writes in *Society in America*: "How fearfully the morals of women are crushed, appears from the prevalent persuasion that there are virtues which are peculiarly masculine and others which are feminine. . . . Christ being the meeting point of all virtues" ([New York: Saunders and Otley, 1837], vol. 25, p. 233).

23. See their writings in *American Sisterhood* and *Feminist Papers*. The Grimké sisters, like most of the women cited, actually treated almost all the issues specified in this argument; I have picked only one expression of each idea for emphasis. Note Sarah Grimké's closing letter salutation: "Thine in the bonds of womanhood" (*Feminist Papers*, p. 316).

24. *A Room of One's Own* (1929; reprint ed., New York: Harcourt, Brace & World, 1957).

25. Betty Friedan, *The Feminine Mystique* (New York: Dell Publishing Co., 1963).

26. Emily Hahn, *Once Upon a Pedestal* (New York: Thomas Y. Crowell, 1974).

27. "A Bright Woman is Caught in a Double Bind," *American Sisterhood*, pp. 285-291.

28. "Psychology Constructs the Female, or, the Fantasy Life of the Male Psychologist (With Some Attention to the Fantasies of his Friends, the Male Biologist and the Male Anthropologist)," *The Norton Reader: An Anthology of Expository Prose*, ed. Arthur M. Eastman et al., 3d ed. (New York: W. W. Norton & Company, 1973), pp. 1010 ff.

29. *Sexual Politics* (Garden City, N.Y.: Doubleday & Company, 1970).

30. *The Natural Superiority of Women* (New York: Macmillan, 1953).

31. Elizabeth Gould Davis, *The First Sex* (New York: G.P. Putnam's Sons, 1971).

32. Carolyn G. Heilbrun, *Toward a Recognition of Androgyny* (1964; reprint ed., New York: Alfred A. Knopf, 1973).

33. de Beauvoir, *The Second Sex*, trans. and ed. H.M. Parshley (1953; reprint ed., New York: Bantam Books, 1961).

34. Margaret Mead, *Sex and Temperament in Three Primitive Societies* (1935; reprint ed., New York: Mentor Books, 1950).

35. "Woman As Nigger, 1969," *American Sisterhood*, pp. 293-298.

36. Rossi, "Social Roots of the Woman's Movement in America," *Feminist Papers*, pp. 248-249.

37. Constance Rourke, *The Roots of American Culture and Other Essays* (New York: Harcourt, Brace and Co., 1942), pp. 84-85.

38. Helen Waite Papashvily, *All the Happy Endings: A Study of the Domestic Novel in America* (New York: Harper & Brothers Publishers, 1956), chapter 1.

39. Earl L. Bradsher, *Mathew Carey. Editor, Author and Publisher. A Study in American Literary Development* (New York: Columbia University Press, 1912), pp. 63-64.

40. Myra Montgomery to unnamed friend. Letter, Manuscripts, The Historical Society of Pennsylvania, 22 November 1808.

41. Nason, *Memoir*, p. 200.

42. [John Swanwick], *A Rub From Snub; or a cursory analytical Epistle: addressed to Peter Porcupine, Author of the* BONE TO GNAW, KICK FOR A BITE,&c. &c. *containing* GLAD TIDINGS *for the* DEMOCRATS, *and a Word of* COMFORT *to Mrs. S. Rowson. Wherein the said Porcupine's Moral, Political, Critical and Literary character is Fully Illustrated* (Philadelphia: Printed for the Purchasers, 1795), p. 79.

Bibliography

Works by Susanna Rowson

The following bibliography is an attempt to provide an up-to-date and usable list of Rowson's works, and to suggest the extent of her production. It includes at least one edition of all the works that appear in current bibliographies, but does not attempt to track down all the editions of any work. The multifarious editions of *Charlotte Temple* and *Charlotte's Daughter* require separate treatment, and the sheet music could also be the subject of a separate bibliographical study. R.W.G. Vail lists 158 editions of *Charlotte Temple* in his fully researched bibliography; Lyle Wright adds ten to Vail's total. Several other Rowson works went through multiple editions. The following pages list the first editions of Rowson's works, those mentioned in this study, and in several instances, the second or third editions of works that received a small number of reprintings. R.W.G. Vail's entry number is given in many cases, and where there is nothing to add to the information, I have relied on Vail. Locations are listed only in cases where a book was not previously located, or is extremely rare. The following bibliographical sources are mentioned:

Allibone, S. Austin. *A Critical Dictionary of English Literature and British and American Authors Living and Deceased. From the Earliest Accounts to the Latter Half of the Nineteenth Century.* 2 vols., 2 suppls. Philadelphia: J.B. Lippincott Company, 1899.

Dunlap, William. *History of the American Theatre and Anecdotes of the Principal Actors.* 2d ed. 3 vols. in 1. Burt Franklin Research and Source Works Series, no. 36. New York: Burt Franklin, 1963.

Durang, Charles. "The Philadelphia Stage: 1749-1821," *Philadelphia Dispatch*, 15 October 1854.

Evans, Charles. *American Bibliography; a Chronological Dictionary of all Books, Pamphlets, and Periodical Publications Printed in the United States from the Genesis of Printing in 1630 Down to and Including the Year 1820.* Chicago: Printed for the Author, Blakey Press, 1903-1959. Subtitle and publisher vary.

Odell, George C.D. *Annals of the New York Stage, 1798-1821,* vol. 2. New York: Columbia University Press, 1927.

Quinn, Arthur Hobson. *A History of the American Drama From the Beginning to the Civil War.* New York: Harper & Brothers, 1923.

Sabin, Joseph. *A Dictionary of Books Relating to America, from its discovery to The Present Time,* Vol. 18. New York: Sabin, 1889.

Seilhamer, George O. *History of the American Theatre: New Foundations.* 3 vols. Philadelphia: Globe Printing House, 1888-1891.

Sonneck, Oscar George, and William Treat Upton. *A Bibliography of Early Secular Music: Eighteenth Century.* Rev. and enlarged, preface by Irving Lowens. New York: Da Capo Press, 1964.

Vail, R.W.G. "Susanna Haswell Rowson, The Author of Charlotte Temple: A Bibliographical Study," *Proceedings of the American Antiquarian Society* 42 (1932), pp. 47-160.

Wolfe, Richard J. *Secular Music in America: 1801-1825. A Bibliography*. Introduction by Carleton Sprague Smith. New York: New York Public Library, Astor, Lenox and Tilden Foundations, 1964.

Wright, Lyle. *American Fiction 1774-1850, A Contribution Towards a Bibliography*. New rev. ed. San Marino, Calif.: Huntington Library, 1960.

Fiction

Charlotte: A Tale of Truth. 2 vols. London: William Lane, Minerva, MDLCXCI. Unique copy of the first edition is in the Clifton Waller Barrett Library at the University of Virginia. Prefatory remarks by "Minerva," presumably a mask assumed by the publisher William Lane, to "Ladies and Gentlemen" readers, assure them that the press's products will be respectable, informative, and entertaining.

————, in *Three Early American Novels*. Ed. William S. Kable. Columbus, Ohio: Charles E. Merrill Publishing Co., 1970.

Charlotte's Daughter: or, The Three Orphans. A Sequel to Charlotte Temple. To Which is prefixed, A Memoir of the Author. Boston: Richardson & Lord, 1828.

The Lamentable History of the Beautiful and Accomplished Charlotte Temple, With An Account of Her Elopement With Lieutenant Montroville [sic], and Her Misfortunes and Painful Sufferings, Are Herein Pathetically Depicted. Philadelphia: Barclay & Co., 1865.

Charlotte Temple: A Tale of Truth. Ed. Francis W. Halsey. New York: Funk & Wagnalls Co., 1905.

————. Ed. Clara M. and Rudolph Kirk. Twayne's United States Classics Series. New York: Twayne Publishers, 1964.

The Fille de Chambre, A Novel, in Three Volumes, by the Author of The Inquisitor, &c. &c. London: Printed for William Lane, at the Minerva, MDCCXCII. Vail (201) lists this first edition as *Rebecca, or the Fille de Chambre*; there was no copy known when Vail prepared his study. Volume 2 of this novel, located at Indiana University Library (vols. 1 and 3 missing), is entitled as above.

————, A Novel. By Mrs. Rowson of the New Theatre, Philadelphia; Author of *Charlotte, the Inquisitor, Victoria*, &c. [1st American ed.] Philadelphia: H.&P. Rice, and J. Rice & Co., 1794.

————. *Rebecca, or the Fille de Chambre*. A Novel. By Mrs. Rowson, Author of Charlotte, The Inquisitor, Victoria, &c. The Second American Edition, Corrected and Revised by the Author. Boston: R.P. & C. Williams, 1814.

The Inquisitor; or, Invisible Rambler. In three volumes. By Mrs. Rowson, author of Victoria. London: G.G.J. and J. Robinson, X.DCC.LXXXVIII. (Vail 191).

————. In three volumes. By Mrs. Rowson, author of Victoria. The first American edition. Philadelphia: William Gibbons, 1793 (Vail 192).

————. In three volumes. By Mrs. Rowson, Author of Victoria. Second American Edition. Philadelphia: Mathew Carey, 1794.

Mentoria; or The Young Lady's Friend: in Two Volumes. By Mrs. Rowson, *Author of Victoria*, &c. &c. London: printed for William Lane, at the Minerva, [1791]. The title page of the first edition does not include a printed date. The date appears to be well established by the evidence Vail cites (195): advertisements and reviews dated 1791. Locations in addition to the New York Public Library, are the Barrett Library, University of Virginia, and the Indiana University Library.

————. By Mrs. Rowson, author of Victoria, &c. &c. Dublin: Printed by Thomas Morton

Bates for P. Wogan, A. Grueber, J. Halpern, J. Moore, R. M'Allister, J. Rice, W. Jones, and R. White, 1791 (Vail 196).

———. In two volumes. By Mrs. Rowson, of the New-Theatre, Philadelphia: Author of *The Inquisitor, Fille de Chambre, Victoria, Charlotte,* &c. &c. Philadelphia: Robert Campbell, M.DCC.XCIV.

Reuben and Rachel; or, Tales of Old Times. A Novel. By Mrs. Rowson, Author of Charlotte, Trials of the Heart, Fille de Chambre, &c. &c. Boston: Manning & Loring, 1798.

———. A novel in two volumes. By Mrs. Rowson, author of Charlotte, Mentoria, Fille de chambre, &c. &c. London: Printed at the Minerva-Press, for William Lane, 1799 (Vail 206).

Sarah, or The Exemplary Wife. By Susanna Rowson, Author of Charlotte Temple, Reuben and Rachel, Fille de Chambre, &c. &c. Boston: Charles Williams, 1813. Rev. from the serial version, *Sincerity,* in *Boston Weekly Magazine,* 4 June 1803-30 June 1804.

The Test of Honour, A Novel. By a Young Lady. In Two Volumes. London: John Abraham, 1789. The running title of this work is *Mary, or the Test of Honour,* and is so listed by Vail (194), who got the title from Knapp. Below the title is a seven-line passage of poetry:

> Take Honour for thy guide, and on just Heaven
> Place thy reliance, there's a secret charm
> In virtuous actions, that o'er awes the wicked,
> And, maugre all the malice of the world,
> Honour thy shield, Religion thy support,
> The shafts of sorrow shall pass harmless by,
> And happiness await thee in the end.

The full imprint reads "Printed by and for JOHN ABRAHAM, at his Circulating-Library, St. Swithin's Lane, Lombard-Street, 1789." A copy—as far as I know, unique—is located at Houghton Library, Harvard University.

Trials of the Human Heart, A Novel. in four volumes. By Mrs. Rowson, of the New Theatre, Philadelphia, Author of Charlotte, Fille de Chambre, Inquisitor, &c. &c. Philadelphia: Wrigley & Berriman, M.DCC.XCV.

Victoria. A Novel. In Two Volumes. The Characters taken from real Life, and Calculated to Improve the Morals of the Female Sex, By impressing them with a just Sense of The Merits of Filial Piety. By Susannah Haswell. London: J.P. Cooke, 1786. Copies at the New York Historical Society and Indiana University Library.

Pedagogical Works

An Abridgment of Universal Geography, Together with Sketches of History. Designed for the Use of Schools and Academies in the United States. By Susanna Rowson. Boston: John West [1805]. Vail (159) notes that the date is not on the title page, and agrees with Nason on 1805, which coincides with the printer's location in Cambridge Street, the address given in the imprint.

Biblical Dialogues Between A Father and His Family: Comprising Sacred History, From the Creation to the Death of our Saviour Christ. The Lives of the Apostles, and the Promulgation of the Gospel; with a Sketch of the History of the Church Down to the Reformation. The Whole Carried on in Conjunction with Profane History. In Two Volumes. By Susanna Rowson. Boston: Richardson and Lord, 1822.

Exercises in History, Chronology, and Biography, in Question and Answer. For the Use of Schools. Comprising, Ancient History, Greece, Rome, &c. Modern History, England, France, Spain, Portugal, &c. The Discovery of America, Rise, Progress and Final Independence of the United States. By Susanna Rowson, Author of Biblical Dialogues, &c. &c. Boston: Richardson and Lord, 1822.

A Present for Young Ladies; Containing Poems, Dialogues, Addresses, &c. &c. &c. As Recited by the Pupils of Mrs. Rowson's Academy, at the Annual Exhibitions. By Susanna Rowson. Boston: John West & Co., 1811.

A Spelling Dictionary, divided into Short Lessons, For the Easier Committing to Memory By Children and Young Persons; and Calculated to Assist Youth in Comprehending What they Read. Selected From Johnson's Dictionary, For the Use of Her Pupils, By Susanna Rowson. Boston: John West, 1807.

————. 2d ed. Portland: Isaac Adams, 1815.

Youth's First Step in Geography, Being a Series of Exercises Making the Tour of the Habitable Globe. For The use of Schools. By Susannah [!] Rowson, Preceptress. Boston: Wells and Lilly, 1818.

Periodicals

The Boston Weekly Magazine; Devoted to Morality, Literature, Biography, History, the Fine Arts, Agriculture, &c. &c. 3 vols. Boston: Gilbert and Dean, 1802-1805. The title pages bear the following verse:

To soar aloft on Fancy's Wing,
And bathe in Heliconia's Spring;
Cull Every Flower With Careful Hand,
And Strew them O'er our Native Land.

See chapter 1, notes, for a discussion of Mrs. Rowson's contribution to this periodical.

New England Galaxy. Boston: 1817-1839[?] Subtitle varies. Mrs. Rowson's contributions are found in early issues under the initials "S. R."

Poetry

Poems on Various Subjects. By Mrs. Rowson, author of the Inquisitor, &c. London: G.G.J. and J. Robinson, M.DCC.LXXXVIII. No copy known (Vail 199). Vail takes this title from Allibone and the imprint from the first edition of *The Inquisitor.*

Miscellaneous Poems. Susanna Rowson, preceptress. Boston: Gilbert and Dean, 1804.

A Trip to Parnassus; or, the Judgment of Apollo on Dramatic Authors and Performers. A Poem. London: John Abraham, 1788. The title page of *A Trip* includes a one-line quotation: "Laugh where we must, be candid where we can.—Pope." The full imprint reads, "Printed by and for John Abraham, No. 3, St. Swithin's Lane, Lombard-Street; and sold by all other Booksellers, in Town and Country. 1788. (Price Two-Shillings.)" There is a copy of this rare work at Houghton Library, Harvard University.

Drama

The American Tar, or the Press Gang Defeated. A "ballet founded on a recent fact at

Liverpool . . . the music entirely new and composed by R. Taylor." Directed by William Francis and performed at the New Theatre, Philadelphia, June 17, 1796 (Sonneck-Upton, p. 22). Vail (160) quotes Seilhamer to the effect that the piece was probably an adaptation from a work by Jacob Morton, and was probably never published. Seilhamer (vol. 3, p. 213) lists the characters as Will Steady, Tom Capstan, Captain Trunion, Midshipmen, Dick Hauser [Mr. Rowson], Susan [Charlotte Rowson] and Jane.

Americans in England, or, Lessons for Daughters. A comedy. Boston: 1796. No copy known (Vail 161). Vail notes disagreement over the possibility of this work having been printed. It was performed at the Federal Street Theater, 19 April 1797, and said to have been produced later under the title "The Columbian Daughter, or Americans in England," a fact which suggests that the play was printed. Seilhamer provides a list of characters, which may denote the flavor of the play. The English characters are Courtland, Folio, Snap, Waiter, Captain Ormsby, Jack Acorn, Thomas, Bailiff's Man, Rhymer, Mrs. Ormsby, Arabella, Betty, and Melissa; the Americans are named Ezekiel Plainly, Horace Winship, and Jemima Winship. Mrs. Ormsby and Jemima Winship were played by Mrs. Rowson, Betty by her sister-in-law, Charlotte Rowson, and Snap by Mr. Rowson (vol. 3, p. 340).

The Female Patriot; or, Nature's Rights. [Altered from Philip Massinger's "Bondman."] Philadelphia: 1794. Vail (184) takes the title from Durang, Knapp, Sabin, and Evans. No copy is known and there is disagreement as to whether the play was printed. Vail cites evidence from Dunlap (an early edition) and Durang that this farce was performed 19 June 1795. Seilhamer's list of characters suggests that Mrs. Rowson stayed pretty close to Massinger: Timoleon, Archidamus, Leothenes, Hernando, Diphilus, Jailor, Graculo, Pymbrio, Pysander, Cleora, Olympio, Statilla, Xanthia. Statilla was played by Mrs. Rowson (p. 181).

Hearts of Oak. [Boston? 1810-1811]. Probably not published (Vail 190). Vail quotes John Bernard (*Retrospections of America 1797-1811* [New York: Harper and Brothers, 1887]), who ascribes this play to Mrs. Rowson, and notes that the play was probably adapted from John Till Allingham's *Hearts of Oak* (Drury Lane, 1803). Allingham's play is a sentimental comedy, with patriotic overtones expressed in the prologue and epilogue. The central action is mainly domestic and involves the departure of one Dorland from his wife Eliza because he had concluded, on seeing her embrace her brother, that she had a lover. There is a money-grubbing land dealer, Ten-Per-Cent, a humorous Irishman, Brian O'Bradleigh, and an orphan heroine (John Till Allingham, *Hearts of Oak. A Comedy. Five Acts.* Drury Lane, London: Alexandra & Fredricksburg, Cotton & Stewart, [1804]).

Slaves in Algiers; or, a Struggle for Freedom: A Play Interspersed with songs, In three acts. [Music composed by Alexander Reinagle]. Philadelphia: Wrigley and Berriman, M,DCC,XCIV, 1794. Vail (208) says this was first performed at the New Theatre, Chestnut Street, Philadelphia, 30 June 1794, and notes Mrs. Rowson's early use of national themes. Seilhamer declares, "The style was wretched, the dramatic quality tawdry, and the sentiment strained and stilted" (vol. 3, p. 156). He claims the play owes its popularity to William Cobbett's attack. Evans assumes a reprinting of *Slaves*, Boston, 1796, from an advertisement (Evans 31130).

The Standard of Liberty: a Poetical Address. Baltimore: 1795. No copy known (Vail 211). Vail takes the title from Knapp and Evans via Sabin, and notes that it probably was printed by George Keatinge, who advertised works by New Theatre playwrights. Published in the *Baltimore Telegraphe*, 31 October 1795, as "The standard of liberty. A poetic tale." Appears in *Miscellaneous Poems*, pp. 94-97.

The Volunteers. A musical entertainment as performed at the New Theatre. Composed by Alex Reinagle. The words by Mrs. Rowson. Philadelphia: Printed for the author and sold at the music shops [1795]. Vail (249) notes that Durang, Seilhamer, and Sonneck agree that the work was performed first at the New Theatre, Philadelphia, 21 January 1795. Doubt exists as to whether there was a separately printed libretto. Evans describes the piece as a farce based upon the Whiskey Rebellion. The available score contains fourteen songs with music, all but one with lyrics by Mrs. Rowson. Copies of the score are located at the Library of Congress and The Historical Society of Pennsylvania.

Songs

"America, Commerce and Freedom." Comp. A. Reinagle. Philadelphia: Carr's Musical Repository [1794] (Vail 216). Date assumed by Sonneck, from ad. The piece was part of "The Sailor's Landlady," produced at the New Theatre, Philadelphia, 19 March 1794. Seilhamer describes this "ballet pantomine" as having been quite popular, and the third of such works by William Francis; the same name appears as the director of *The American Tar* (pp. 151-152).

———. Comp. A. Reinagle. Baltimore: Carr's Musical Repository, [1794-1796].

———. "New Song." Sung by Mr. Darley. [Philadelphia]: M. Carey, [1794] (Evans 27648).

"Captn Truxton or Huzza! for the Constellation," Sung Mr. Tyler at the Theatre with the greatest applause. New York: Printed and Sold at J. HEWITT'S Musical Repository, [ca. 1799] (Evans 36246). "Captain Truxton," "Huzza for the Constellation," and "Truxton's Victory," while all commemorate the same occasion, and are dated the same year, have different words.

"Charity." [An ode. Music by John Bray] (Vail 220). Part of an elaborate religious performance for the anniversary of the Boston Fatherless and Widow's Society. Performed at Boylston Hall, Boston, 11 October 1820.

"Child of Mortality." Duett and Chorus. Written by Mrs. Rowson. Composed by John Bray. Portsmouth, N.H.: T.H. Miller [ca. 1824] (Vail 222); (Wolfe 1276).

"The Columbian Sailor." Written by Mrs. Rowson, Composed by J. Bray. Philadelphia: G.E. Blake, [1816?]. Vail (223) dates this song [1816-1820?]; Wolfe (1284) gives it as [1816?]. It was number 6 of Blake's Musical Miscellany.

"Come Strike the Silver String. A Sacred Song." Written by Mrs. Rowson. Composed by Oliver Shaw. Providence: Oliver Shaw [1817-1823]. Wolfe (7935) narrows Vail's "1818-1825" to "1817-1823." Reissued in Shaw: *Sacred Songs, Duetts, Anthems, &c.* Providence [1823].

"A Dirge" [to George Washington]. Words by Mrs. Rowson, of Medford. In *Sacred Dirges, Hymns, and Anthems, Commemorative of the Death of General George Washington, The Guardian of His Country, and The Friend of Man. An Original Composition.* By a Citizen of Massachusetts [Oliver Holden]. Boston: I. Thomas and E. and E.T. Andrews, [1800] (Evans 37635-37638).

"Drink to Me Only With Thine Eyes" (Vail 226). Three four-line stanzas. "This first verse also is from the original song" [by Ben Jonson], the last two verses by Mrs. Rowson. Published in *Miscellaneous Poems*, p. 198.

"He is Not Worth the Trouble." Written by Mrs. Rowson. Composed by J. Hewitt. Boston: J. Hewitt, [18—?]. Vail's entry for this song lists the place and publisher as "New-York: Firth & Hall No. 1 Franklin Sq.," and dates the song [1832?] on the evidence that the publisher appeared at the given address between 1832 and 1847. The copy I have bears the above information, and is dated "ca. 1813."

"How Cold and Piercing Blows the Wind." A Favorite Ballad, Sung with great applause by Mrs. Graupner at the Philharmonic Concert, Boston. The Words by Mrs. Rowson. Music by J. Hewitt. New York: J. Hewitt's Musical Repository and Library, [1809]. Wolfe (3721) gives the date as [1809]; evidence from an advertisement of 12 September 1809 in the *New York Evening Post* features it among "new songs just published." Wolfe's entry has Mrs. Rowson listed as Mrs. Rawson. My copy has her name correct.

"Huzza for the Constellation." Sung by Mr. Fox at the Theatre. Printed and sold at B. Carr's Musical Repository, Philadelphia, & Carr's, Baltimore, & P. Hewitt's, N. York [1799] (Evans 36247).

"Hymn to the Deity." (Vail 228). Twelve four-line stanzas. Published in *Miscellaneous Poems*, pp. 53-58.

"Hymn." [For Washington?] *Hymns and Odes Composed on the death of General Washington*. Portsmouth: 1800.

"I'd Rather Be Excus'd." Composed by Mr. Hook. Boston: J. Hewitt, [1814-1815]. (Wolfe 4086).

    Reissued from same plates; Boston: E.W. Jackson [1821-1824] (Wolfe 4086A). Reissued from same plates; Music Saloon 325 Broadway [n.d.], ca. 1825 (Wolfe 4086B).

    In The *Songster's New Pocket Companion*, Boston: 1817 (Wolfe 4087).

"Independent and Free," From the AMERICAN TAR or the PRESS GANG DEFEATED. Sung by Mr. Rowson at the New Theatre Philadelphia. The Words by Mrs. Rowson, the Music by R. Taylor. Printed for the Author . . . & Sold at Carr's Repository's [1796] (Evans 47929), (Sonneck, p. 207). Location, Historical Society of Pennsylvania.

"The Independent Farmer." A song. Three twelve-line stanzas. Published in *Miscellaneous Poems*, pp. 191-193 (Vail 231).

"I Never will be Married." The words by Mrs. Rowson. The music by Mr. Hook. London: Polyhymnian Company. [1790-1820] (Vail 229).

"In Vain is the Verdure of Spring." A new song composed by Mr. Carr. The words by Mrs. Rowson [Philadelphia:] Printed and sold by G. Willig, [1797-1798?]. Vail (230) notes that the Willig music store appears in the Philadelphia directories between 1797 and 1854, and the fact that Nason dates this song prior to 1799. Wolfe (10186) says "[1799-1802]," and lists "Mrs. I. Rowson" as lyricist.

"Kiss the Brim and Bid it Pass." A new song. Written by Mrs. Rowson. The music composed by P.A. Von Hagen. Boston: P.A. Von Hagen's Piano Forte Warehouse [1802]. Vail (232) and Wolfe agree on date, Vail by means of ads, Wolfe (3292) from copyright granted Von Hagen, 21 August 1802.

"The Little Sailor Boy." A Ballad Sung at the Theatres & other Public Places in Philadelphia, Baltimore, New York &c. by Messrs Darley, Williamson, Miss Broadhurst, M. Hodgkinson. Written by Mrs. Rowson. Composed by B. Carr. Printed and sold at the Authors Musical Repository, Philadelphia, J. Carrs, Baltimore & J. Hewitts New York [1798] (Vail 233; Evans 34489). See Vail and Sonneck-Upton for the many editions of this song, and see Wolfe for problems in dating.

"Ma Jolie Petite Fille." A New Song. Set to Music by Mr. R. Taylor—the words by Mrs. Rowson/Of Medford, near Boston. In The *Philadelphia Repository and Weekly Register* 1, no. 26 (9 May 1801), fol. p. 205.

"National Song for the 4th of July the Birthday of American Independence." Words by Mrs. Rowson of Boston, Massachusetts, the music composed by Dr. Arnold. Boston: G. Graupner [181—]. Vail (235) gives the date [1818]; Wolfe (269) says [1815].

"Ode. To the Memory of John Warren." Published in *An Oration Occasioned by the*

Death of John Warren . . . Delivered . . . by Josiah Bartlett . . . Boston: C. Stebbins, 1815 (Vail 236).

"Original Ode." Boston Fatherless and Widow's Society Order of Performance at Park St. Church, 16 October 1825. Annual Meeting. Boston, 1825.

"Orphan Nosegay Girl." The words by Mrs. Rowson. Boston: G. Graupner. Vail (237) dates [1818-1825]; Wolfe (7466), [1803-1806]. Vail notes that Graupner appears in the Boston directory between 1805 and 1825.

> A second state of the preceeding. In Shaw, "A Selection of Progressive Airs and Songs." Dedham, 1810 (Wolfe 7467A).

"Parody on the Marseilles Hymn, adapted for the sons of Columbia." Three eleven-line stanzas. Published in *Miscellaneous Poems*, pp. 186-188 (Vail 238).

"Peace and Holy Love, a Sacred Song"; Sung by Master Ayling, at the Handel & Haydn Society: Written by Mrs. Rowson, the Music Composed by John Bray. Boston: S. Wood [1820] (Vail 238); (Wolfe 1323).

> Reissued on the same plates, imprint altered to: "Boston: Published by E.W. Jackson [1822-1826] (Wolfe 1323A). My copy has S. Wood scratched out and E.W. Jackson apparently written in.

"Soft As Yon Silver Ray That Sleeps." A song, With an accompaniment for the piano forte. The words by Mrs. Rowson. The music composed by J. Bray. Boston: G. Graupner. Vail (240) gives the date of this song as [1814-1825]; Wolfe (1346) says [1820-1825]. Wolfe lists seven issues of this song, the lyrics for which, as he and Vail both note, are from Anne Radcliffe's *The Mysteries of Udolpho*. Only the one version is ascribed to Mrs. Rowson.

"A Soldier is the Noblest Name." [First published in *The Highland Reel*. A comic opera, in three acts. As performed with universal applause, at the Theatre—Federal—Street. By John O'Keeffe. Boston: Printed [by Joseph Bumstead] for Wm. P. and L. Blake, 1797 (Vail 241). Produced at the New Theatre, Chestnut St., Philadelphia, 5 April 1794; music by Alexander Reinagle.

"Song." [First line:] "Fragile sweets, how frail ye are." Three eight-line stanzas. Published in *Miscellaneous Poems*, pp. 184-185 (Vail 242).

"Song." [First line:] "The rose just bursting into bloom." Two eight-line stanzas. Published in *Miscellaneous Poems*, pp. 204-205 (Vail 243).

"Song." [First line:] "Welcome is the morning light." Three eight-line stanzas. Published in *Miscellaneous Poems*, pp. 206-207 (Vail 244).

"Song." [First line:] "When far from freedom's happy court." Two ten-line stanzas. Published in *Miscellaneous Poems*, pp. 194-195 (Vail 245).

"Song." [First line:] "When hoarse winds roar, and lightnings gleam." Two eight-line stanzas. Published in,*Miscellaneous Poems*, pp. 199-200 (Vail 246).

"Song. Written for the celebration of the Birthday of George Washington, Esq." and sung on that occasion, in Boston, February 11th, 1798. Air—Anacreon in Heaven. Three eight-line stanzas. Title from *Miscellaneous Poems*, pp. 178-179 (Vail 247).

"Truxton's Victory." A Naval Patriotic song. Sung by Mr. Hodgkinson. Written by Mrs. Rowson, of Boston. [Boston: Printed by Thomas & Andrews, 1799?]. Imprint in ink (Vail 248); (Evans 36248); (Sonneck-Upton, p. 438). Sonneck notes that "Truxton's Victory" was advertised in March 1799 as "published, at P.A. von Hagen, jun. and Co's, No. 55, Marlboro' Street . . ." Boston.

"When the Cloud Has Pass'd Away." Air, in *A Sacred Concert*, in Two Parts/ To Be Performed on Sunday Evening Dec. 9, 1821. by the "Neponset Sacred Music Society" at their Hall Near Milton Bridge. Order of Performance. Words by Mrs. Rowson, Music by John Bray. Vail locates at The American Antiquarian Society; my copy from Barrett Library, University of Virginia.

"Where Can Peace of Mind Be Found." A Duett. Written by Mrs. Rowson. The Music Composed by John Bray. Boston: G. Graupner [1821]. Wolfe (1356) notes that the copyright was granted Graupner in 1821.

"Will Not Dare Not Tell." A New Song Written by Mrs. Rowson. The Music Composed by P.A. von Hagen. Boston: P.A. von Hagen's Piano Forte Warehouse, [1802] (Vail 251; Wolfe 3296). Wolfe notes copyright granted von Hagen September 1802; both he and Vail cite advertisements that support date.

"Will You Rise My Belov'd." Words by Mrs. Rowson—Adapted to the Music of "Will You Come to the Bower." Boston: G. Graupner. Vail (252) gives the date as [1818-1825]; Wolfe (6061) as [1811?].

Works Referred To

Adams, Oscar Fay. "Susanna Haswell Rowson." *Christian Register*, 17 March 1913, pp. 296-299; 3 April 1913, p. 321.

Angoff, Charles. *A Literary History of the American People*. 2 vols. in 1. New ed. New York: Tudor Publishing Co., 1935.

Anthony, Katherine. *First Lady of the Revolution: The Life of Mercy Otis Warren*. Garden City, N.Y.: Doubleday & Company, 1958.

Baker, Ernest A. *The History of the English Novel: The Novel of Sentiment and the Gothic Romance*. Vol. 5. London: H.F.&G. Witherby, 1934.

Benson, Mary Sumner. *Women in Eighteenth-Century America: A Study of Opinion and Social Usage*. New York: Columbia University Press, 1935.

Bernard, John. *Retrospections of America: 1797-1811*. Ed. Laurence Hutton and Brander Matthews. New York: Harper & Brothers, 1887.

Blakey, Dorothy. *The Minerva Press 1790-1820*. London: Oxford University Press, 1939.

Boyd, Elizabeth. *The Happy-Unfortunate, or the Female-Page*. Ed. William Graves. Garland Series, Foundations of the Novel. New York: Garland Publishing, 1972.

Bradsher, Earl L. *Mathew Carey. Editor, Author and Publisher. A Study in American Literary Development*. New York: Columbia University Press, 1912.

Bradstreet, Anne. *The Works of Anne Bradstreet*. Ed. Jeannine Hensley, Adrienne Rich. Cambridge, Mass.: Harvard University Press, 1967.

Brown, Charles Brockden. *Alcuin: A Dialogue*, 1935; reprint ed. with afterwords by Lee R. Edwards. New York: Grossman Publishers, 1971.

Brown, Herbert Ross. *The Sentimental Novel in America, 1789-1860*. Durham, N.C.: Duke University Press, 1940.

Brown, William Hill. *The Power of Sympathy, or, the Triumph of Nature. Founded in Truth, in The Power of Sympathy and The Coquette*. Ed. William S. Osborne. Masterworks of Literature Series. New Haven, Conn.: College and University Press, 1970.

Buckingham, Joseph Tinker, *Personal Memoirs and Recollections of Editorial Life . . .* Vol. 1. Boston: Ticknor, Reed, & Fields, 1852.

Burney, Frances. *Evelina, or the History of a Young Ladies Entrance into the World*. Ed. Edward A. Bloom. London: Oxford University Press, 1968.

The Cambridge History of American Literature. Colonial and Revolutionary Literature; Early National Literature. Vol. 1. Ed. William Peterfield Trent, John Erskine, Stuart P. Sherman, Carl Van Doren. New York: G.P. Putnam's Sons, 1917.

Charvat, William. The Profession of Authorship in America, 1800-1870. Ed. Matthew J. Bruccoli. Foreword by Howard Mumford Jones. Columbus: Ohio State University Press, 1968.

———. Literary Publishing in America, 1790-1850. Philadelphia: University of Pennsylvania Press, 1959.

Cobbett, William [Peter Porcupine, pseud.]. A Kick For a Bite; or, Review upon Review; with a Critical Essay, on the Works of Mrs. S. Rowson, in a Letter to the Editor, or Editors, of The American Monthly Review. Philadelphia: Thomas Bradford, 1795.

Cowie, Alexander. The Rise of the American Novel. New York: American Book Co., 1948.

Dall, [Caroline Wells Healey]. The Romance of the Association; or, One Last Glimpse of Charlotte Temple and Eliza Wharton. A Curiosity of Literature and Life. Cambridge: Press of John Wilson and Son, 1875.

Davis, Elizabeth Gould. The First Sex. New York: G.P. Putnam's Sons, 1970.

de Beauvoir, Simone. The Second Sex. Ed. and trans. H.M. Parshley, 1953; reprint ed., New York: Bantam Books, 1961.

Deegan, Dorothy Yost. The Stereotype of the Single Woman in American Novels: A Social Study with Implications for the Education of Women. New York: King's Crown Press, Columbia University, 1951.

Eastman, Arthur M., et al., eds. The Norton Reader: An Anthology of Expository Prose. 3d ed. New York: W.W. Norton & Company, 1973.

Fiedler, Leslie A. Love and Death in the American Novel. New rev. ed. New York: Dell Publishing Co., 1969.

Field, Vena Bernadette. Constantia: A Study of the Life and Works of Judith Sargent Murray 1751-1820. University of Maine Studies, 2d ser., no. 17. Orono: University of Maine Press, 1931.

[Foster, Hannah]. The Boarding School; or, Lessons of a Preceptress to her Pupils: consisting of Information, Instruction, and Advice, Calculated to Improve the Manners, and form the Character of YOUNG LADIES. to which is added, A Collection of LETTERS, Written by the PUPILS. to their Instructor, their Friends, and each other. By a Lady of Massachusetts; Author of The Coquette. Boston: I. Thomas and E.J. Andrews, 1798.

———. The Coquette, or, The History of Eliza Wharton. A Novel Founded on Fact, in The Power of Sympathy and The Coquette. Ed. William S. Osborne. Masterworks of Literature Series. New Haven, Conn.: College and University Press, 1970.

Friedan, Betty. The Feminine Mystique. New York: Dell Publishing Co., 1963.

Goulianos, Joan, ed. By a Woman Writt: Literature From Six Centuries By and About Women. Baltimore: Penguin Books, 1973.

Hahn, Emily. Once Upon a Pedestal. New York: Thomas Y. Crowell, 1974.

Hale, Nancy. New England Discovery: A Personal View. New York: Coward, McCann, 1963.

Hall, Ernest Jackson. "The Satirical Element in The American Novel." Ph.D. diss., University of Pennsylvania, 1922.

Halsey, Francis W. "Historical and Biographical Introduction," Charlotte Temple: a Tale of Truth. New York: Funk and Wagnalls Company, 1905.

Hart, James D. The Popular Book. A History of America's Literary Taste, 1950. Reprint ed., Berkeley: University of California Press, 1963.

Heilbrun, Carolyn G. Toward a Recognition of Androgyny. New York: Alfred A. Knopf, 1973.

Heilman, Robert Bechtold. America in English Fiction, 1760-1800: The Influences of the American Revolution. Baton Rouge: Louisiana State University Press, 1937.

Jones, Mary Gwladys. *Hannah More*. Cambridge: Cambridge University Press, 1952.

Kable, William S. "Introduction," *Three Early American Novels*. Columbus, Ohio: Charles E. Merrill Publishing Co., 1970.

Kettler, Robert Ronald. "The Eighteenth-Century American Novel: The Beginning of a Fictional Tradition." Ph.D. diss., Purdue University, 1968.

Knapp, Samuel L. "A Memoir of the Author," in *Charlotte's Daughter: or, The Three Orphans. A Sequel to Charlotte Temple*. Boston: Richardson & Lord, 1828.

Literary History of the United States: History. Ed. Robert E. Spiller, Willard Thorp, Thomas H. Johnson, Henry Seidel Canby, Richard M. Ludwig. 3d ed., rev. New York: Macmillan, 1964.

Loshe, Lillie Deming. *The Early American Novel*. New York: Columbia University Press, 1907.

MacCarthy, B.G. *The Female Pen*. 2 vols. New York: William Salloch, 1948.

Mackenzie, Henry. *The Man of Feeling*. Ed. Brian Vickers. London: Oxford University Press, 1967.

Manvill, P.P. *Lucinda; or, the Mountain Mourner. Being Recent Facts, in a series of Letters, from Mrs. Manvill, in the State of New York, to her sister in Pennsylvania*. 2d ed., rev. Ballston Spa, N.Y.: William Child, 1810.

Martin, Terence. "The Emergence of the Novel in America. A Study in the Cultural History of an Art Form." Ph.D. diss., Ohio State University, 1954.

———. *The Instructed Vision; Scottish Common Sense Philosophy and the Origins of American Fiction*. Indiana University Humanities Series no. 48. Bloomington: Indiana University Press, 1961.

Martin, Wendy. "Seduced and Abandoned in the New World, 1970: The Fallen Women in American Fiction." *The American Sisterhood: Writings of the Feminist Movement from Colonial Times to the Present*. Ed. Wendy Martin. New York: Harper & Row, Publishers, 1972.

Martineau, Harriet. *Society in America*. New York: Saunders and Otley, 1837.

Mates, Julian. *The American Musical Stage Before 1800*. New Brunswick, N.J.: Rutgers University Press, 1962.

Mead, Margaret. *Sex and Temperament in Three Primitive Societies*. New York: Mentor Books, 1950.

Melville, Herman. *Redburn, His First Voyage. Being the Sailor-boy Confessions and Reminiscences of the Son-of-a-Gentleman, in the Merchant Service*. Ed., Harrison Hayford, Hershel Parker, G. Thomas Tanselle. Vol. 4 of Northwestern-Newberry Edition. General ed. Harrison Hayford. Evanston, Ill.: Northwestern University Press, 1960.

Millett, Kate. *Sexual Politics*. Garden City, N.Y.: Doubleday & Company, 1970.

Montagu, Ashley. *The Natural Superiority of Women*. New York: Macmillan, 1953.

More, Hannah. *Works: Strictures on the Modern System of Female Education–Sacred Dramas*. Vol. 6. New York: Harper & Brothers, Publishers, 1855.

Morgan, Robin, ed. *Sisterhood is Powerful: An Anthology of Writings from the Women's Liberation Movement*. New York: Vintage Books, 1970.

Mott, Frank Luther. *Golden Multitudes: The Story of Best Sellers in the United States*. New York: Macmillan, 1947.

———. *A History of American Magazines, 1741-1850*. Vol. 1. New York: D. Appleton & Company, 1930.

Murray, Judith Sargent. "On the Equality of the Sexes." *The Feminist Papers: From Adams to de Beauvoir*. Ed. Alice S. Rossi. New York: Columbia University Press, 1973.

Nason, Elias. *A Memoir of Mrs. Susanna Rowson, with Elegant and Illustrative Extracts*

From her Writings in Prose and Poetry. Albany, N.Y.: Joel Munsell, 1870.

Neal, James. *An Essay on the Education and Genius of the Female Sex. To Which is Added, An Account, of the Commencement of the Young Ladies' Academy of Philadelphia, Held the 18th of December, 1794. Under the Direction of Mr. John Poor, A.M. Principal.* Philadelphia: Jacob Johnson & Co., 1795.

Orians, G. Harrison. *A Short History of American Literature. Analyzed By Decades.* New York: F.S. Crofts & Co., 1940.

Papashvily, Helen Waite. *All the Happy Endings: A Study of the Domestic Novel in America, the Women Who Wrote It, the Women Who Read It, in the Nineteenth Century.* New York: Harper & Brothers Publishers, 1956.

Parker, Gail, ed. *The Oven Birds: American Women on Womanhood, 1820-1920.* Garden City, N.Y.: Doubleday & Company, Anchor Books, 1972.

Pattee, Fred Lewis. *The First Century of American Literature, 1770-1870.* New York: D. Appleton-Century Company, 1935.

Petter, Henri. *The Early American Novel.* Columbus: Ohio State University Press, 1971.

Plumb, Harriet Pixley. *Charlotte Temple, A Historical Drama, Three Acts With Prologue.* Chicago and London: Publishers Printing Co., T. Fisher Unwin [1899].

Quinn, Arthur Hobson. *American Fiction: An Historical and Critical Survey.* New York: Appleton-Century-Crofts, 1936.

Richardson, Charles F. *American Literature 1607-1885.* Vol. 2. New York: G.P. Putnam's Sons, 1889.

Richardson, Samuel. *Clarissa, or the History of a Young Lady.* Ed. George Sherburn. Boston: Houghton Mifflin Co., 1962.

———. *Pamela, or Virtue Rewarded.* Ed. William M. Sale, Jr. New York: W.W. Norton and Co., 1958.

Rossi, Alice S., ed. *The Feminist Papers: From Adams to de Beauvoir.* New York: Columbia University Press, 1973.

Rourke, Constance. *The Roots of American Culture, and Other Essays.* New York: Harcourt, Brace and Co.. 1942.

[Sansay, Leonora]. *Laura. By a Lady of Philadelphia.* Philadelphia: Bradford & Inskeep, 1809.

Sargent, Mary E. "Susanna Rowson." *Medford Historical Register,* 7 April 1904, pp. 24-40.

Scott, Anne Firor. *Women in American Life. Selected Readings.* New York: Houghton Mifflin Co., 1970.

Sedgwick, Catherine Maria. *The Poor Rich Man, and The Rich Poor Man.* New York: Harper & Brothers, 1836.

Sewall, Samuel. "Talitha Cumi," *Sewall Letter Book, Coll. Mass. Hist. Soc.,* ser. 6, vols. 1-2, 1886-1888.

Smith, Thelma M. "Feminism in Philadelphia, 1790-1850." *Pennsylvania Magazine of History and Biography* 68, no. 3 (July 1944), pp. 243-268.

Sonneck, Oscar George. *Early Opera in America.* New York, London, and Boston: G. Shirmer, 1915.

Southworth, E.D.E.N. *Self-Raised, or From the Depths.* New York: Grosset & Dunlap, 1864.

[Swanwick, John]. *A Rub from Snub; or a cursory analytical Epistle: addressed to Peter Porcupine, Author of the* BONE TO GNAW, KICK FOR A BITE, &c. &c. *containing* GLAD TIDINGS *for the* DEMOCRATS, *and a Word of* COMFORT *to Mrs. S. Rowson. Wherein the Said Porcupine's Moral, Political, Critical and Literary character is Fully Illustrated.* Philadelphia: Printed for the Purchasers, 1795.

Tompkins, J.M.S. *The Popular Novel in England, 1770-1800.* London: Constable & Co., 1932.

Twain, Mark. "The Literary Offenses of Fenimore Cooper." *The Portable Mark Twain.* Ed. Bernard de Voto. New York: Viking Press, 1946.

Violette, Augusta Genevieve. *Economic Feminism in American Literature Prior to 1848.* University of Maine Studies, 2d ser., no. 2. Orono: University of Maine Press, 1925.

Wasserstrom, William. *Heiress of All the Ages: Sex and Sentiment in the Genteel Tradition.* Minneapolis: University of Minnesota Press, 1959.

Watt, Ian. *The Rise of the Novel: Studies in Defoe, Richardson and Fielding,* 1957; reprint ed., Berkeley: University of California Press, 1967.

Whittier, John Greenleaf. *Whittier on Writers and Writing: The Uncollected Critical Writings of John Greenleaf Whittier.* Ed., Edwin Harrison Cady and Harry Hayden Clark. Syracuse, N.Y.: Syracuse University Press, 1950.

Wollstonecraft, Mary. *A Vindication of the Rights of Woman, with Strictures on Political and Moral Subjects.* Ed. Charles W. Hagelman, Jr. New York: W.W. Norton & Company, 1967.

[Wood, Sally Sayward Barrell Keating]. *Dorval; or the Speculator. A Novel. Founded on Recent Facts. By a Lady. Author of "Julia."* Portsmouth, N.H.: Nutting & Whitelock, 1801.

————. *Julia and the Illuminated Baron. A Novel. Founded on Recent Facts. . . . By a Lady of Massachusetts.* Portsmouth, N.H.: United States Oracle Press, 1800.

Woolf, Virginia. *A Room of One's Own.* New York: Harcourt, Brace & World, 1957.

Wyman, Margaret. "The Rise of the Fallen Woman." *American Quarterly* 3 (1951), pp. 161-177.

Works Consulted

Adams, Elmer C., Warren Dunham Foster. *Heroines of Modern Progress.* New York: Macmillan, 1939.

[Anon]. "Rights of Women." *Philadelphia Minerva,* 17 October 1795.

Bowne, Eliza Southgate. *A Girl's Life Eighty Years Ago. Selections from the Letters of Eliza Southgate Bowne.* Introduction, Clarence Cook. New York: Charles Scribner's Sons, 1888.

Brooke, Frances. *The History of Lady Julia Mandeville.* 5th ed. 2 vols. London: J. Dodsley, 1769.

Brooks, C. *History of the Town of Medford, Middlesex County, Massachusetts, From Its First Settlement, in 1630, to the Present time, 1855.* Boston: James M. Usher, 1855.

Brown, Charles Brockden. *Arthur Mervyn, or Memoirs of the Year 1793.* Ed. Warner Berthoff. New York: Holt, Rinehart and Winston, 1962.

————. *Edgar Huntly; or, the Sleep Walker.* London: Richard Bentley, 1842.

————. *Memoirs of Carwin the Biloquist,* in *Three Early American Novels.* Ed. William S. Kable. Columbus, Ohio: Charles E. Merrill Publishing Co., 1970.

————. *Ormond, or the Secret Witness.* Ed. Ernest Marchand, 1937; reprint ed., Hafner Library of Classics, no. 24. New York: Hafner Publishing Company, 1962.

————. Wieland; Or the Transformation, in Three Early American Novels. Ed. William S. Kable. Columbus, Ohio: Charles E. Merrill Publishing Co., 1970.

Cady, Edwin H. The Light of Common Day. Realism in American Fiction. Bloomington: Indiana University Press, 1971.

Cone, Helen Gray, Jeannette L. Gilder. Pen-Portraits of Literary Women By Themselves and Others. Vol. 1. New York: Cassell & Company, 1887.

Defoe, Daniel. The Fortunes and Misfortunes of the Famous Moll Flanders. New York: Heritage Press, 1942.

Dexter, Elizabeth Anthony. Colonial Women of Affairs: A Study of Women in Business and the Professions in America Before 1776. Boston: Houghton Mifflin Co., 1924.

Donahue, Jane. "Colonial Shipwreck Narratives: A Theological Study." Books at Brown 28 (1969), pp. 101-119.

George, Margaret. One Woman's "Situation." Urbana: University of Illinois Press, 1970.

Gidez, Richard Banus. "A Study of the Works of Catherine Maria Sedgwick." Ph.D. diss. Ohio State University, 1958.

Guest, Boyd. "John Neal and 'Women's Rights and Women's Wrongs.' " New England Quarterly 18 (1945), pp. 508-515.

Hixon, Donald L. Music in Early America: A Bibliography of Music in Evans. Metuchen, N.J.: The Scarecrow Press, 1970.

Hogan, Charles Beecher, ed. The London Stage 1660-1800. A Calendar of Plays, Entertainments and Afterpieces Together with Cast, Box-Receipts and Contemporary Comment. Compiled from the Play-bills, Newspapers, and Theatrical Diaries of the Period: 1776-1800. Part 5. Carbondale: Southern Illinois University Press, 1968.

Howay, F. W. "A Short Account of Robert Haswell." Washington Historical Quarterly 24 (1933), pp. 83-90.

Howells, W.D. Heroines of Fiction. 2 vols. New York: Harper & Brothers Publishers, 1901.

Inchbald, Elizabeth. A Simple Story. Ed. J.M.S. Tompkins. London: Oxford University Press, 1967.

Johnson, R. Brimley. The Women Novelists. London: W. Collins & Co., 1918.

Jones, Howard Mumford. "American Prose Style: 1700-1770." Huntington Library Bulletin, no. 6 (1934).

————. "The Importation of French Literature in New York City," Studies in Philology 28 (1931), pp. 235-251.

Kirk, Clara M. and Rudolph. "Introduction," Charlotte Temple: A Tale of Truth. Twayne's United States Classics Series. New York: Twayne Publishers, 1964.

Lennox, Charlotte. The Female Quixote, or the Adventures of Arabella. Ed. Margaret Dalziel. London: Oxford University Press, 1970.

Mease, James M.D. The Picture of Philadelphia. Philadelphia: B. & T. Kite, 1811.

Mills, W. Jay. Through the Gates of Old Romance. Philadelphia: J.B. Lippincott Co., 1903.

Mitchell, Juliet. Woman's Estate. New York: Pantheon, 1971.

More, Hannah. Coelebs in Search of a Wife; Comprehending Observations on Domestic Habits and Manners, Religion and Morals. The Complete Works of Hannah More. Vol. 2. New York: Harper & Brothers, 1855.

Nye, Russel Blaine. The Cultural Life of the New Nation, 1776-1830. New York: Harper & Brothers, 1960.

[Prévost, Antoine Francois]. History of Manon Lescaut and of the Chevalier des Grieux. Paris: Société Des Beaux-Arts, 1915.

Rees, James. *The Dramatic Authors of America*. Philadelphia: G.B. Zieber & Co., 1845.

Rosenbach, Abraham Simon Wolf. *Early American Children's Books*. Portland, Maine: Southworth Press, 1933.

Rousseau, J.J. *Eloisa: Or, a Series of Original Letters*. 3d ed. 4 vols. London: T. Becket and P.A. De Hondt, 1764.

[Sedgwick, Catherine Maria]. *Hope Leslie: or, Early Times in Massachusetts*. By the Author of "The Linwoods," "Poor Rich Man," "Live and Let Live," "Redwood," etc. 2 vols. New York: Harper & Brothers, Publishers, 1872.

Smith, Charlotte. *Emmeline, The Orphan of the Castle*. Ed. Anne Henry Ehrenpreis. London: Oxford University Press, 1971.

———. *The Old Manor House*. Ed. Anne Henry Ehrenpreis. London: Oxford University Press, 1969.

Snow, Caleb H. *A History of Boston; The Metropolis of Massachusetts, from its Origin to the Present Period*. Boston: Abel Bowen, 1825.

Snow, Edward Rowe. *Women of the Sea*. New York: Dodd Mead & Company, 1962.

Spargo, John. *Anthony Haswell, Printer-Patriot-Ballader. A Biographical Study*. Rutland, Vt.: Tuttle Co., 1925.

Spiller, R.E. *The Cycle of American Literature: An Essay in Historical Criticism*. New York: Macmillan, 1955.

[Stanton, Elizabeth Cady]. *Elizabeth Cady Stanton As Revealed in Her Letters, Diary and Reminiscences*. Ed. Theodore Stanton and Harriot Stanton Blatch. 2 vols. New York: Harper & Brothers, Publishers, 1922.

Stein, Roger B. "Seascape and the American Imagination: The Puritan Seventeenth Century." *Early American Literature* 7, no. 1 (1972), pp. 17-37.

Steiner, George. "The Americanness of American Literature." *Listener* 62, no. 158 (1959), pp. 95-97.

Taft, Kendall B. *Minor Knickerbockers*. New York: American Book Co., 1947.

Utter, Robert Palfrey, Gwendowyn Bridges Needham. *Pamela's Daughters*. New York: Macmillan, 1936.

Van Doren, Carl. *The American Novel, 1789-1939*. Rev. ed., New York: Macmillan, 1940.

Watkins, Walter Kendall. "The Great Street to Roxbury Gate, 1630-1830." *Bostonian Society Publications*, 2d ser., no. 3 (1919), pp. 89-126.

Wegelin, Oscar. *Early American Plays. 1714-1830. A Compilation of the Titles of Plays and Dramatic Poems Written by Americans born in or Residing in North America previous to 1830*. 2d ed., rev. New York: Literary Collector Press, 1905.

Whitmore, Clara H. *Woman's Work in English Fiction, From the Restoration to the Mid-Victorian Period*. New York: G.P. Putnam's Sons, 1910.

Williams, John [pseud. Anthony Pasquin]. *The Children of Thespis*. London: Kirby and Co., 1792.

[Wollstonecraft, Mary]. *The Emigrants*. Dublin ed., 1794; reprint ed. with intro. by Robert R. Hare, Gainesville, Fla: Scholar's Fascimiles and Reprints, 1964.

Wright, Lyle. "Propaganda in Early American Fiction." *Papers of the Bibliographical Society of America* 33 (1939), pp. 98-107.

———. "A Statistical Survey of American Fiction, 1774-1850." *Huntington Library Quarterly* 2, no. 3 (1939), pp. 309-318.

Index